EARLY CHILD|

NANCY FILE & CHRISTOPHER P. BROWN, EDITORS

To look for other titles in this series, visit www.tcpress.com

continued

Music Therapy With Preschool Children on the Autism Spectrum

Moments of Meeting

Geoff Barnes

TEACHERS COLLEGE PRESS

TEACHERS COLLEGE | COLUMBIA UNIVERSITY

NEW YORK AND LONDON

Published by Teachers College Press,® 1234 Amsterdam Avenue, New York, NY 10027

Front cover photo by SanyaSM / iStock by Getty Images.

"Blackbirds" from *Wing Over Wing* by Julie Cadwallader Staub. Copyright 2019 by Julie Cadwallader Staub. Used by permission of Paraclete Press.

Library of Congress Cataloging-in-Publication Data

Names: Barnes, Geoff (Geoffrey P.) author.
Title: Music therapy with preschool children on the autism spectrum : moments of meeting / Geoff Barnes.
Description: New York, NY : Teachers College Press, 2022. | Series: Early childhood education series | Includes bibliographical references and index. | Summary: "In vivid narratives, readers follow individual preschoolers through their challenges and their steps toward shared attention, interpersonal interaction, and communication during music. This book explores connections among students, teachers, and a music therapist; raises key issues about autism supports and therapies; and offers encouraging alternatives to prevailing educational and therapeutic methods."—Provided by publisher.
Identifiers: LCCN 2022021127 (print) | LCCN 2022021128 (ebook) | ISBN 9780807767085 (paperback) | ISBN 9780807767092 (hardcover) | ISBN 9780807781098 (ebook)
Subjects: LCSH: Music therapy for children. | Autistic children—Treatment.
Classification: LCC ML3920 .B22 2022 (print) | LCC ML3920 (ebook) | DDC 615.8/5154—dc23/eng/20220525
LC record available at https://lccn.loc.gov/2022021127
LC ebook record available at https://lccn.loc.gov/2022021128

ISBN 978-0-8077-6708-5 (paper)
ISBN 978-0-8077-6709-2 (hardcover)
ISBN 978-0-8077-8109-8 (ebook)

Printed on acid-free paper
Manufactured in the United States of America

Contents

Introduction
"My Name Is . . ."

It's 5 minutes before the class music session, and I'm taking my guitar out of its case and setting up my amplifier. Soon I will begin to sing the "Hello Song" to welcome six preschoolers in this class for children on the autism spectrum, part of a thriving early childhood program that serves 237 youngsters, ages 3–5 years. Children with and without a range of diagnosed disabilities learn in 12 classrooms at this free public preschool. In the preceding years, the parents and school had sought additional services for some of the students on the autism spectrum who needed more-extensive educational supports and related therapies. In response, the preschool developed a specialized class with a smaller size of 6 to 8 students, hired additional staff, and provided special education services and extended hours for children on the spectrum requiring very substantial supports. This is the classroom that I work in.

I provide weekly music therapy sessions to add to the special education services and therapies—including speech, vision, occupational and physical therapy—available to the children. The following chapters describe and reflect on video excerpts from 16 classroom music therapy sessions over the course of 2 years, using pseudonyms for the individuals involved. I am not able to portray a universal depiction of the widely varying abilities and experiences of all preschool students on the spectrum—some of whom already demonstrate substantial language and academic skills—in differing classrooms, communities, and states. Instead, I seek to share the story of children in one specific classroom who are starting a new year facing significant challenges in the beginning steps of personal interactions and communication.

THE "HELLO SONG"

My initial goal for this November 19th session is to lead an opening song that involves the children in friendly interactions and vocal/verbal communication. With my singing and guitar playing, I want to greet and give attention to each of the children one by one—Dylan, Gabriel, Emily, Caleb, Erik, and James. And I will try to encourage their steps in interpersonal interaction, such as each child saying their own name. I will also invite peers to greet their classmate with a wave or a "hi." This is my plan. How will it go?

Dylan's Response

Julie, a teaching intern, sits on the floor and turns toward Dylan, one of the class members, while I'm getting ready to begin. She is eye level with him in his chair as she asks, "What's your name?" and takes Dylan's hand and taps it on his chest in a "me" gesture.

Dylan is a handsome young boy with brown eyes and dark brown hair. He has just turned 3 and is beginning his first weeks at the preschool. Dylan's family speaks English and Arabic. What is it like for a 3-year-old boy to be learning two languages and cultures while living with the impacts of autism? He's already captured my attention and affection this semester with his vitality and surprising thought-provoking actions. His occasional use of spoken words contrasts with many of the children in this classroom who are not using verbal communication.

Responding to Julie's question, "What's your name?" Dylan looks back at her, reaches out his pointer finger, touches near her neck, and starts to reply. He says, "What's . . . ," and then he pauses.

He becomes quiet before he again slowly speaks, "My . . . name . . . is . . . ," then he halts. He looks over to the side. His steps in verbal communication are encouraging to hear, and they build anticipation among the teachers of this class in which the majority of students are not yet speaking.

"What is your name?" Julie asks Dylan again.

"My . . . name . . . is . . . , " he begins again. He stops. He seems a centimeter away from saying his name, but he doesn't go on. Silence hangs in the air and extends until it's as though his interactions and talking with Julie disappear.

Julie taps him on the arm and answers, "Dylan!" for him. Her voice sounds upbeat but also strained. I think that she and others of us in the group were really hoping that Dylan would be able to take the next step and say his name.

She moves over and sits next to another student.

Dylan rubs his face with his hands as if he were trying to wash off a spot.

Like an afterthought, he says quietly and slowly to himself, "My . . . name . . ." and then his voice fades.

A few moments later, I pull my guitar strap over my shoulder and gently strum the first chords of the upcoming "Hello Song." I look at each of the six preschoolers in the circle, and I remember influential teachers in my life whose presence and actions communicated caring and peace even before they spoke or officially began an activity. Now, I'm trying in my own way to start our music session by communicating a spirit of caring and play and my interest in getting to know each of the children. Initially, I sing the chorus to the whole group, "Hello, everybody, yes indeed! . . . It's good to see you!" Then I turn to one of the children, Caleb, and sing, "What's your name?" He responds by saying the hard-C sound that starts his name. Speaking this beginning consonant is a new step for him, and the teachers and I enthusiastically respond. Caleb smiles.

Suddenly, Dylan speaks up and interjects, "Good job!" He looks animated and buoyant. His praise comes as a clear and well-synchronized contribution to the group. I'm appreciative and also surprised by Dylan's ease and spontaneity in saying, "Good job!" when moments before he appeared to shut down on the brink of communicating his own name.

I continue singing the "Hello Song" with its familiar structure of a repeated chorus for the whole class. Then I resume greeting each child and giving them chances to say their names. Gabriel and Emily, who are the next two children in the circle, however, do not say their names and, in fact, do not say a word. They are watching me but are quiet. At this stage, I am still trying to gauge what forms of vocal, verbal, or nonverbal communication we can nurture with them.

Now I come to Dylan's turn during the "Hello Song." I'm hoping that some of the animation and spirit of his "Good job!" response to another student will carry over into his own turn. Will it help him say his own name in our greeting song?

"And what's your name?" I sing. And I add in spoken language, "Hello! What's your name?"

"My . . . ," Dylan begins.

Then assistant teacher Elizabeth directs his hand to his chest, attempting another physical gesture for "me." However, Dylan responds by ceasing to talk altogether. He begins to lean his head down toward his lap. Elizabeth guides him back upright, saying for him, "My name's Dylan." Her prompts are simple and direct. But in reaction, Dylan seems to shut down. He again lowers his head, this time almost touching his forehead to the floor.

How should we respond? Surprising myself, I try something different. I say, "Is your name Frank?" Dylan brings his head back up, acquiescing to Elizabeth's tug on the back of his shirt. "Are you Frank? Are you Bill?" I ask. By saying clearly wrong names, I'm hoping that unexpected humor might spark his interest and motivate him to speak up to correct me. Some children relish the chance to announce the right answers when an adult is playfully suggesting wrong ones. Maybe Dylan will abruptly look up, smile, and say his name to let us know. Julie asks at the same time, "What's your name?" But Dylan turns his face away, looking in the opposite direction from Julie.

Julie says to Elizabeth: "We've worked a lot on this, this week . . . I have, with him." Then Julie moves her head side to side indicating that Dylan usually hasn't said his name at these other moments either. "He said it to me once," she says, while looking directly toward Elizabeth, as if appealing for help.

Reflecting on What Happened

Five times Dylan begins to speak up. He comes close to saying, "My name is Dylan," several times, but each time he stops at the brink, although he energetically says, "Good job!" when another classmate takes a turn. In many moments during the early weeks of the school year, he seems to show alternating combinations of lively abilities and puzzling difficulties, which causes me to wonder how I can better offer music activities to support him? Songs that invite participation and turn taking can spark communication and interpersonal exchange with many children, but Dylan's response this morning raises questions. Can Dylan say his own name when asked? Julie thinks she heard him do it once. I haven't seen that yet. Is he experiencing our requests to speak his name and the personal interactions involved as unwelcome intrusions that he wants to avoid? For Dylan, is there something about self-identification that might be problematic rather than clear?

During this morning's session, I witness some of challenges facing Dylan, his preschool classmates, and the adults who care for them, and I want to learn from the questions that arise: How can the teachers and I help the children to reach their potential and to develop their abilities along with their connections with people? What can participation in our music group reveal about the difficulties and possibilities of fostering communication, shared learning, play, and caring?

I've undertaken research about our music therapy group in order to better understand and to respond to these questions. By studying the video recordings of our interactions, and by viewing teacher interviews, field notes, and school reports, I aim to describe and analyze specific moments from our music group in detail for this book. My goal is also to explore the meanings of these interactions and to reflect on comparisons with related research and therapeutic approaches. I believe that this will yield knowledge that will be helpful to me and may be useful to teachers, music therapists, parents, and classroom researchers who are interested in learning more about the potential of music to support the development of young children on the spectrum.

GAINING KNOWLEDGE THROUGH PARTICIPATIVE ACTION RESEARCH

To come to know children in a preschool class in greater depth and for a longer duration, I advocate a participative action research approach, which combines practitioner research and qualitative case-study research. Practitioner research has been defined as individuals closely examining their own work and studying the services and organizations that they participate in. The goals of practitioner research are to improve skills and to develop and share knowledge (Aigen, 2014; Ansdell & Pavlicevic, 2001; Cochran-Smith & Lytle, 2009; Newman & Leggett, 2019).

Recent years have seen the rising influence of quantitative methods in the fields of education and music therapy. Quantitative research often concentrates on a few variables and many cases, using repeated prescribed procedures and gathering numeric data and generalizing the results across groups of people. However, I use qualitative case-study research methods because I believe that teachers and music therapists can be helped by in-depth descriptions of a specific setting (in this case a preschool classroom with additional services for students on the spectrum) and practice (a music therapy group that uses changing strategies over time to adapt to the evolving needs and interests of the children during 2 years). Immersing oneself in a particular classroom, learning from personal involvement, and experimenting with a range of methods offers a needed complement to the currently prevailing randomized controlled studies that are often larger, briefer, and focused on the repeated testing of a method. Readers of practitioner qualitative research also can benefit from more-personal, descriptive inside perspectives that bring them close to classroom life—seeing the children's actions, hearing their voices. Educators Marilyn Cochran-Smith and Susan Lytle (2009) write, "With narrative inquiry, validity rests on concrete examples (or 'exemplars') of actual practices presented in enough detail that the relevant community can judge trustworthiness and usefulness" (p. 43). Accordingly, in the chapters of this book, my goal is to portray and discuss 16 such concrete examples derived from video recordings of class music sessions over 2 years. I want to convey the challenges and possibilities of encouraging the interests and participation of young children on the spectrum in a preschool music group. Like other qualitative case-study researchers, I undertake reflective and systematic analysis to gain knowledge about the experiences of participants within an existing interactive setting rather than in a more controlled or laboratory environment.

MOMENTS OF MEETING

The vivid narratives and transcriptions of psychiatrist and child researcher Robert Coles (1996) have encouraged me during my research. He sought to unite the rational discussions of the scholar "with the passion and affection of the friend who cares and is moved" (p. 11). In addition to envisioning a researcher who is an involved caring coparticipant, Coles also characterized his methodology as an attempt to tell the stories of meeting the children, and continuing to get to know them and to reflect about their changing actions and words over time. About his book, *The Call of Service*, Coles (1993) wrote:

> This book offers many such stories and conversations and observations . . . In relating my own experiences and memories, I write as a witness trying to do justice through narration to lives I have met . . . This is research, I think it is fair to say, living up to its literal meaning of an inquiry made again and again, during meetings and more meetings with those whose deeds, finally, are the subject matter of this book. (pp. 29–30)

Coles's efforts to understand these continuing exchanges and meetings also inspire my interest in telling the stories of the specific small "moments of meeting" with the children in the music group. As I describe in the coming chapters, I believe that the preschool children's early steps in shared attention, interaction, and communication are nurtured during these moments of meeting.

By focusing attention on specific small moments within the music group, I also take part in wider traditions that closely examine pivotal and problematic moments as entryways to learning about interactions between people. Child psychiatrist Daniel Stern (2000) video recorded and analyzed the second-by-second preverbal interactions between mothers and infants occurring through gaze, facial expressions, and vocalizations. Stern became intrigued with the lasting impact of "moments of meeting" during shared activity, emotion, and contact between caregiver and child. He asserted that these small exchanges play a crucial role in the development of relationships and capabilities.

What is actually happening in moments of meeting has fascinated people across a range of time and disciplines. Philosopher Martin Buber (1937) stated that "all real living is meeting" (p. 11). Psychotherapist Carl Rogers (1957) spoke of "a real experiential meeting of persons, in which each of us is changed" (as cited in Kirschenbaum & Henderson, 1989, p. 48). During 14 years of working with children with autism and developmental disabilities, music therapists Paul Nordoff and Clive Robbins (2007) described "meeting the music child" in emerging steps in communication and interaction during shared musical play. In the kindergarten classrooms of teacher Vivian Paley (1997, 2010), it is in moments of play that the children's developing interests and relationships with each other are often clearly revealed. As music therapist Deforia Lane (2016) shares songs at University Hospitals of Cleveland, the patients and family members and medical staff experience the caring of human connection. In varying ways, people from a number of fields of endeavor have expressed an idea crystallized by psychotherapist Irvin Yalom (2017): The heart of a therapeutic encounter is in moments of authentic deeply human meeting between people. These perspectives—from psychotherapy, developmental psychology, music therapy, and early childhood education—have corresponded with my belief in the importance of focusing attention on small, easily overlooked, and sometimes unspoken "moments of meeting." However, I want to re-envision these moments of contact with young children on the spectrum in our preschool class: I believe that it is vital to focus on a broader range of moments of meeting that occurred during our music therapy group. These moments included not only the breakthroughs and positive signs of development, but also the questions, problems, and everyday challenges that we encountered within the group.

CONCENTRATING THE FOCUS ON KEY PARTICIPANTS

As I look back to review the 43 video recordings involving 14 children during my 2 year's research of classroom music sessions, I know that it will be impossible to describe and examine *all* of the experiences and people in the music group during these years. I need to find a way to concentrate the focus of what I will describe and share with others. So, I will center this book on the three children who remained in the classroom for the majority of both years—Dylan, Emily, and Gabriel— along with three key staff members—David, Elizabeth, and Rachel. I will follow them through time, transcribing and discussing video excerpts from the music therapy sessions spanning both years.

Beginning to Learn About the Children

Before entering preschool, Dylan, Emily, and Gabriel had each been diagnosed with autism based on pediatricians' assessments and diagnostic tests and on evaluations completed with the preschool's speech therapists, behavior analysts, and other specialists. The three children's ages at the beginning of the study were:

- Dylan: 3 years, 1 month;
- Gabriel: 3 years, 2 months;
- Emily: 3 years, 3 months.

Dylan, Emily, and Gabriel were part of a diverse class: Eleven of the 14 children who participated came from bilingual families whose native languages included Filipino, Arabic, Spanish, Hebrew, Thai, and Russian. As Rachel, an assistant teacher in the classroom, expressed informally in an interview, "So we had a bunch of kids who were bilingual . . . or actually, not lingual, in a [conventional] way . . . since most of them did not speak." Parent reports and school evaluations indicated varied communication challenges among Gabriel, Emily, and Dylan. Gabriel demonstrated significant language and communication delays in both Spanish and English and did not yet use spoken language. Emily currently did not usually use expressive language in Filipino or English. Dylan's profile was different: At home (in Arabic) and in the classroom (in English), he was demonstrating his emerging abilities in speaking and understanding language. But in formal assessments, he was not able or willing to complete any of the test items that required receptive or expressive language. Emily, Dylan, and Gabriel could also sometimes appear withdrawn or disinterested in social interactions, often seeming not to give attention to the classmates and teachers around them.

Therefore, one early challenge that I faced: How could I help nurture the development of shared attention and joint activity, which are foundations for learning and social interactions and communication? How could the teachers and I build upon the children's interests and support their involvement in shared activities through play, movement, eye contact, gestures, or language? Another challenging question arose during my music sessions: How much did accompanying intellectual impairment impact the preschoolers in this class? Even within the initial small class group of six, there was substantial variability in the children's comprehension, language use, and practical skills in everyday tasks. It was difficult to discern how much the delays in language ability and in cognitive, social, and practical skills might be the result of the intertwined factors of autism, second-language learning, underlying intellectual impairment, and other issues.

In addition to learning about challenging questions, as the weeks went by, I also started to become more familiar with Emily's, Gabriel's, and Dylan's skills, interests, and abilities. While Emily initially seemed to be a nearly silent but alert observer, I learned from her family that she showed interest in music at home, was responsive to audio recordings, and made sing-song sounds while playing. This book chronicles how Emily's involvement with songs, musical instruments, and vocal expressions started to grow in our class, and began to motivate her attention, interpersonal interactions, and communication. With Dylan, I eventually discovered that his reading skills were more advanced than many typically developing students' abilities. His attraction to written language along with his responsiveness to visual materials and the tactile feel of instruments eventually became pathways toward increasing interpersonal contact and exchanges. Gabriel's vitality was sparked by chances to move, sway, and bounce. His reoccuring disengagement or low energy would change into action and personal connections through the rhythms and the music. These examples of Gabriel's, Dylan's, and Emily's active participation emerged gradually, however, after early phases when it was hard to foster connection and engagement in shared play.

I write about the children's interests and abilities to give a more balanced representation of their mixture of engagement and difficulties during class. I also want to foreshadow a major theme of this book: the possibilities for developing relationships with preschoolers on the spectrum while tapping into their enthusiasms during shared music experiences. Autism researcher Barry Prizant (2016) writes,

"With enthusiasms, by definition, you already have something they're interested in, so use that to maximize learning" (as cited in Murray Law, 2016, p. 54). Music engenders enthusiasm for many children. And it can help motivate interpersonal connections and learning. As we tapped into music's potential, our preschool music group was taking part in a wider tradition stretching back to Leo Kanner's reports of autism in 1943, in which he presented 11 case studies of children on the spectrum. Kanner repeatedly referred to the musical interests and capabilities of many of these youngsters. Building on young people's curiosity about and attraction to music can be a promising way for schools to strengthen children's engagement and development.

What Terms Are People Using When They Write About Autism?

People have differing preferences today when writing or speaking about individuals who have a diagnosis of autism. There are many autistic self-advocates, professionals, and family members who prefer identity-first language (e.g., "autistic person"; cf. Botha et al., 2021; Bottema-Beutel et al., 2021). From this perspective, being autistic is essential and inherent to a person's identity. Autism is a different way of experiencing and interacting with the world, with each person having a combination of abilities, interests, perceptions, and challenges in contrast with defining autism by impairments or negative impacts. There are also family members, helping professionals, and individuals on the spectrum who prefer person-first language (e.g., "person with autism"). This viewpoint advocates recognition and respect of a person, first, rather than leading with a label, in an effort to emphasize that there's much more to an individual than their diagnosis (Gray, 2020; Kenny et al., 2016).

Because of the wide variation among those on the autism spectrum, a plurality of terms and beliefs may continue to be used in writing and talking about autism, which may change over time. In this book, I will endeavor to use an individual's preferred autism terms when known, and in cases in which an individual's language preference is not known to me, I will use varying terms including identity-first and person-first language. I will also use "on the autism spectrum," which some surveys have indicated may currently be a less polarizing alternative (cf. Bury et al., 2020; Kenny et al., 2016). My intent is to write about the spectrum in a way that is respectful, considering people's differing viewpoints.

Furthermore, this book does not aim to encapsulate the experiences of all children on the autism spectrum in early education. The range of abilities, interests, and life circumstances of autistic preschoolers varies widely—in this educational center and in many communities beyond it. Children's individuality and their varied experiences will not be encompassed in sufficient detail in any one account or research study. Instead, my goal is to portray and learn from one specific local class of children who were in the earliest stages of communication and intellectual development.

Introducing the Teachers

During the 2 years of my research, eight staff members took part in the music group for brief periods of time, including three teaching interns, a one-to-one aide, and an additional assistant teacher in the 2nd year. However, there were three primary staff members who remained with the class for the majority of the 2-year period: David, the lead teacher, and Rachel and Elizabeth, the assistant teachers. In future chapters, there are instances when I describe David, Rachel, and Elizabeth simply as teachers, rather than restating their respective titles and roles.

David had been working with children on the autism spectrum for 12 years. When my study began, he was 36 years old and the father of three young children. He shared with me that his daughter had Down syndrome and had responded positively to music therapy as part of her early intervention services. David was a kind, skilled, supportive person to work with. So was Elizabeth, the veteran assistant teacher and parent who had been working with children on the spectrum for 16 years. Rachel, the other assistant teacher, was also a parent and an experienced early childhood educator. I realize how fortunate I was to have had the chance to work with these professionals, who treated me as a valued member of their team. Daily, they played an essential collaborative part in encouraging the children's involvement in music. When the teachers told me that music therapy was becoming a favorite time of the week for them and for the children, it reinforced my energy and commitment. I continue to appreciate the chance that I had to work with them!

ABOUT THIS BOOK

"I tell the story of our year together because teachers, educators, parents, and others are always in need of personal, direct accounts from the classroom," wrote educator Daniel Meier (1997). I hope this book, in its own way, will meet today's need for a detailed account of the collaboration of a music therapist and teachers to support preschool children's early steps in shared attention, interaction, and communication through participation in music. This book is organized chronologically: The chapters describe and analyze successive video excerpts of music therapy sessions from October through May during 2 consecutive school years. At the end of each chapter, Suggestions for Reflection are offered to highlight particular developments and dilemmas and to invite discussion of issues that arose during the music sessions. The book's concluding chapter summarizes the challenges that the children, teachers, and I faced, and the developments in our abilities and connections with each other which emerged during the music therapy sessions.

What Can This Book Contribute?

This book is the first 2-year descriptive research study of a music therapy group with preschool children on the autism spectrum in a U.S. public school. I hope that, because a sustained inside view of music therapy in this context has not been published before, my work will raise awareness of the potential of music to engage children who experience substantial challenges, and who also display considerable capabilities, during preschool learning. The book is intended to bring attention to the earliest steps in shared attention, communication, and interaction with young children on the spectrum. These early developments are often less understood and represented in research because these initial actions may be small, complex, or preverbal. Research that gives a personal and descriptive account and extends for 2 years can promote understandings that will contrast or complement broader randomized controlled and often-depersonalized studies of shorter duration, which are currently given precedence by many journals and publishers.

What Brought Me to This Classroom?

Several experiences in my own background led me toward working with this group of children and teachers. I grew up in a small town in Indiana, much different from my eventual working environment, and moved to Massachusetts for college studies. After 4 years, I was planning to undertake graduate studies at Oxford University, thinking I might become a writer and college professor. But my path changed. Instead, I began working near the Truxton Circle neighborhood of Washington, DC, at a nonprofit organization, So Others Might Eat (SOME), which provided meals and medical services to people who were homeless. My change of direction was sparked by an article in a faith-based news-letter that asked, "Do you want to help others?" I found myself drawn to this simple question, as if it activated instincts inside me to become more involved in responding to people's basic needs.

Helping to serve meals to 600 people each day at SOME, I met many people who continue to influence me—Juan, Fraser, Russ, Christine, Jennings, Glen, Armando—as I witnessed their actions in facing the ad-versities in their lives, even when their situations were very difficult. Years later, I began working with children diagnosed with cerebral palsy, Down syndrome, intellectual disabilities and other developmental differences. I also started to offer music therapy sessions with preschoolers on the au-tism spectrum. Even though the children's realities were much different from those of the individuals at SOME, I carried with me the idea that there is far more potential within people than the world often recognizes, and that I could support people who were taking steps in facing life's fun-damental challenges.

After volunteering at So Others Might Eat for a year, I was hired. This began 15 years of my working with several grassroots organizations in Washington, DC: a shelter for women who were homeless, an after-school program for children and adolescents from low-income families, and a service-learning center that organized volunteer opportunities and educational programs for college students. At the same time, I was also exploring music—writing songs in collaboration with fellow musician Mark Chinen. In addition, I started to work with an organization called Arts for the Aging, which gave me opportunities to share music with people in psychiatric hospitals, Alzheimer's groups, treatment centers, and intergenerational day programs for children and adults.

In fact, I began to believe that involvement in music might be the deepest way for me to connect with and support people. When I was able to join with others during music making—people singing, play-ing instruments, heads nodding, feet tapping in time, bodies swaying or dancing—the distance between us seemed to lessen and there were opportunities for shared benefits and enjoyment. As I encouraged and facilitated people's involvement in music and formed relationships through this, I became inspired by music's power to promote the health and development of people with a range of abilities and disabilities. Neurologist Oliver Sacks (2007) wrote that it was through music that he was able to connect with members of a group of young people on the autism spectrum whom he had previously been unable to get to know. Sacks not only identified music's ability to open doorways for initial contact, he also expressed the continuing possibilities and benefits of music for many different people across a wide range of health and wellness needs: "In therapeutic terms, this is an extraordinary modality . . . because [for some people] it can bring ability where there's been disability, and freedom where people have been locked-in, and it gives delight to people, there's something intrinsically joyful about music" (Sacks, as cited in Wacks & Klotz, 1996).

I came to Boston to pursue training in· music therapy—to combine my hope of helping others with my interests in music. I undertook studies through Antioch University, Berklee College of Music, and Lesley University. After completing coursework for my master's degree and 1,200 hours of clinical training and then passing the national examination, I became a credentialed music therapist (MT-BC, music therapist, board certified). During subsequent years of study for my PhD, I began working with the preschool that would eventually become the site of my research for this book. With the permission of many families and the cooperation of teachers, I was excited to undertake doctoral research that would not seem dry or remote but closely relevant to my ongoing professional work. And I looked forward to the benefits that increased reflection through video analysis would bring. I still recall something that lead teacher David said to me before my work in the preschool class began: "The children may cry a lot during the early sessions when you start to lead the group. So, don't be worried. It often takes the kids a while to get used to a new person or new things." Well, I worried anyway. A classroom filled with the sounds of crying would be hard on everyone involved. However, I believed then, as I still do, that music can help nurture, support, and engage people. This conviction had formed from my experiences sharing music with groups for the previous 10 years and during my 18-year work life with people with a range of differing ages and needs. As I looked ahead toward the coming months with the preschoolers, what I did not know yet was how many new difficulties, discoveries, and moments of connection lay ahead.

SUGGESTIONS FOR REFLECTION

Before closing this chapter, I want to express my belief that teachers and related service providers working in a particular community know the most about the distinctive needs and potentials in their own classrooms. So, I raise the topics below in the spirit of sharing ideas about fostering engagement with young children, while encouraging helping professionals' own initiatives and reflections in early childhood classrooms. I hope that these suggestions may support you in exploring the following approaches:

- **Focusing on your own classroom and specific context**, setting, and situation. Your immersion in that local context opens the way to being responsive to the needs of your specific community and classroom and to giving further attention and review to your work.
- **Building relationships with the individual children in the class and the other teachers, one-to-one aides, and specialists.** Each of the varied class members plays a key role in enabling the group to nurture abilities and participation.
- **Learning by doing.** Gaining understanding from personal experience is a vital complement to the study of others' writing and research about educational and therapeutic approaches with young children on the autism spectrum. This book advocates learning from the questions and insights that arise when leading a class by taking time to review and analyze the interactions in your daily life in school.
- **Undertaking research in your classroom for the purpose of *discovery* and developing your understanding, and sharing the insights with others** as an alternative to the goal of testing and confirming preselected methods and hypotheses.
- **Exploring the possibility of making video recordings of class activities after receiving the permission of families, children, and school**. Video recordings give you multiple opportunities to review and see more clearly and in more detail the responses of the children and your staff team during class sessions. This enables further reflection, analysis, and adjustment of classroom practices to meet the needs of participants. Reaching out to parents, guardians, and school staff to ask their permission for filming specific activities is essential and can also enhance our learning as educators and group leaders.
- **Incorporating music therapy in early childhood education and school-based autism services.** One of my central goals is to encourage educators and other adults to bring into play the powers of music to increase young children's participation, motivation, and abilities to learn during class. As touched upon earlier, the potentially pivotal impact of music for

some children is highlighted in the words of neurologist Oliver
Sacks (2007). Have you experienced related moments that
reveal music's influence on and appeal for the children in your
class?

- **Giving thoughtful attention to the challenges and
  problems that arise, not only to the successful efforts
  and outcomes.** Over time, deeper understanding comes from
  paying attention to and reflecting on interactions and attempts
  that don't go as planned and that raise questions for us. I
  believe that we can help each other when we share information
  about the difficulties and questions that we encounter in
  addition to the approaches that can help foster engagement and
  learning.

Part I

THE FIRST SCHOOL YEAR OF MUSIC THERAPY WITH THE CHILDREN

CHAPTER 1

Gabriel and "Ten Fingers"
November 19

"But it's time . . . ," I say, reaching for a picture from my bag, "to do a little . . ." Then I pause. I look toward the six preschoolers seated in front of me—James, Caleb, Gabriel, Emily, Dylan, and Erik—and three adult teaching staff—Julie, Elizabeth, and Kristy. I show them a drawing with printed text underneath that depicts two people who are dancing or walking together. I don't yet say the final part of my sentence. Leaving out the missing last word can create the feeling of a guessing game. This may arouse the children to react or speak up. I look around at each class member in the circle to invite vocalizations, eye contact, or body motions in response to the activity picture that I'm showing.

"Move-em . . . ," Dylan slowly says, starting to pronounce the sounds in the printed word beneath the drawing.

"Yes, Movement!" I say, with pleasure. If previously he's surprised me by not saying his name, despite our urging—here I'm happy that he volunteers to speak up and to try to sound out the word underneath the picture. Since I haven't spoken that word yet, this brings a welcome dawning of awareness for me that at age 3, Dylan has an ability to sight read words! This is a skill that is in advance of a number of his peers throughout the preschool.

"Movement," affirms teaching intern Julie as she smiles at Dylan.

I continue displaying the picture and word to the students, while moving it around the circle to show each student a close-up view. When I bring it in front of Emily, she doesn't seem to look. She herself, however, is in the midst of movement, holding up the sole of her small foot toward me, tugging on her toes with her hand like she is doing a yoga stretch. Is this just "off-task" behavior? Is it simply a physical release of energy? Or is this Emily's own movement response to the "movement" drawing and Dylan's speaking the word?

The student next to her, Gabriel, doesn't seem to respond to the picture in any way. He is slumped down across his seat as if resting on a recliner. As I bring the picture into his line of sight, he remains motionless. Gabriel has recently become 3 years old. He seems bigger than his classmates. For example, a year earlier, his head's circumference placed him in the 98th percentile for children his age. And yet in other ways he seemed so young during previous class sessions, perhaps because of his sudden ebullience when happy and his tempestuous upsets when frustrated.

Today he is wearing a cream-colored long-sleeve shirt, which contrasts with his dark curly hair and brown skin. His family speaks Spanish and English. At this moment, Gabriel is also wearing a bright blue weighted vest. The weights are sewn into the vest's lining and result in steady light pressure on the body. This use of weights is intended to help children with sensory processing disorders, autism, or ADHD to decrease hyperactivity or repetitive movements and to improve children's ability to pay attention and relax while sitting. Weighted vests are usually used at the recommendation of a classroom's occupational therapist. Before the music therapy session, the staff had already placed the blue weighted vest on Gabriel because earlier in the day he had been agitated. He had been making repeated distress-filled "eeee" sounds, kicking his feet, and rubbing his eyes.

Now, as the music therapy session continues, he no longer seems upset, but now he doesn't appear alert or attentive. For more than 30 seconds at the beginning of this movement activity, he remains nearly motionless, with his legs spread out in front of him and both his arms seemingly inert in the same position: elbows on the chair's armrests with his left hand held up, palm open, as if he were nearly asleep in a waiting-room chair.

I start to lead the activity called "Ten Fingers," which is a chant with accompanying movements. This is not like an ancient plainsong chant of monks or the shouted chants of a crowd at a sports event. It's more akin to kids chanting during jump rope. But my tempo is closer to slow tai chi movements. I make the pitch of my voice rise and fall to the rhymes, like weaving a story or poem.

I find that this hybrid of rhyme, movement, and singsong speaking can sometimes engage members of the class, especially as a change of pace from faster music segments during a session. In the next few pages, I'd like to detail several of the challenging and encouraging events during this chant/movement activity.

I reach my hands forward to show my 10 fingers extended, palms facing the group. I begin, "I have . . ."

But just then, Emily gets out of her chair and starts walking away from the group.

"Emily," says Julie, moving forward to get hold of Emily's elbow, "Emily sit." Julie steers Emily back into the chair, which she reluctantly assents to after a few fervent protesting vocalizations.

Meanwhile, I continue, "I have 10 fingers," as I stretch my hands toward the children, wiggling all fingers. "And they belong to me." I bring both my hands toward me and cross them on my chest.

In these few moments, I'm starting to get the beginnings of the group's attention as I see four of the six children (Erik, Dylan, Caleb, and James) looking at my movements, sitting up in their chairs, and focusing on the activity. I'm not sure about Gabriel and Emily.

Actually, I am pretty sure about Gabriel—he is still slumped back in his chair, and his head tilts backward far enough that I can hardly see his face. Julie is propping up his hands halfway in an attempt to get him to follow along with the movements and rhyme.

But with his elbows still resting on the armrests of the chair and his hands being held upward by Julie, I somehow imagine a stagecoach passenger getting robbed in an old cowboy movie, hands propped up in an "I surrender" gesture. The four children who are sitting up and giving their attention aren't moving their hands or arms along to the chant either. Then I see Erik bringing his hands to his chest, joining in the motion that I showed for "they belong to me." Ah, nice to see this!

I pause. I circle my fists around each other, like two planets orbiting, saying, "I can make them do things." I'm enjoying moving my arms and shoulders. Then I see a few of the children also move or make sounds. Dylan leans toward me in his chair. Erik starts rotating his hands around each other, following my motions.

"Good job, Erik!" I say. "C'mon James, you know this one!"

Gabriel begins to make an "eeee" vocal sound. He extends his legs and feet into the circle. Otherwise, he is still unmoving.

But this is about to change. I say, "I can shut them up tight," bracing my hands on my legs, and squeezing my fists tight. My face is animated with pretend strenuous effort, my voice adding a forceful sound, "oooo-oughhhhh."

This is the moment when Gabriel starts to become active. Like someone doing leg lifts, he begins to raise up and pull back his feet, which had been languidly extended into the circle. He simultaneously raises his midsection, shoulders and head more upright.

"Try this, Dylan," I say, with another "ouggghhhhh." I have a funny-looking pinched-together expression on my face as I tighten my fists. I continue, "I can open them . . . ," as I soundlessly slowly spread my hands wider and wider apart.

Gabriel is sitting forward in his chair now. When he initially sits upright again, it takes him a moment to focus. But now he is looking directly at me, a smile on his face and an expectant gaze.

I barely whisper the word "wide." Teachers Julie and Elizabeth join me in softly and slowly extending the word, saying, "wi——de." I really extend my arms, chest open. I take time.

The room is quiet for a moment. The only sound is the very faint voice of Emily vocalizing a sound like "wa-wa" in a tiny voice (which, in retrospect, I recognize as a possible approximation of the "w" starting sound of the word "wide").

Then I say, "I can put them to-gether . . ." Pause. Then I give a sharp clap of my hands!

Caleb brings his hands together just as I've done, and he actually claps three times. Erik opens his arms wide too and brings his palms together as I clap.

Gabriel has moved up in his seat, giving another clear smile, and he starts swinging his legs up and down underneath his chair a few times in apparent excitement. I am smiling too, and I am experimenting with saying and doing the rhymes and movements in a way that is some-how fresh for me. I'm enjoying a sense of anticipation myself. Now the majority of the children and staff are sharing a common focus in the group activity.

After clapping my hands together, I keep my two palms touching, extending my joined hands outward toward the group, held still with deliberateness and intention.

Caleb imitates me, hands held together. James also has hands to-gether, but they are near his face, and James is smiling, almost as if he is on the verge of laughing.

My smile is like that too. I say, "And make them both . . ." and I lean forward, separating my hands and slowly stretching each of them around my sides and behind my back.

"Hide," says Julie, very softly, barely audible.

I don't yet say the end of the line, "hide." I am still focusing on try-ing to communicate nonverbally, "Can you see this; will you join me?" I am still trying to invite responses from the children, hoping that the pause may again prompt them to fill-in-the-blank with a sound or a movement.

Erik reaches both his hands behind his back, following my actions. Assistant teacher Elizabeth says, "Yeah, Erik!"

James also approximates this motion by bringing his hands to his sides. "Good job," says Kristy, his classroom aide.

A little later than the others, Emily starts to angle her outstretched arms behind her head, a response that is also possibly a variation of my reaching-behind-the-back motion.

"I can make them jump . . . high!" I say with an ebullient "j" sound for "jump," and my voice projects a high-pitched shaking quality on the word "high!" I raise both my hands straight up into the air, moving my arms and shoulders with rapid force.

One of the children squeals. It is Gabriel who makes a high-pitched giggly sound, his face bright, his body bouncing. His attention, movements, and vocalizing represent a palpable shift from his earlier passivity. Julie seems to catch his new liveliness too, making her own "woo-woo" sound while taking Gabriel's arms and shaking them.

"I can make them go . . . low," I say, moving my arms down toward the ground, drumming my fingers on the floor, quickly up and down.

Erik touches the floor with his fingers too.

Elizabeth directs Dylan's arm toward the ground. He touches down but then pops immediately back up.

"Try it, Caleb," I say, trying to encourage the other children too. "Can you come low with me?"

And Caleb does! He bends down and touches his hands to the floor.

Kristy says, "Good job, James," as he joins in too. Kristy sounds genuinely pleased and surprised that he joins in the motions voluntarily.

Now Dylan, perhaps influenced by seeing the actions of his peers and hearing the praises given by adults, vigorously reaches back down to the floor and joins me and the other children.

I look around the circle and for a moment most of us are doing the same thing, although Gabriel gets some very direct physical persuasion from Julie to bend over.

"Everybody's doing great!" I say.

Then, as we near the end of the movement chant, I say, "I can put them together . . . and put them . . . just . . . so." My fingers are interlaced and now placed in my lap. I am sitting upright.

There are 4 seconds of quiet in the group, after I say "just . . . so." Then I softly say, "Good!" and I start to turn toward my bag to get out the picture symbol and objects for the next activity. Somehow, creating shared quiet space sometimes also promotes the attention and engagement of the children and teachers, in alternation with the music, words, and movements.

REFLECTIONS AFTERWARD: GABRIEL'S AGITATION, LETHARGY, AND ACTIVE MOVEMENTS

As I described earlier, Gabriel had been wearing a weighted vest designed to foster calmness, because before the music session he had showed agitation: making distress-filled sounds, rubbing his eyes, and kicking his feet against the floor. Then after two songs, as we began the "Ten Fingers" movement activity, Gabriel had become relaxed but also lethargic. He reclined in his chair, not responding, and looked almost to be in a trance when I showed him the picture of the activity. He remained passive and immobile for the first 45 seconds, and then his level of arousal changed. As the "Ten Fingers" chant and movements continued, he sat up (body posture), smiled (facial expression), directed his gaze and his attention toward me and toward the movements (shared attention), vocalized a high-pitched giggle (preverbal communication), and moved his arms and body in response to the activity.

Over-arousal and Under-arousal

Preschoolers on the spectrum, like Gabriel, can experience distinctive issues related to level of arousal. An estimated 80% of children diagnosed with autism may have co-occurring challenges in dealing with sensory input (Case-Smith et al., 2015). Three primary types of sensory processing issues have been identified:

1. *Hypersensitivity*, or over-responsivity, which refers to elevated reactions to stimuli (e.g., distress from specific sounds, heightened sensitivity or discomfort with certain kinds of touch)
2. *Hyposensitivity*, or under-responsivity, which describes slow or reduced response to sensory input
3. *Seeking*, which denotes pursuit of sensory stimulation (e.g., rocking, spinning, or repetitive movements)

Gabriel's agitation and subsequent inertia could be viewed as examples of the opposites of hyper- and hypo-responsiveness. In addition, some children, like Gabriel, have shown alternating patterns of both over- and under-arousal, resulting in fluctuations that can be challenging for individuals, families, and professionals. In a study by Baranek et al. (2006), 38% of the children on the spectrum evidenced both hyper- and hypo-responsiveness.

Self-Regulation and Emotional Regulation

Gabriel's changes from agitation to passivity to subsequent attention could also be understood as examples of the problems and potentials of self-regulation. Self-regulation involves people's ability to manage their emotions, cognitions (e.g., attention), actions, interpersonal interactions, and arousal level (Laurent & Gorman, 2018). When children on the spectrum experience difficulties regulating their sensory experiences and levels of arousal, or when they become distressed, fearful, or disengaged, it can interfere with education and growth. Conversely, more pleasurable and comfortable levels of arousal can play an important part in assisting children's ability to learn, interact, and communicate.

The SCERTS model for working with children on the autism spectrum has made emotional regulation, an aspect of self-regulation, a central part of its clinical and pedagogical approach (Prizant et al., 2006). The acronym SCERTS refers to social communication (SC), emotional regulation (ER), and transactional support (TS), which are viewed as three primary dimensions that need to be addressed to promote the development of children on the spectrum. In describing the ER component, the authors state that "emotional regulatory capacities enable a child to be organized and focused, to problem solve, to communicate, to maintain social engagement, and to be 'available' for learning" (p. 4). Specific examples of emotional regulation goals at a prelinguistic level include expanding a child's repertoire of alerting strategies (e.g., taking part in jumping or movement-based song routines) for a child who is typically in a low state of arousal. For a child who is typically in a high state of arousal, developing a repertoire of calming techniques can help (e.g., holding a favorite object or engaging in rhythmic motions or movement activities). Other emotional regulation strategies for cognitive and language development may focus on introducing activity schedules with pictures and written words to symbolize sequences and transitions of upcoming class events. Supporting a child's ability to acquire and use language to identify emotions or make requests can also assist with emotional regulation (e.g., learning to ask for a break from an activity when a child begins to become overwhelmed).

The SCERTS model emphasizes the benefits of fostering more-optimal states of arousal in order to facilitate the growth of social and communication skills.

Gabriel's Cyclical Pattern and His Response to Rhythmic Chants, Movement, Facial Expressions, and Sound Effects

Reflecting on the sequence of Gabriel's changing response levels, I saw a reoccurring pattern in some of the early sessions with him: Even if he had been anxious beforehand or during the early parts of class, he usually became more at ease during the music group, with its consistent opening routines and the exchanges with teachers, peers, and me. Nevertheless, sometimes he could veer toward lethargy, perhaps caused by boredom, release, or difficulties with using spoken language or understanding the picture symbols or printed vocabulary that we tried to introduce. So, I think that the music, the routines, and social exchanges could calm Gabriel, but he actively began to attend and respond when we added movement (like opening my arms wide or squeezing my fists together tight), along with heightened facial expressions (my face animated with pretend strenuous effort) and sound effects ("ooo-oughhhhh," I said, after "I can shut them up tight").

Analyzing this excerpt with Gabriel has helped me realize with greater clarity that cultivating more-balanced states of arousal—thereby fostering readiness for learning and interaction with children like Gabriel—was a central goal in my music therapy work in this classroom. I relied on music's ability to alter arousal level, mood, emotion, attention, and behavior (cf. Juslin & Sloboda, 2010) in my attempts to help Gabriel and each of the class members.

THINKING ABOUT GOALS—GRAVITATING TOWARD COLLECTIVE AND EMERGENT LEARNING

When fellow music therapist Sharon Gan offered written feedback about my November 19th session with the preschoolers, she wrote, "I would like to know your music therapy goals/objectives with Gabriel." This made me pause and reflect. Teachers and school-based therapists are trained to begin with SMART goals—specific, measurable, attainable, relevant, and time based—for one individual child. And school professionals are often urged to focus on stimulating this child's concrete behaviors. For example, here is a sample music therapy goal if a therapist wanted to help a young girl develop her verbal communication and her ability to memorize personal information: "Given music mnemonic strategies (song melody presentation), Justine will recite her phone number through song independently with 100% accuracy in four of five trials" (Coast Music Therapy, n.d.) Yet because I was leading group music therapy sessions, I was channeling more energy toward the plans for the class as a whole rather than initially focusing on individual objectives.

Over time, I gained awareness about the needs and interests of each child in the class. And I sought to adjust group activities to give opportunities for social interaction and communication that were tailored for each of the preschooler's distinct abilities and limitations. But this took time and emerged gradually. Overall, I perceive that my initial approach was often more collective than individually centered. I was seeking to promote shared engagement, reciprocal interactions, group cohesion, and opportunities to communicate, socially interact, move, and enjoy music and self-expression. I also aimed to have the music help facilitate social and emotional learning, and foster self-regulation and mutual regulation, while offering chances for active participation in a group with varying abilities and needs.

Subtle and Small Early Steps of Communication

Early on, however, I was receiving only subtle, and usually preverbal, signs that my efforts were having an impact on the preschoolers. When I spread my arms open and whispered the word "wide," Emily vocalized the sound "wa-wa" in a tiny voice, leading me to believe that she was approximating the starting "w" sound of the word "wide" while also imitating the hushed voice volume that I used. When I placed my hands behind my back and encouraged the group to join me in my motions later in the session, Emily started to angle her outstretched arms behind her head in what also seemed to be an idiosyncratic approximation of my movement. These moments could be easily overlooked or interpreted differently, but I have come to believe that they were small, just-perceptible signs of vocal approximation and motor imitation for Emily.

Classmates Erik, Caleb, and James also joined in the movements of the chant activity: clapping and opening arms wide. In addition, the visual pictures and words prompted Dylan's spoken communication: "Move-em," he says, approximating the sounds of the printed letters. Retrospective video analysis helped develop my awareness of some of the children's small early steps in communication and interactive movement, even as it has shown me evidence of Gabriel's agitation, dormancy, *and* moments of balanced arousal and attention.

Developmental Level and Communication Abilities

To what degree might cognitive delays have been affecting Gabriel's ability to participate in class? Maenner et al. (2020) estimate that 33% of children on the autism spectrum may have co-occurring intellectual disability. During our weekly music therapy sessions, was Gabriel experiencing more difficulty than the other members of his class in understanding the activities and in preverbal communication? School reports stated that Gabriel, at 38 months old, tested at an 18- to 24-month level for cognitive abilities and displayed speech and language skills at the 3- to 21-month level—which were notably lower than a number of preschoolers in his chronological age group. While standard assessments have limitations for measuring the abilities of people who may have incomplete understanding of assessment tasks (or the motivation or current communication skills to engage in the tasks), these results suggested that Gabriel might be impacted by significant cognitive and communication delays. But how many of Gabriel's challenges which I observed during music sessions could be ascribed to developmental differences from his classmates or, conversely, to my limitations in finding the best ways to engage him, or to other possible explanations?

In retrospect, I believe that Gabriel's absence of verbal communication during most of the music therapy sessions contributed to my uncertainty about the extent of his cognition, and this may have narrowed my abilities in interacting with him. More than one-third of children diagnosed with autism have been estimated to be minimally verbal or nonspeaking (Koegel et al., 2020). So as I looked ahead to future music sessions, I faced a question: In addition to encouraging verbal or vocal communication, could I also find nonspeaking ways to engage Gabriel and other minimally verbal students, as we had to some extent with the movements, sound effects, and facial expressions during the "Ten Fingers" activity?

SUGGESTIONS FOR REFLECTION

- **What actions and ideas can support preschool children on the spectrum in dealing with experiences of over- or under-arousal?** What activities might be incorporated into a child's home and school environments to enhance their emotional and self-regulation and their ability to attend to shared learning and interpersonal exchanges?

- **When intellectual disability or communication delays are impacting children in the class**, what are ways to adapt educational approaches in efforts to promote the children's participation, preverbal communication, and engagement? One strategy to consider is combining rhythmic verses and playful preverbal sounds and facial expressions while encouraging shared accompanying body movements. These interwoven activities can stimulate shared attention, interpersonal interactions, and children's learning of early language and concepts.

CHAPTER 2

Emily's Turn
December 3

December comes, and the cloudy winter skies appear motionless, like a hazy blanket covering the sky. But perhaps this morning's scattering of snow is a sign of a coming change. In our classroom music group, five children and three teachers gather in a circle. It's about to be Emily's turn in the "Hello Song," as I welcome each child one by one. Her dark brown hair is straight and short, and she has bangs down to her eyebrows. She is 3 years and 4 months old and is the smallest person in the class. Of the 14 different children who will attend this class over the next 2 years, she will be one of three girls to participate. Currently in the United States, autism is about four times more likely to be diagnosed in boys than in girls.

According to school records, Emily has initially responded to her teachers' attempts to involve her in activities by looking away, leaving the area, throwing items, or having outbursts of frustration. Her parents have expressed concern that she has very limited use of language in English or Filipino, which is spoken in her home. Formal assessments present a mixed picture, finding that Emily often does not exhibit joint attention or social interaction for communication but that she will sometimes attend to music and singing.

If melodies and sounds can attract Emily's attention, I'm hopeful that the combination of music and familiar actions during activities, like our opening "Hello Song," may help spark Emily's communication and connections with the people in this preschool class. This is my aspiration not only with Emily but also with each of the children in the group.

In today's session, lead teacher David has brought in additional visual supports to include in the song—the printed words *My name is* and a photograph of each child—to help the class members better understand and participate in the process of saying their names. Shortly before Emily's turn in the "Hello Song," David reaches over her head to place the printed words and photograph in front of Dylan, whose turn is first. As David lifts these visual supports over Emily's head, she arches her neck and torso quickly backward, and then swings sideways in order to see David maneuvering them into Dylan's view. Then she looks at the photograph and printed words.

When her own turn begins, David attaches Emily's photograph with Velcro onto a sign made of thick laminated paper cardstock, and he reaches forward to present it to her. But before he can complete this action, Dylan speaks up. He says in a loud clear voice: "My name is . . . Em-lee." If this had been a play at the theater, Dylan would have been stealing Emily's line. His unexpected pronouncement causes one of the teachers, Rachel, to give an infectious laugh, and others in the group smile. In the midst of laughing, Rachel shakes her hair, and looks at Dylan and Emily and says, "He's gonna help you, he's gonna help you out today, Emily!"

But Emily starts looking across the circle, away from the adults and peers. Her gaze doesn't return to the group. She doesn't appear to react to Dylan saying her name, the adults' laughter, or Rachel's words.

Her face looks expressionless. But her quick movements, just moments ago, to twist her body in order to see the photograph and printed words make me think that she is still observing us while appearing to look remote. Her legs are curled together and her right hand remains at her side as if she's sitting on her hands.

In a moment, I lean forward toward Emily, trying to connect with her, and I sing: "And what's your name?" From behind Emily, David reaches forward and holds the printed words in front of her and shows Emily's photograph. I gesture toward her and ask again, "What's your name?"

Emily glances down at the words and her picture for a millisecond and quickly turns her head away to the side. Her speedy movement reminds me of a child turning her head away from a spoonful of undesired food. She then steadily looks away to her right. She makes no sound. Her expression has a neutral unchanging quality of someone who is looking past you.

David takes Emily's left hand and guides it toward each printed word, in turn, as he says, "My . . . name . . . is . . . Eh (he utters the initial vowel sound of her name, then pauses), . . . Emily."

But she does not look at the pictures, or acknowledge the closeness of David's physical presence, either to complain or to show pleasure.

She does not push him away—she just doesn't seem to be reacting. When David lets go of her hand, she lets it plop down onto the armrest. Her hand slides down the side of her chair, like a fish that had been caught and then released back into the water.

In the temporary quiet, Dylan then says, with great volume and zest, "My name is . . . David!" while suddenly reaching up his arm and pointing directly at lead teacher David. Dylan is smiling and excited. And I'm surprised again. How do I make sense of this aspect of today's music session? In previous weeks Dylan has seemed unable or unwilling to complete this part of the hello song during his own turn. Yet now he's completing it with seeming ease, paying attention to his peer's turn, and saying Emily's name. And then he says David's name and points to him, demonstrating a synchronized leap into self-initiated communication, along with a pointing gesture and responsiveness to social interactions.

Dylan and David look at each other directly for a moment. David looks down, smiles, and shakes his head, in a seeming mixture of appreciation and perplexity for Dylan's spur-of-the-moment verbal communication, which robustly interrupts Emily's turn.

To try to return the attention back to Emily, I start singing "Let's say hello to Emily," as I encourage the children and adults to respond to her by looking toward her, waving hello, or giving a verbal welcome like "Hi." Emily's gaze now follows me as I look at her and wave. She looks directly toward me and we look at each other for 2 seconds. I say, "Hi, Emily," and so do the teachers.

Assistant teacher Elizabeth leans forward and touches Emily's left arm, lifting underneath her elbow. Emily ignores this attempt to prompt her to wave hello. She keeps her hands laying on the armrests. In fact, Emily doesn't turn around to see who has touched her. Then she looks off to her left, away from people again.

So, amidst the laughter and my excitement about Dylan's lively response, I have a perplexing mixture of feelings when I think about my early interactions with Emily this morning. I have regrets that my attempts to prompt her vocal or verbal response during the "Hello Song" seem to have such slight impact, and I feel uncertainty about the best ways to help her develop vocal and gestural communication. Yet I also have an impulse to keep trying, and I am grateful for the visual supports and caring involvement offered by the teachers. And I feel a strong continuing desire to learn more about the possibilities of forging connections with the children.

EMILY'S INITIAL REACTIONS AND MY EARLY QUESTIONS

After our music session, I look further into research about children on the spectrum in order to try to develop my understanding and support of Emily. Four of the topics that I find there—about atypical facial expressions, averted gaze, and difficulties with shared attention and communication— raise questions about Emily's reactions and experiences.

Atypical Facial Expressions

Emily's face remains almost expressionless during the time that we attempt to encourage her to say her name today. She does not seem to directly react to Dylan's boisterous declaration that "my name is Em-lee," and she appears impassive as teachers and I try to engage her during her turn. This contrasts with Dylan's reactions in earlier sessions—clearly frowning when unhappy or lighting up when excited.

Is Emily's apparent blank expression during moments of the music session an example of the reduced facial expressions or flat affect attributed to some individuals diagnosed with autism, discussed in studies like Weiss et al. (2019)? Or do her expressions appear atypical because they do not follow conventional forms of acknowledging people who are close by? Will I be able to learn what she is thinking or feeling? Early in my relationship with Emily, I know that I often feel my difficulty in understanding her emotions, and her likes and dislikes, as I see her facial expressions.

Averted Gaze

Another interconnected aspect of Emily's response is her turning her gaze to the side or into the distance. She steadily looks away from us and from her photograph and the printed words, as soon as it is her turn during the "Hello Song." Does the term *averted gaze*, which I find in research on autism, describe Emily's looking away and seeming to ignore people? Is she experiencing an aversion to being asked her name, and is her response akin to Dylan's past reaction of dropping his head down into his lap? Yet Emily's responses also seem distinctively different from Dylan's as she remains upright and appears almost vigilant as she looks away.

Research by Konstantareas and Homatidis (1992) has remained on my mind and has troubled me about the possible negative impact of gaze disconnection. This study investigated the following question:

Do the parents of children with autism spend more time with their child (than a comparison selection of parents of typically developing or developmentally delayed children) because of their child's compelling specific needs? Or do the parents spend less time because their child's limited eye contact, smiling, and vocalization reduces the mutual play and communication that stimulates parents' more sustained interactions with a child? The parents of autistic children in this Ontario study reported having shorter interactions with their children than the comparison groups of parents of typically developing children or children diagnosed with cognitive delays. The study's authors also discussed parental difficulties when a child on the spectrum seemed to reject or become distressed by attempts to interact. If the results of this research have any wider applicability, it makes me wonder whether limited contact through gaze (along with other differences in social communication like fewer instances of vocalizing and proximity seeking) can create risks for a cycle of reduced interactions between parents and children, and between me and the children in the preschool class.

Difficulties With Shared Attention

Emily's looking away might also be related to joint attention difficulties, which many researchers view as a crucial early characteristic of autism (Adamson et al., 2019; Mundy, 2018). Health professionals and educators have asserted that sharing attention with another person is foundational for social development, learning, and language development, and takes place via gestures and eye gaze toward a social partner or an object during a common activity. When Emily doesn't appear to attend to the people or printed words and picture presented, or to share a common focus with class members on objects or activities, her actions can be understood as limitations in shared attention that have been exhibited by other children on the autism spectrum in previous studies.

Questions remain in my mind, however. Was Emily also revealing signs of covert attention, of noticing and absorbing what was happening, without giving the appearance of doing so? Even when she looked away from our attempts to prompt her to say her name, I sensed her awareness and alertness amidst behaviors that suggested she was ignoring us. There seemed a peripheral indirect watchfulness that enabled her to shift into showing her interest, as when she quickly swiveled her head and twisted her torso to visually track the printed text and picture when David first presented these to Dylan.

Psychologist Annie Rogers (1995) describes a similar indirect form of attention during her therapy sessions with 5-year-old Ben: "I don't look directly at him. On the periphery of my horizon of awareness, I pick up every gesture and every shift of breath. I have learned that this way I know far better what someone is thinking and feeling" (p. 123). Rather than in the direct/head-on gaze that is often thought to communicate interest and intimacy in Western cultures, Annie feels connection side-by-side with Ben, perceiving him out of the corners of her eyes. In a related way, I felt that Emily was sometimes "attending" and peripherally picking up group members' gestures and actions, though she was not showing her attention directly.

The possibility of attuning to people without depending only on eye contact was familiar to me because my own father was blind. I had learned about a person's ability to hear and sense what other people were doing and communicating in ways that were different than direct visual attention.

Issues with Communication

In what ways do core challenges in communication, which are defining characteristics of autism, impact the interaction between Emily and me during the "Hello Song"? Looking back, I think that during the early sessions of the year, I did not fully understand the difficulties of spoken communication for Emily, a 3-year-old preschooler whose family's first language was Filipino, and who was also facing significant language development delays because of the ways that autism was affecting her. School reports state that Emily currently says only a few words, in both Filipino and English. Her parents say that she sometimes "sings" in Filipino. But they report that the words are not comprehensible to them, although she approximates the intonations of the melodies. Typically developing toddlers at this age might have a vocabulary of several hundred words. So, using spoken words to exchange information and to respond to questions appears to be a fundamental challenge for Emily and for her parents, teachers, and me, as we try to connect with each other.

I also ask myself: How do I begin to more clearly understand her use of nonspeaking actions to communicate? When she appears to shut down during her turn, is she effectively communicating her disinterest or her dislike of the task of saying her name? Or do her responses suggest that the social-language routine in the "Hello Song" is something that she's still figuring out and deciding whether to participate in?

SUGGESTIONS FOR REFLECTION

These end-of-chapter questions focus on two aspects from today's session: Dylan's unexpected speaking up during Emily's turn, and Emily's silence and turning away.

- **Why do you think that Dylan might have been able and willing to say a classmate's name and a teacher's name** today, although in previous sessions he seemed unable or unwilling to say his own name?
- **Could it have been the addition of the printed words and pictures** that prompted Dylan's further verbal communication and peer awareness of Emily as well as his self-initiated interaction with a teacher, David? Or was it somehow more attainable or more preferable for Dylan to say others' names rather than his own?
- **Was disinterest the reason for the moments when Emily looked away** and didn't seem to respond? Was she resisting and refusing a non-preferred task when she was given the chance to say her name, to see and learn the printed words, *My name is . . .* , or to use a waving "hi" gesture to other people in the class group?
- **Were Emily's silent responses related to her lack of familiarity or current ability with verbal communication skills**, reading of English printed words, or using the gestures involved in the "Hello Song"?
- **Was "lack of response" only one possible interpretation of Emily's actions**, which might also be envisioned as Emily's version of indirectly observing and waiting prior to more active forms of participation? How should we understand the contrasts between moments when she clearly engages in visual attention (e.g., Emily looks directly toward my face as I wave to her; we look at each other for 2 seconds) and other instances when she definitely looks away and seems to disregard adult attempts to prompt her communication?
- **Have you experienced questions similar to these listed above when interacting with the children whom you know?** What ideas or strategies have been helpful to you when you are trying to make contact with a child, and when you are trying to understand what is causing a child's response or seeming lack of reaction?

CHAPTER 3

The "Instrument Song"

Shaking and Moments of
Meeting—January 28

We're about to invite the children to play handheld percussion instruments. I'll also play guitar and sing for this "instrument song," which is an ongoing part of each class session. I enjoy the challenge of learning and introducing new songs from a variety of folk, rhythm and blues, and international traditions. If the "Hello Song" and the "Goodbye Song" are meant to give children familiar routines, the various instrument songs are designed to introduce new music each month while giving children a consistent structure of choosing and playing instruments. And the children are able to engage in self-directed play with shakers, tambourines, bells, cabasas, gourd shekeres, wooden clappers, and other options.

The instrument song also creates an opportunity for all the class members to play together simultaneously. In many language-based activities or turn-taking games, only one person at a time is encouraged to communicate in order to minimize confusion: "For someone's turn must always and exclusively be in progress" writes sociologist Erving Goffman (1964, p. 136). But in music making with rhythm instruments, it's possible for every person in the group to simultaneously participate and play. Throughout the song, all the children can explore making sounds, moving, and responding to the actions, rhythms, and sounds of the other class members.

Prior to this whole-group play, we're starting today's class with a turn-taking opportunity. Six of the children are present on this January morning: Carlos, Gabriel, Dylan, Rowen, Caleb, Emily, and James. Five staff members are here: lead teacher David; assistant teachers Elizabeth and Rachel; Lisa, a teaching intern; and Kristy, a personal aide for James.

Several days earlier, Caleb's father had mentioned that their family had a child-sized guitar at home. Today, I'm happy that Caleb has brought it to class, and the teachers and I experiment with including it during the beginning of the instrument song as a way of connecting his music making at home and at school.

I start sliding his small black guitar out from a soft carrying case and bring it toward Caleb. Classmates Emily, Dylan, Gabriel, Rowen, and Carlos each lean forward to get a closer look. Four of the them watch Caleb for 51 seconds as he strums. Their sustained shared attention is conspicuous in a group of children who often may not appear to be giving attention to the actions of classroom peers or adults. But as Caleb strums the guitar, Emily and Rowen gaze toward him and then reach out their hands to touch the guitar too. Dylan leans far forward, smiles, and literally licks his lips. Gabriel views Caleb's playing with a happy expression. The children's focus lasts not for an instant, but for about 1 minute, in varying degrees among the individuals in the group, as Caleb strums and I sing and finger the chords for a familiar children's song.

CHOOSING A MUSICAL INSTRUMENT TO PLAY

After a while, it's time to start offering chances for all the children to pick their own instrument to play. I ask the teachers and assistants to offer two choices of rhythm instruments to each of the children near them. Choice making is one of the children's communication goals (e.g., "will communicate choices by using gestures, objects, or picture symbols"). In addition, children may simply enjoy the process of selecting their own instrument and may be motivated to play the one that they chose.

While we begin passing out instruments, lead teacher David gives Rowen an opportunity to strum Caleb's guitar, largely because Rowen has just taken a new and unusual step for him: verbalizing his request by saying, "Me too!"

Soon afterward, Dylan takes an unusual step also, bending forward and appearing to try to make eye contact with Rowen, while saying to him, "Hi!" I have rarely seen Dylan make an overt attempt to communicate with a classmate. Is there something about watching Rowen play the black guitar that motivates Dylan to try to socially interact?

Peer interaction can be a challenging area for children on the spectrum. Researchers Phillip Strain et al. (2008) write, "Whereas most preschoolers are quite reciprocal in their interactions with peers (Guralnick, 2001), young children with ASD seldom initiate social interactions (Strain & Hoyson, 2000) and tend not to respond to the initiations of others"

(p. 254). In this moment, it is notable that Rowen does not acknowledge Dylan's "Hi" in any way. However, it is significant and intriguing that Dylan has made a direct attempt to initiate interaction with a peer.

Emily Reaches for Both

When it is Emily's turn to choose between a small yellow shaker and a tan tambourine, she swiftly and wordlessly grabs for both.

"Which one do you want?" asks teaching intern Lisa. "Pick one! Which one do you want?"

Again Emily quickly grasps for both. So, Lisa tries a different approach, presenting the instruments sequentially. She intends to first offer Emily the tambourine and, next, the shaker. But Emily immediately begins beating the tambourine after it is shown to her, making me wonder. Does she actually have a preference between instruments? Does she understand or is she willing to follow the routine of selecting one choice from a field of two objects? What *has* come across clearly, however, is her interest and her direct visual attention in this moment toward people (me, Caleb) and objects (guitar, shaker, and tambourine). It is a marked difference from the turning-away behaviors that she had sometimes exhibited in earlier sessions.

Dylan's Clear Choice

I step toward Dylan to offer him a choice of instruments. I bend my knees, lowering my body until I am at his eye level. "Dylan," I say, to get his attention, and he looks.

All six of the children have turned to look at the interaction. I'm not sure why this moment catches their attention. Perhaps it is because I've stepped forward from where I usually sit in the circle, and I am bending down and moving in closer.

I offer Dylan a choice of a big yellow shaker or a wood castanet attached to a wooden spoon handle (which I call the "clacker" because it click-clacks when shaken). Without words, I lightly shake the wood clacker on his right side, pause, and then play the big yellow shaker on his left side, so that he can distinctly hear the two options.

Dylan doesn't move but looks at the two. Then, he reaches forward and grasps the castanet clacker. Dylan turns the clacker in his hands examining it. Then he shakes it with vigor.

"Oh!" I say, "That was a clear choice!" Assistant teacher Rachel simultaneously says, "[Good] choice," and smiles. We are both happily surprised in this moment that he reaches out to choose an instrument and to join in the activity, because in earlier weeks he has often ignored our offered objects and attempts to interact.

Gabriel's Yellow Mini Maraca and "Stimming"

Gabriel has silently and steadily focused on the choice-making interaction with Dylan. Then I reach toward Rachel and pass her a yellow mini maraca and a ring with small bells, and I ask, "Can you give Gabriel a choice?"

Rachel holds them both in front of him, "Gabriel, which one?"

He reaches out quickly and takes the small yellow maraca with his left hand.

"Oohh!" says Lisa encouragingly, from across the circle.

"He likes the yellow one," says Rachel, confirming his choice and consciously modeling verbal communication about preference ("likes") and color ("yellow").

Gabriel begins to rock the maraca side to side, rotating his wrist, moving it back and forth past the palm of his other hand (with an unusual scrunched-up expression while he seems to be squinting or closing one eye). Then he lifts the mini maraca up toward his face and rubs it against the side of his head. Sometimes his feet are waving as he does this. His facial expression and physical movements reflect contentment, and he is not experiencing the distress or lethargy we sometimes see with him. But Elizabeth, the teacher sitting nearest to him, becomes concerned after a while by his repetitive and slightly unusual-looking motion of squinting and rocking the mini maraca back and forth past one of his hands, like a pendulum of a clock. She views his fast "tick-tock" motion as "stimming," or perseverative self-stimulatory body movement. Determining what constitutes perseverative stimulation involves perception and opinion. Is a child's movement in some way purposeful or benign, or does it interfere with a child's ability to constructively take part in activities or interact with others? Is Gabriel's playing responsive to the music or unrelated to it? Early on, it is hard to know. But I notice that Elizabeth begins to be bothered by some of Gabriel's repeated movements, and this impacts their interaction later in this episode, as we'll see.

Carlos's Surprising Decision

Carlos is the last child to pick an instrument. Elizabeth is so sure which instrument he will want that she had asked me earlier to keep it in reserve as an option for him. She thinks he is going to choose the brown shekere—a West African percussion instrument that consists of a hollowed gourd, surrounded by beads and white cowrie seashells woven into a net covering it. The net of shells can be slid over the surface of the dried gourd, creating a distinctive gentle sound. Or the whole gourd can be shaken energetically or clapped to produce a variety of sounds.

Elizabeth holds the brown shekere and a purple mini maraca in front of Carlos and says, "Which one do you want?" Without hesitation Carlos reaches far across to his right to choose the purple mini maraca. Elizabeth shrugs in a comical way, and David, Rachel, and I laugh.

"You never can tell!" I say.

Rachel looks to Elizabeth and says, "[Well] *I'll* take the big one [the shekere]!"

Rachel turns and shares a smile with David. "I like this!" she says, "I'm gonna have to go get myself one of these." She gazes down and examines it just as the children had done when we'd passed instruments to them. Then she does an impromptu dance in her chair, shaking her hair, her torso, and the shekere, while smiling and looking at Elizabeth, who joins her in a momentary shimmy.

I really enjoy the spirit and humor that Rachel, Elizabeth, and David bring to the group. Their mutual liking and rapport promote an ease, security, and sense of fun and support within the group. A couple of the children smile during this brief playful adult exchange.

BEGINNING "FREE AT LAST"

Getting down from the chair that I usually use, I sit on the floor in front of the children. I start to sing, "Free at Last," which I've chosen as today's instrument song. The school has recently observed the Martin Luther King federal holiday, and I want to honor the legacy of Dr. King with music. I'll play the energetic expressive song that he had referred to in his "I Have a Dream" speech.

Emily's Initial Playing

When I start the rhythmic beat of the song on my guitar and begin to sing, Emily sits up from where she'd been reclining in her chair. She shrugs off the assistant teacher's hand, which has been holding the tambourine with her. Emily takes hold of both the yellow shaker and the tambourine herself and starts rapping the shaker against the head of the tambourine.

"Yes!" I say looking at Emily, glad to see her playing with energy along with the music. She bangs the shaker onto the tambourine roughly in time to the rhythm of the song—an encouraging sign of shared attention and coordinated interaction. Emily continues to join in for about 25 seconds, sustaining her involvement.

Dylan's Intermittent Play, Reaching for Different Instruments, and Tug-of-War

Dylan, meanwhile, has been quietly exploring the castanet clacker with his fingers. When I first begin to sing, his hands begin roaming over the clacker faster, and his legs kick. However, Rachel attempts to get him to more actively shake his instrument. So, she models what she wants by pulsing her shekere in front of him in a lively, steady beat and then nonverbally suggesting that he do the same with his clacker. Dylan responds by putting his hand on top of her shekere, stopping the sound, and then he reaches backward, seeming to hand Rachel his clacker.

Trying to figure out why he's doing that, Rachel asks, "Wanna trade?"

But Dylan complicates things by instead reaching over to try to take a different bell-shaker out of a classmate's hand.

"No, can't have that one. [You] want this one?" says Rachel, offering him the shekere.

Dylan takes it and plays exuberantly for 4 seconds but then he pauses and turns around to Rachel. He seems to be gesturing to get a different instrument again.

"C'mon, pick *one*," says Rachel. "You get *one*!"

He takes the clacker, taps the wooden parts together, trying different sounds and motions. In a few moments, he becomes quite still, looks pensive, and curls his tongue into a *U* shape. David leans over, takes the clacker, which is now resting in Dylan's lap, and begins to play it beside him, urging him to resume playing again.

For a moment longer, Dylan looks in a trance and then suddenly reaches out to try to take the castanet clacker away from David. But David doesn't release it. Dylan tries to pull the clacker toward him. David holds on. Dylan uses both hands. David maintains his hold. Dylan makes eye contact with David. David gives one more shake emphatically (is he nonverbally saying, "Shake it!"?) and then releases the instrument to Dylan, who then plays the clacker with speed and force, similar to the way that David has modeled.

In the preceding moments, it has been an odd tug-of-war between Dylan and David. David is often gentle with the children and gives a lot of himself. But he also has considerable firmness and strength. In this interaction, he doesn't look too irritated, but he does look resolute and unwilling to have the instrument taken away when Dylan tries to take it back. Is David just acting from instinct? Or is he also trying to get Dylan to communicate with words or use nonverbal means like eye contact in order to get the shaker (and, by extension, other things he wants during the school day) rather than simply grabbing it and taking it from someone else?

A Surge in Energy and Instrument Playing

When he gets the castanet clacker back, Dylan pumps it up and down with fast arm movements, with a smile on his face.

Around that time, I'm also feeling some of the hope and strength that "Free at Last" gives me. I feel invigorated by the excitement that Dylan is showing. I also feel a surge rising within me as I think about the meaning of this song and how its words ring out at the climactic end of Dr. Martin Luther King's "I Have a Dream" speech.

I sing, "One of these mornings and it won't be long!" I bring added force in my guitar playing and emotion in my voice. "Thank God Almighty, we're free at last!"

I hear one of the boys, James, vocalize loudly and he bounces in his seat.

Rowen bends down, picks up some small jingle-like bells, and lifts the bells high up into the air as my own voice is rising.

Emily reaches under her chair, finds her yellow shaker again, and starts beating her tambourine with it energetically. She hits accented rhythms that fit well with the song as she plays.

I continue, "You're gonna look for me but I'll be gone——Thank God Almighty *we're* free at last!"

Dylan shakes his instrument fast and loud.

Rachel says, "Attaway, Dylan . . . Wow . . . Good job!"

Dylan turns around to look toward Rachel and David. Rachel's lively syncopated rhythms, and David's strong steady beat, are attracting Dylan's curiosity. His inquisitive turning around to look, and fast shekere playing, are connected to the teachers' playing. It seems an example of the way that teachers and peers can influence each other in a group.

During this part of the song, it feels as though the children, teachers, and I are joining together to create a heightened energy and synchronicity in the music. In a poem called "Blackbirds," by Julie Cadwallader Staub (2019), she sees birds rounding a curve, up in air, "the whole flock taking a long, wide turn as if of one body and one mind." The birds become, for her, a reminder that there are times,

> when, even more rarely, we manage to unite and move together
> toward a common good,
> and can think to ourselves:
> ah yes, this is how it's meant to be.

During "Free at Last," the children and adults simultaneously get into motion, play instruments, and, I think, briefly manage "to unite and move together toward a common good." I feel the fulfillment and well-being expressed in the poem: "This is how it's meant to be." One of my aspirations is to experience connection and meaning with the children and teachers in the group, and I feel that happening during this song.

As I've looked back, I've also wanted to try to understand why the song "Free at Last" so personally moves me when I play it with the group. I am striving to help children who face restrictions and struggles, and in personal ways I am very aware of my own struggles and limitations. I know that people in the wider world are also striving to be free, although they often face great restraints and obstacles. And I find this song inspiring, with its history and its connection to the suffering of people and their efforts to be free—possibilities for liberation now in our present times, not only in the future, celebrated in King's speech. I am hoping that the music we play together in the group and the relationships we develop will help each of us take steps toward growth—and toward some degree of freedom even amidst the difficulties in our lives.

ACTIVE PLAY WITH THE INSTRUMENTS INTERMINGLING WITH DROPPING SHAKERS AND IDIOSYNCRATIC OR REPETITIVE ACTIONS

Along with moments of cooperative lively instrument playing during the session, we also see examples of children dropping instruments, manipulating them in unconventional ways, and resisting or protesting adult directions. These moments—of stopping, dropping, idiosyncratic play, and resistance—are also part of the reality of the session. They, too, seem important to represent and try to understand. Let me describe two such instances.

Emily's Drops and Toe Pick Up

During an early verse of "Free at Last," Lisa reaches forward to prompt Emily to tap the yellow shaker onto the tambourine again. But Emily lets the shaker slide down onto the floor. Lisa picks it up and begins shaking it with Emily, hand-over-hand. Emily reasserts her own grip and takes the shaker and plays on her own for a time. Lisa pats Emily's shoulder, but then Emily lets the shaker fall back down onto the floor. After a moment, she picks it up and begins playing again. Lisa tousles Emily's hair in a gesture of apparent affection and appreciation for Emily's independently picking up the shaker and resuming active playing. But again, Emily lets go of the shaker after Lisa touches her. And Emily lets it tumble down onto the carpet. This time, after some maneuvering, Emily manages to pinch the shaker between her big toe and second toe, and she lifts it up with her toes and brings it into her outstretched hand—dexterous and ingenious in its own way, though it's not what we're expecting.

As the song proceeds, Emily's instrument drops look inadvertent sometimes and intentional at other times. Emily's facial expressions do not give us clear clues about what she is feeling or intending. I sense that some of the drops seem to reflect Emily's resistance to being directed. But I am also left with questions. Does Emily actually like Lisa's affection and therefore keeps dropping her shaker—and resuming play—in the hopes of getting more affirming touch and praise? Or does Emily dislike Lisa's touch and therefore indirectly communicates "Stop that" by dropping her instrument? Or is Emily simply experimenting with the sounds and sights of dropping instruments to the ground, which might be interesting to her although it isn't what the adults want?

Gabriel's Wrist Twisting/Squinting and His Protest

In another part of the song, as I began to describe earlier, Elizabeth perceives that Gabriel is getting stuck in a repetitive movement, and she intervenes to introduce alternatives. She models shaking up and down with the yellow mini maraca shaker and initially holds Gabriel's left hand to stop his pendulum swinging/squinting motion. She also offers him a second alternative instrument, the bells, and begins to shake them with him, with his left hand. Gabriel accepts her touch and bell-shaking, but he soon tries to resume a one-handed version of his own wrist twisting/squinting motion with the mini maraca. After he does this several times, she takes both the instruments from him.

Gabriel sits up, turns sideways, and looks up at her. After a few moments' pause he says something like, "Hey!" His tone of protest is unmistakable, a clarity of intentional communication that is not often common with him.

"You wanna play?" Elizabeth says, and then she leans in closer to Gabriel's ear and whispers something else that I can't quite hear. However, it appears that she may be insisting that he not keep repeating the same movement, which she perceives as perseverative. He vocalizes a frustrated yelp, kicks his feet, curls his knees up, and puts his head down into his shirt. When the song nears its finish, he lethargically and unhappily allows Elizabeth to shake the maraca with him.

Off Task? Or Pauses and Variations in Play?

During the interactions that I describe above and the "tug-of-war" between Dylan and David, I see the classroom teachers trying to guide children away from actions like grabbing an instrument or dropping it on the floor. Teachers can also get bothered by children's overly repetitive movements, or by their seemingly passive inactivity. For me, however, the issues that arise in these moments can be viewed in multiple ways. Certainly, I don't want children hijacking instruments from peers or staff. Nor would I relish class members regularly dropping instruments and having them crack on the floor.

But perhaps moments of "doing nothing" (silent motionless pauses) as well as "odd" idiosyncratic explorations are part of the process of playing and learning? Can unusual play be a natural part of experimenting rather than simply "stimming"? I notice that Emily and Dylan, particularly, appear to handle the instruments in alternating cycles of active play followed by silent pauses. There are also times when they will touch the instruments with their fingers in ways that are different from steady rhythmic shaking or beating. Music needs space, silence, breathing room, as well as sound, rhythm, and movement.

Recognizing the Realities of Alternating Participation and Resistance/Withdrawal

Emily's dropping the shaker to the floor also brings to mind a related idea discussed by trailblazing music therapists Paul Nordoff and Clive

Robbins (2007): that intimacy and shared musical play may often be followed by actions that break off that musical contact, or by behaviors of withdrawal or rejection. These alternating contrasting patterns of approach/avoidance and closeness/distance are fundamental parts of the development of relationships and music participation according to Nordoff and Robbins's model:

> With many children a progressive response is generally preceded and or followed by one that is resistive in some way . . . Paralleling the ascent of the levels of participation, resistiveness is seen to move from shutting out the therapy situation, withdrawing from it, or actively rejecting it, to appear in successively higher forms as evasion, manipulation, assertiveness, and expressions of oppositional competent independence. (p. 373)

The alternating patterns of participation and resistiveness described by Nordoff and Robbins offer additional ways to understand previous instances of Dylan's combinations of energetic engagement and later putting his head down into his lap. Emily's blend of zestful playing and shaker-dropping during "Free at Last" also represents another example of the fluctuations between active involvement and sudden disengagement. One possible difference I see during our sessions with the preschool children: While Nordoff and Robbins describe successive *stages* that emerge over the course of weeks, we are sometimes seeing co-occurring mixtures or rapid cycles of engagement/withdrawal and interpersonal connection/disconnection within the same session and sometimes within the same song!

I think this is a powerful insight for teachers, music therapists, and family members: to realize that these contrasting changes between contact/separation, approach/avoidance, and intimacy/remoteness may not simply represent problems ("off task," stimming, dropping, stopping) or failures or inadequacies on the part of the caregivers. These changing dynamics may also be more sympathetically and accurately viewed as inherent interwoven parts of the process of developing relationships. As in games like peek-a-boo, children and caregivers may actually be developing their play together in successive cycles of withdrawal from and return to personal contact and shared play.

Free Play Compared with "Teaching"

I think the moments with Emily, Dylan, and Gabriel during the instrument song also raise questions about how to balance the multiple goals of the adult leaders. How much emphasis do we give to *instructing* compared with *free play*? School staff members David, Lisa, and Elizabeth often gravitated toward teaching the children how to play the instruments in appropriate intended ways. The adults were urging the children to vary their actions in active play rather than perseverate on the same motions or remain in passive inaction. And in some instances, these were worthwhile goals. Yet, wasn't it also beneficial to give children opportunities for free play of the instruments, not shaped by adults—so that preschoolers could have the time and permission to initiate and control their own ways of exploring, sometimes unconventionally? This freedom seems important and not as fully included in school curriculums that are becoming increasingly prescribed and less child-directed in this preschool and in many other communities. In a larger sense, Dr. Martin Luther King's dream invokes the music of "Free at Last" to advocate for the possibilities of freedom "to make real the promises of democracy." And, I believe, we make real the promises of education too when we allow children more opportunities for freedom and self-direction.

Gabriel's Attempt to Pass the Bells to Dylan

There's a subsequent moment that I'd like to mention. It happened when Gabriel was content and participating (after an earlier period of being upset) and he appeared to offer a ring of bells to a peer. Let me explain what led up to this attempt. I had spontaneously transitioned into a traditional children's song as an additional handheld-percussion song because the children looked ready to continue playing instruments. I also felt that segueing without delay into an upbeat familiar song might help Gabriel more quickly get over his upset and re-engage in the activity. Fortunately, Gabriel did eventually recover his good humor and begin to play the maraca independently and, occasionally, with motions that were different from the one that Elizabeth hadn't liked. He was smiling again. At one point, Elizabeth gave Gabriel both the maraca and the bells to play. He looked mystified at first. Then he held the bells toward Dylan's arm. He seemed to be attempting to pass the bells to Dylan, although Dylan didn't appear to notice or accept it. Earlier, it had been Dylan who had tried to interact with a peer, Rowen, leaning near and saying, "Hi!" Now, it was Gabriel who reached toward Dylan and seemed to attempt to give him an instrument. Although the circle of communication was not completed—classmates did not acknowledge or respond to Dylan and Gabriel's overtures in these instances—we were seeing some beginning attempts at peer interaction during the instrument songs.

ENERGIZING, CHAOTIC, AND PROMOTING PEER ATTENTION, CHOICE MAKING, AND SOCIAL COMMUNICATION

It could often be invigorating when the group played instruments. The handheld percussion and up-tempo songs attracted class members' attention and offered children on the spectrum accessible opportunities to engage in a shared activity. Both adults and children joined in with gusto, at times. But group instrument play could also become disjointed or only loosely coherent. Sometimes I wondered if we were just making noise without particularly interacting with one another.

In the session described above, however, I've come to appreciate the interactions that *were* being generated during the instrument songs. Rowen, Emily, and others gave their attention to a peer, Caleb, as he strummed the guitar. His classmates moved closer to him and reached out to try to do what he was doing. Dylan, Gabriel, and each of the group members then chose percussion instruments when the adults offered them, and then the children played, at times, with intention and enjoyment during the song. Rachel, David, and Elizabeth noticed, praised, and guided their student partners. Dylan, Emily, Gabriel, and the other children interacted with the teachers, sometimes in curiosity and pleasure, sometimes in protest. Dylan's fast shekere rattling and his smiling sparked a renewed force in my singing and guitar playing. Then, in turn, other group members responded (Emily, Rowen, David, and Rachel) by picking up the pace of their instrument playing, adding their own rhythms. A number of varied interpersonal interactions were taking place.

Instrument playing has been viewed as one of the three primary ways that participants interact during music making: through vocalizations, instrumental play, and body movements in response to music (Nordoff & Robbins, 2007). Through these three forms of musical activity, participants and music therapists begin to know each other in "an initial level of encounter" (p. 3) and may subsequently "broaden and stabilize the working contact" (p. 398).

So today's music session underlines a point that I'd like to emphasize about working with Emily, Dylan, Gabriel, and the other children: Our preschool class found that exploring musical instruments together could offer an engaging avenue for shared play and connection for children at the earliest phases of communication development, and we discovered that instrument play could also facilitate simultaneous communication and participation for multiple class members. Like joining in vocalizing and movement during music, playing instruments together can help foster a sense of belonging and an awareness and interest in other people in the group, which may counterbalance isolation or disconnection that class members sometimes experience.

Meeting and making contact through the songs and the instrument playing are aspects of this January music therapy session that I have sought to further understand through researching others' perspectives. How have innovators who considered child development and interpersonal relationships thought about questions such as: What is actually happening as we try to get to know another person? What is realistically possible?

"Moments of Meeting" and the Boston Change Process Study Group

The word *meeting* can denote an appointment, a gathering for business, religious, or social purposes. It can also refer to a social encounter or the act of coming together in shared experience, as in "a meeting of hearts and minds." It is these latter meanings—meeting as encounter and shared experience—that I want to more fully understand by learning from the ideas of several pathfinders.

Psychiatrist Daniel Stern (2000) and colleagues (Boston Change Process Study Group, 2002) studied "moments of meeting": synchronized or coordinated movements, vocalizations, gazes, or expressions of emotion between parents and infants. Such exchanges came when an infant's smile unexpectedly emerged, or when a parent's surprising vocal or facial expression disrupted the usual dynamic between parent and child. And this interaction spontaneously generated laughter or varying emotions between them. Stern et al. (1998) asserted that long-lasting change (in both children and adults) often took place at this fundamental preverbal "implicit" level of interaction rather than at the spoken "explicit" level (Fosshage, 2005). "Moments of meeting" played a key role in bringing about changes in relationships, according to Stern et al. (1998), increasing the relatedness between parent and infant and encouraging children's development. Within the music therapy group with preschoolers, we too were endeavoring to cultivate moments of shared interaction, coordinated or alternating vocalizations, gazes, movements, and expressions of emotion, and we believed that these would promote the children's development and relatedness.

1957 Dialogue Between Martin Buber and Carl Rogers: Possibilities and Limits in Meeting

Philosopher Martin Buber (1937) and psychotherapist Carl Rogers (1957) explored the potentials and limitations of interpersonal meeting during a public dialogue on April 18, 1957, at the University of Michigan. In his influential book, *I and Thou*, Buber had stated, "All real living is meeting" (p. 11). During the Michigan public forum, transcribed in *Carl Rogers: Dialogues* by Kirschenbaum and Henderson (1989), Rogers spoke of "a real experiential meeting of persons, in which each of us is changed" (p. 48), a mutual "meeting of persons no matter what the psychiatric labels" (p. 53).

Rogers asked Buber if he saw similarities between a therapeutic relationship and the intimate I-Thou relationship that Buber had described in his religious and philosophical writings: a personal interconnectedness possible not only with God but, at times, between persons when they were able to meet as partners in dialogue rather than treating each other as tools to be manipulated.

While acknowledging therapy as dialogue, Buber focused on essential differences between the therapist and the person needing help. Buber imagined an interaction with "a sick man" in which this person's impairment might prevent a meeting of equality and mutuality:

> Out of a certain fullness you give him what he wants in order to enable him to be, just for this moment, so to speak, on the same plane with you. But even that is very—it is a tangent. . . . It is not the situation as far as I see, not the situation of an hour; it is a situation of minutes. And these minutes are made possible by you. Not at all by him. (Kirschenbaum & Henderson, 1989, p. 45)

The disparities inherent in therapy, in Buber's conception, were a reminder of "the problem of limits" in human dialogue and in humans' ability to truly meet each other. As an example, he stated that he could talk to a person with schizophrenia

> as far as he is willing to let me into his particular world . . . [although] in general he does not want to have you come in . . . But he lets some people

in. And so he may let me in too. But in the moment when he shuts himself, I cannot go on. And the same, only in a terrible, terribly strong manner, is the case with a paranoiac. He does not open himself and does not shut himself. He *is* shut. (Kirschenbaum & Henderson, 1989, p. 54)

This was particularly important, Buber asserted, because there were people in the larger society also who were shut off from others, limiting the possibilities for genuine encounter: "This is a problem for the human in general" (Kirschenbaum & Henderson, 1989, p. 54).

The exchange between Rogers and Buber surfaced questions that I carried with me in my work with the children and that I continue to contemplate today. Were the reciprocity, shared vitality, and cooperation that I wanted to foster in the group a realistic possibility with this classroom of children on the autism spectrum? In other words, were moments of meeting possible "no matter what the psychiatric labels," as Rogers had said? Or were the children "shut" in ways that would prevent this?

If I viewed the interactions in our preschool music group from Buber's perspective, I might assess them as only "a situation of minutes" or a "tangent" rather than as examples of mutual encounter. Considering the specific realities in this group of young children on the spectrum, however, I believe that the shared music play, social interactions, peer attention, choice making, and communication during the instrument songs did represent genuine encounters and small but important early developmental steps. And our group experiences differed from Buber's assertion that "these minutes are made possible by you. Not at all by him." It was not solely my actions as a music therapist that caused responses in the children. The interactions in the group were emerging from a mixture of influences—from the impulses and initiatives of individual children, and from the actions of peers and teachers in the group, which were often just as impactful as mine as an activity leader.

Moments of shared interaction were beginning to develop with children in the preschool music therapy group, and we also faced elemental continuing questions. Would we be able to find ways to help Dylan develop the interpersonal and communicative abilities that we'd glimpsed in flashes, or would he again withdraw? Could we make further contact with Gabriel and assist in the development of intentional communication? Could we attract Emily's attention and involvement in new activities or would she turn away or keep her distance? Similar questions came to me when I thought about each child in the class.

SUGGESTIONS FOR REFLECTION

- **What are some of the particular experiences that you remember** in your moments of meeting with children? People who consider child development, therapy, and education (such as Daniel Stern, Martin Buber, Carl Rogers, Vivian Gussin Paley, and many others) have sought to understand such moments of shared interaction involving gaze, facial expressions, body language, vocal and verbal communications, movements, and expressions of emotion. Have you found that moments of meeting are possible "no matter what the psychiatric labels," as Carl Rogers has said? Or do you think that sometimes children might be "shut" in ways that prevent this, corresponding to Martin Buber's assertion, "When he shuts himself, I cannot go on"?

- **How do you try to make contact and begin to interact and communicate?** As you get to know the children on the autism spectrum in your classroom, neighborhood, or family, are you aware of them being willing and able to make contact with you and others? What are the challenges that arise?

- **As you reflect on Paul Nordoff and Clive Robbins' ideas about music encouraging meeting and contact, what are some of the children's reactions to music that you have seen evoked?** When children on the spectrum start to become interested and interact during music, why does music motivate or enable their involvement?

- **Which of these factors seem to attract children's participation**: the music's melody; the rhythms; the options to receptively listen or to actively play instruments; the mixture of repeated familiar parts and variations; the flexibility to change the speed and mood of the music; the sense of connection that can come when jointly playing instruments, moving, or vocalizing together?

- **What are helpful ways to respond** when children's actions can intermingle shared play and odd explorations, "stimming," stopping, dropping, resistance, or withdrawal?

- **Do we accept idiosyncratic explorations or "off task" or "resistive" actions** as reflecting the alternating closeness/distance and engagement/withdrawal that are often part of developing relationships and learning? Rather than focusing on stopping these actions, do we seek to attract children toward more interactive and reciprocal forms of play and interpersonal contact? Or is it best to take direct steps to curtail interfering behaviors, or should adults try to redirect or suggest alternatives in order to show children ways to take steps in joint attention, socializing, and communicating?

CHAPTER 4

Playing the Chime

Dylan's "Give It to Me" and Emily's Energetic Participation—February 25

SPEAKING AND NOT SPEAKING

Six children, three teachers, and I are sitting in a semi-circle at the beginning of our music session on February 25. Before her turn in the "Hello Song," Emily is quiet, unstirring. She looks across the group and doesn't appear to be looking at what is happening during my interactions with other students. I sing, "What's your name?" to her classmate Rowen. He vocalizes "ree-ree" three times and I'm not quite sure what he means. He becomes quiet.

Emily Surprises Us

Then Emily speaks, saying his name, "Ro-wen," suddenly. She swivels toward lead teacher David, who simultaneously looks at her and says with enthusiasm, "Good job, Emily!" "Yes!" I add, "Emily! That is it!"

I have rarely heard her speak before. I'm still trying to learn how to support her communication. Until this moment, it hasn't been clear to me if Emily really has an interest in the "Hello Song," or if she knows the names of her peers, or if she listens during their turns. Yet by saying Rowen's name, she shows that she is following the interactions. Despite her indirect gaze and body orientation, she is watching her peer's turn and knows his name.

This is a heartening small surprise that I'm glad to see, because so far during this school year, I've often been puzzled, trying to figure out how to encourage peer interactions in the group. Some days I wonder if I'm trying the wrong approaches. Do I need to first focus more on encouraging and appreciating some of the children's precursors to peer interaction, such as peer awareness and shared attention in a common activity, before being able to witness more conventional forms of peer interaction such as waving hello, saying "hi," or saying names?

But during this particular February session, as we give our attention to Rowen again, I am still feeling a mixture of hope and determination, along with my questions. And I'm concerned that Rowen might feel that his turn has been overshadowed by Emily's verbalization and our subsequent praise of her. I'm also curious if the energy and encouragement that we have given Emily may spur Rowen's communication too. So, I gesture toward him once again, strum the guitar and say, "You can say Rowen!"

He scoots forward to the edge of his chair and says "Rowen!" very clearly!

Then he leans further toward me and looks at me with a smile.

"Rowen!" I sing, celebrating.

Lead teacher David says, "Good job!" and gives Rowen a flurry of rapid pats on his chest. I also affirm, "Good job! Rowen!"

"Give me five," I exclaim, and I hold out my palm for him to tap. He reaches out and touches my palm.

This feels new and exciting to hear Rowen and Emily verbally communicating names during the "Hello Song." It is also good to see Emily demonstrating her awareness of her classmate, and to connect with Rowen by tapping our palms together in a high five.

Vocalizations but Not Name

Next, I pivot toward Emily to focus on her own turn during the song. I sing, "Hello . . . What's *your* name?"

She doesn't respond. She looks over to the side, away from her classmates and teachers. She lowers herself back down into her chair, wiggles her feet, and makes a nonverbal sound with an unusual high intonation, "wa—oh." In retrospect, I wonder if this is an approximation of "he-llo." Or is it sound making that may not have a conventional meaning? Or could Emily be intentionally using an unusual voice? Her tone reminds me of times when my own children have felt compelled to answer a question that I've asked, and they have responded with a peculiar-sounding voice that reflects a measure of resistance or subversion along with compliance with my request.

David reaches over, takes Emily's hand, taps it on her chest, and says, "Em-i-ly."

Instead, she starts making fast repeated sounds like, "Ji joe ee joe ji."

He moves closer to her, points to his mouth: "Eh, Eh," he says, enunciating the beginning sound of her name, "Emily . . . You say Em-i-ly."

She makes another series of babble-like sounds that don't seem to resemble the sound of her name. We keep trying a little longer but Emily doesn't speak further, and then David says, "Emily . . . you said 'Rowen' so well!"

Just as our efforts are ending, Dylan speaks up and says, "Emily." Then he looks up, smiles, and claps his hands.

"That's right, Dylan!" I say, acknowledging Dylan's clear speaking of her name.

Dylan: "Here We Go" (Again)

Moments later, I greet Dylan as part of his turn during the "Hello Song," and I move toward him and sing, "And what's your name?"

He does not speak in response. Assistant teacher Rachel taps him on his back three times quickly and whispers, "What's your name?" He squints his eyes closed, and he raises his left hand to rub his eyes.

I pluck the guitar strings, and I ask him again. Rachel guides his hand to pat his chest for each syllable of the words, "My name is . . ."

But he starts to make his body go limp and begins sliding down his chair. As he slides, he sticks his feet out into the center of the group. For some reason, my instinct is to respond playfully to his feet. I reach my hand and fingers forward toward his oncoming feet—as if to nip them with my hands, crocodile-style. He suddenly changes from limp to athletic, pulling his feet away with speed from my approaching hand. He also smiles at me and looks up directly at my face, briefly, for the first time since his turn began.

"What's your name?' I say again, in an upbeat tone, as if this is a do-over. But Dylan's eyes go down toward the floor. Rachel also tries to engage him again, but he is silent.

Then he says, "Here you go," in a throaty gravelly sounding voice directed toward his shirt. Momentarily encouraged by his spoken response, Rachel and I try once again. But soon he stops speaking. His head bends down, and his body becomes motionless. After that, I'm sensing that he's not likely to say his name at this moment, and so I begin to move my attention to the next child in the circle.

THE GOODBYE CHIME

In the subsequent segments of the music therapy session, we focus on three activities: an action song with accompanying movements, a musical call-and-response game, and a song with rhythm instruments. Then it is nearing the ending activity for the session.

"All right, it's time for the goodbye song," I say.

The children are looking at me quietly. The only sound is the steady tapping of Dylan's right foot on the floor, like a metronome keeping time.

"Bye," Emily says. There is a second's pause, followed by pleased affirmations from the classroom staff. Kristy, James's classroom aide, smiles and laughs. David nods.

"Bye," I say, with appreciation. Emily has verbally communicated in such a quick, natural way!

"Bah," interjects Rowen, kicking his feet up and down, and then he half-stands in his chair. Is he again following Emily's lead by verbally approximating "Bye" after she does? It is good to hear the children taking initiative to verbally communicate!

"Time to say bye to Geoff," says David, acknowledging and extending Emily's and Rowen's one-word utterances into a sentence.

I pause for a second or two of open space.

Then I show the children the chime—a silver-colored tone bar that is 4 inches long, mounted on a wooden base. In the past month, I've been offering each child, in turn, an opportunity to tap the chime with a small wooden mallet as part of our goodbye song.

As I tap it softly to begin the song, the chime's ring lingers in the air for a few seconds. The children are quiet, listening.

"Give It to Me"

I start to sing, "It's time to say goodbye," and I tap the chime again with the small mallet. The bell-like sound rings and again stays in the air, like a miniature clock tower striking.

Dylan starts to bounce up and down in his chair.

Emily stands up and walks directly toward me, reaching out for the chime.

Simultaneously, from his seat, Dylan says, "Give it to me." He tilts his head back and smiles and strokes his hand down his raised chin and neck, as if contemplating a snack.

David directs Emily back to her chair until it is her turn.

"Give it to me," Dylan says again. He soundlessly claps his hands together in front of his chest four times, and he lifts his face upward in a continuing smile. He half-stands in his chair and asks for the chime again.

"Okay, Dylan, we're going to come 'round your way soon . . . hold on . . . ," I say. I stand up and I walk to the first student to my left, Gabriel, to begin giving each child in the semi-circle a turn to tap the chime.

I kneel in front of Gabriel, extending the wooden mallet and the silver chime tone bar out to him, and I sing, "Goodbye, Gabriel."

When I hold out the mallet toward him, Gabriel covers his face with his hands. He doesn't reach out for the mallet or the chime. I wait for a moment. Then, he removes his hands from his face. He sits up, reaches out, takes the mallet in his right hand, and strikes the chime. Quite hard, actually.

Carlos, another classmate, says loudly, "Hey!" Perhaps he's startled by Gabriel's louder-than-expected strike of the chime, much sharper than my soft tap. I pause for a moment, and then Gabriel reaches out to give the mallet back to me, and looks intent, as if considering what has just happened.

"Good job, Gabriel," I say.

I bring the chime toward Dylan. When I offer the mallet to him, he takes it quickly. His immediate engagement starkly contrasts his earlier-in-the-session evasion or inability about saying his name. He looks at the mallet, then the chime, as he energetically brings the mallet down onto the chime tone bar one, two, three times in quick succession. We make sounds together—Dylan is tapping the chime as I sing, "Good job, Dylan!"

When I lean toward him to retrieve the mallet, he reaches forward to try to keep playing. I am so glad to see his excitement and motivation. Yet I also want to give each child in the group the assurance of getting an approximately equal turn, so I retrieve the mallet and begin to move toward the next child.

As I do this, I can faintly hear the teachers talking, quietly remarking about Dylan's much-greater-than-usual excitement and repeated attempts to play the chime. Assistant teacher Rachel says, "Only . . . only when this comes out" as she gestures toward the chime with her open palm. She sounds both impressed and mystified.

Emily: Intent Energetic Participation

Though Dylan gets very animated during the chime song, some of the other children who are listening appear to be distinctly calm but attentive while hearing the chime and the gentle singing. They seem to be absorbing the ceremonial pace of the activity. So, a little later, after other children's turns, when I approach Emily, she is quiet and almost motion-less. But when I hold out the chime tone bar to her, both her hands dart forward. They spring out from behind a big fold in her sweatpants where they had been resting. She moves forward to the edge of her chair, and I sing, "Now, it's Emily!" Up to the level of her forehead, she raises the mallet high and brings it down onto the chime with concentration. Her face looks absorbed, alert, and serious. She then looks down at the mal-let with an expression that might have been surprise or wonder. Rachel laughs spontaneously, and Gabriel smiles. I am smiling, too, at Emily's intent energetic participation and our cooperation together—my offer-ing the chime, she reaching out for it, my singing, her playing. I like the sudden speed, urgency, and determination of her actions. I really enjoy even the studiousness of her expression, amidst the more overt enjoy-ment that others seem to be experiencing watching her.

Then Emily lifts the mallet toward her chest to examine it. I feel that we need to give a turn to the last child in the circle, so I reach out to get the chime back. Emily grabs both ends of the mallet with her right and left hands to prevent me from retrieving it. My hand and Emily's hands grasp and rotate. We determinedly-but-gently arm-wrestle for the mallet.

"Okay, okay, okay," I say softly.

We continue our mutual grip on the mallet.

"Okay, let go, Emily," I say, and she finally eases her hold on it, and I bring the mallet back.

Suddenly, she reaches her hands forward again rapidly two more times to try to get the chime and mallet. Then she moves back in her seat and claps her hands together sharply.

David looks toward her, smiling, saying, "Grabby girl!" after her repeated reaching out to get the mallet and her clapping her hands together. In retrospect, that clap may have been a gesture to request more, or perhaps it was a sign of her frustration at my ending her turn. But I also want to make sure to give a chance to one more class member, who hasn't had an opportunity to play the chime yet.

Though I am about to shift our focus to the next child, I also want to clearly affirm Emily: "You did really well," I say, "really well!" I reach forward and lightly touch the top of her head.

Afterward, she abruptly begins to smile broadly and twist in her chair, a giddy-looking expression of emotion on her face that is very unusual for her. This is accompanied by vocalizing, which almost sounds like an "eeek" or a giggle. Is this a delayed emotional expression related to her just-completed turn? For a few moments, at least, we are witnessing a clear smile and happy-sounding vocalization that represent such a difference from the seeming absence of facial expression or emotion glimpsed in the previous November session—and often during current sessions.

REFLECTIONS ABOUT PERIPHERAL ATTENTION AND UNCONVENTIONAL SIGNS OF PEER AWARENESS

When I later reviewed the video recording of this class session, my attention was initially drawn to the "Hello Song" when Emily had unexpectedly said her classmate's name, "Rowen." In doing this, she revealed that she had been paying attention to the group activity and was aware of her peer, although she had seemed to be remote and looking away. This strengthened my earlier impression that her indirect attention—by almost imperceptible side-glances and by listening—often did not include conventional attending behaviors like direct visual gaze or forward-facing body orientation, as I discussed in Chapter 2. She was orienting to people through peripheral attention and ear contact rather than through eye contact and facing directly toward them. *Peripheral attention* is the descriptive term that I have conceived after observing Emily and other children in the group. The possibilities of indirect but attentive interactions are described with humor in a book titled *How to Talk Minnesotan: A Visitor's Guide*, in which Howard Mohr (1987) depicts "Minnesota body language" and "rules" of conversation:

> Two standing Minnesotans never face each other during conversation . . . A simple discussion between two standing Minnesotans about the weather or the Twins' chances of getting out of the cellar would be conducted at a full 180 degrees—both would be staring off into the distance as they talked to each other . . . Two Minnesotans in a living room for conversation will both sit on the sofa, one at each end, facing forward, with only an occasional side glance . . . If a person looks directly at you and locks on to your eyes while he talks, we take that as a sign that he's selling something or not from around here, or both. (pp. 180–181)

It is not only Minnesotans who interact with each other indirectly! I don't wish to diminish the possible benefits for children on the spectrum to also learn direct forms of interrelating. But I feel that the actual shared attention of children like Emily is underestimated if one focuses only on children's eye contact, front-facing posture, or other direct conventional expressions of attention. Author Donna Williams (2017), who has written vividly about her own experiences of autism, once described her childhood perspective in this way: "My use of peripheral vision said 'keep enjoying your own world without invading mine and I'll keep spying on you'" (The Getting of Language section, para. 1). Donna, like Emily, was sometimes giving attention to events and interactions at the edge of her vision, rather than using forward-focused direct gaze. When Emily said her classmate's name during this February "Hello Song," she showed her peripheral attention to her peer and to adult class leaders. She also evidenced her understanding of the next step in this social routine for the "Hello Song," and she demonstrated her ability to use spoken language to communicate.

After Emily voiced his name, Rowen communicated more readily and clearly—saying his own name, making direct eye contact, and sharing a high five with me—although earlier his response had been brief and hard to decipher. This suggested the possibility that peer influences might be operating within the group, sometimes before I was aware of overt signs confirming it.

Yet when we asked Emily to say her own name, she did not. She didn't simply ignore us this time during her turn, as we had experienced in previous sessions. She emitted a series of vocalizations in response, although it was difficult to discern the meaning of these vocalizations.

Spontaneously, Dylan then spoke her name, saying, "Emily." As in previous sessions, however, when we asked him to say *his* name, *he* did not. He covered his face with his hand and looked down at the floor. He began to slide off his chair, and he showed continuing evasion and/or difficulties in identifying himself in a conventional social interchange. But his avoidance/inability coexisted with capacities in verbal expression evident in phrases that he initiated, such as, "Here we go."

It was only later that I noticed a pattern: Rowen initially hadn't said his own name, but then Emily spoke his name. Then Emily didn't say her own name, but Dylan spoke her name. Several of the children seemed more willing or able to say their peers' names than their own.

Peer awareness—and attention during a classmate's turn and verbal communication of a peer's name—were being engendered during the "Hello Song." In contrast, the goal of children's self-identification as part of a social-greeting routine was not being achieved with a number of the children.

The Goodbye Chime That Motivated New Attempts to Interact and Communicate

Sometimes the sound and appearance of a certain instrument captured the attention and interest of the children and helped evoke increased communication and interaction. In this session and in the months ahead, the tone bar chime was one of the instruments that particularly elicited children's interest and communication. During music therapist Juliette Alvin's (1991) sessions with children on the spectrum, it was her cello that offered them a motivating way to interact with her. With Emily, Dylan, and Gabriel, I saw new willingness and ability to interact when I introduced the chime as part of the "Goodbye Song." Emily and Dylan reached out and communicated with gesture and spontaneous speech in order to play the chime. This was unusual. We'd seen them turn away from attempts to encourage their participation, despite intensive adult efforts. Gabriel's response to the chime was less overt, but he gradually became engaged.

In these moments, the children were communicating verbally ("Give it to me"), nonverbally (Emily standing and reaching for the chime), and through movement (bouncing, clapping, accepting the offered chime, grasping the mallet, lifting arms high to play). They were actively participating in a shared musical interaction. Children in the group were also often giving their attention to peers' turns with the chime. Emily's saying "Bye" soon after I introduced the song was also surprising. She briefly initiated speech—well synchronized and matching with the social goodbye context—although she was seldom using verbal communication previously in the classroom.

Group Work

The children's actions on February 25th were shaped within a group. Working with a group involved distinct differences from one-to-one work, which I will discuss in the next section. Groups offer structured opportunities for children on the autism spectrum to interact with several peers and adults—interactive possibilities that are more varied than those available within a one-to-one adult-child intervention. The presence of a music therapist, teachers, and peers provides multiple social partners and models. Groups can also initiate chain-reaction or multiplier effects, in which one child's or adult's action can trigger additional social or communicative reactions from other group members. Related descriptive terms from autism research literature include *emotional contagion*

(Scambler et al., 2007) and *chains of interaction* (Greenspan & Wieder, 2006). For example, in the "Hello Song" previously described, it was immediately after Rowen's classmate Emily said his name, and after she received our enthusiastic praise, that Rowen himself began to use verbal communication (saying his own name), eye contact, and interaction through touch (sharing a high five). Multiplier effects could operate in different directions within the music therapy group—amplifying both desired actions (interaction and communication) and unintended reactions (crying, withdrawal). A further feature of group work in the classroom was that it gave the preschoolers opportunities to practice and develop social and communication skills in their own daily classroom environment, with familiar peers and teachers. Although there were advantages to group work with the children, I also wished that I could have had the opportunity to work with them individually too. One-to-one music sessions could have additionally helped me come to know each of their unique needs and abilities in further detail.

CONTRASTING APPROACHES TO TREATING AUTISM

To promote further understanding of important differences in varying approaches to early childhood activities, in the following sections, I examine three pairs of contrasting terms from research and clinical literature: *behavioral* and *developmental*; *skill based* and *relationship based*; and *directive* and *responsive*.

Behavioral Treatments

A National Research Council report (2001) summarizing decades of autism research stated that the majority of educational and therapeutic programs for children on the spectrum have stemmed from two major theoretical frameworks: behavioral and developmental.

Behavioral treatments have traditionally concentrated on observable and quantifiable aspects of behavior and overt actions rather than inner psychological activities. Behaviorism is based on the work of John Watson (1913), B. F. Skinner (1966), and others. Watson stated that the principal goal of behaviorism was "the prediction and control of behavior" (p. 158) in accordance with standardized criteria. In early education, behavioral goals center on assessing behavioral excesses (abnormal in kind or in frequency, e.g., hyperarousal, repetitive compulsive movements) and behavioral deficits (absent or infrequently used abilities, e.g., attention or interaction with others). Behavioral techniques are then implemented to increase a child's deficit skills and decrease the behavioral excesses.

Applied behavior analysis (ABA) is a prominent approach that strives to modify behavior through the use of carefully repeated drills and rewards: deciding the appropriate antecedent and consequence for a target behavior, and systematically instructing the target behavior, and consistently assessing the child's progress (Cooper et al., 2020). Several contemporary behaviorally based programs such as Pivotal Response Treatment (Koegel & Koegel, 2019) and the Early Start Denver Model (Rogers et al., 2012) have augmented one-to-one directive methods with inter-responsive methods in naturalistic or group settings.

Developmental Approaches

Developmental approaches often focus on *emerging internal* processes (e.g., emotion, motivation, maturation, potentials) as well as *existing external* behaviors. Developmental theories examine several interrelated areas—social, emotional, cognitive, and communicative development—and have stemmed from the work of Jean Piaget (1964), Lev Vygotsky (1987), and others. Developmental educational and therapeutic programs for children on the autism spectrum typically place more emphasis on supporting a child's engagement in interactions and learning, and these programs place less emphasis on children giving correct responses to discrete tasks (Prizant et al., 2000). Strategies often use a less directive style in teaching and incorporate more child-centered activities, with increased choice making, individualized interactions, and joint play. For example, parents and practitioners are urged to follow a child's lead initially rather than primarily relying on methodically instructing the child to master adult-defined objectives. The goals in the DIR model (developmental, individual difference, relationship based) of Greenspan and Wieder (2006) include tailoring interventions to a child's particular strengths and limitations, eliciting and responding to children's emotions and individual interests, and developing relationships in spontaneous child-centered interactions. The SCERTS model of Prizant et al. (2006), which I touched upon in Chapter 1, is another example of a developmental approach. It advocates responding to a child's attentional focus and facilitating a child's initiatives within activities, in addition to working toward goals based on the child's individual abilities and needs. SCERTS draws from both behavioral and developmental research and methods and seeks to combine goal-directed learning with responsiveness to children's preferences in naturally occurring settings.

Skill-Based Treatments

Two other contrasting terms, *skill-based* and *relationship-based*, have also been used to describe different emphases among educational and therapeutic programs.

Skill-based treatments for children with autism have been characterized as promoting children's learning of specific functional skills rather than focusing on children's development of relatedness or bonding with others (Simpson et al., 2005, p. 47). Skill-teaching strategies such as discrete trial teaching (DTT) are based on adult direction and a child's response in one-to-one learning contexts. Traditionally, trainers have been instructed to prompt specific "on-task" responses and ignore or redirect children's "off-task" responses. Children's progress has been assessed by tallying the total number of correct responses during predetermined teaching programs, and by adults counting the frequency of particular child behaviors (e.g., vocalizations, words). Proponents of skill-based programs, such as ABA and DTT, have viewed their practices as scientifically based, and have regarded the majority of other treatments for autism as lacking scientific evidence.

Relationship-Based Approaches

Relationship-based approaches emphasize building supportive connections among caregivers, children, and peers as crucial to developing communication, interpersonal interaction, and broader growth and learning. Proponents recommend giving opportunities for choice making, turn taking, and shared control between adult and child or peer partners rather than primarily centering autism treatment on an adult's modification of a child's behavior. Prizant et al. (2000) underline the benefits of shared control as they discuss communication:

> Natural interactions among friends and peers are largely based on reciprocal sociocommunicative exchange and sharing of control. Typical peer interaction does not allow for one partner to dominate or control the other partner . . . When an interaction is dominated by one partner, the other partner often loses interest or interactional breakdowns occur. (p. 216)

From a relationship-based perspective, the intensive use of repetitive drills in traditional behavioral programs is viewed as possibly limiting children's engagement in interactions and communication, particularly self-initiated spontaneous interactions and communication

(Greenspan & Wieder, 2006; Prizant, 2016). Caregivers are urged to create jointly directed activities that are naturalistic and appealing to children on the spectrum.

The decisive impact of relationships and interpersonal interactions in facilitating learning and development has been emphasized in the psychotherapeutic and early-childhood-developmental perspectives of Carl Rogers (1957), Daniel Stern (2000), Jack Shonkoff and Deborah Phillips (2000), Lauren Lowry (2018), and others. I will mention a few aspects of Carl Rogers's person-centered approach that have particularly resonated with me. Rogers asserted that the personal relationship between the teacher and learner was a primary catalyst for students' change and development. In his essay "The Interpersonal Relationship in the Facilitation of Learning," Rogers (1989) stated that the same essential qualities in relationships that led to psychotherapeutic change also facilitated learning: positive regard (caring, acceptance, trust), authenticity, and empathetic understanding. He urged people to develop these facilitative attitudes, which would have more impact than the choice of a particular instructional technique. Society should "give strong positive attention to the human interpersonal side of our educational dilemma . . . Better courses, better curricula, better coverage, better teaching machines will never resolve our dilemma in a basic way" (p. 320). Instead, Rogers's student-centered approach advocated increased opportunities for learner-selected and learner-controlled exploration and interaction. "Discovery learning" and "active learning" express this idea that student-chosen activities and experimentation are crucial in children's engagement in their education. This differs from "banking" models of education in which teachers or therapists deposit information to students (Bybee, 2020; Freire, 1970).

Directive or Responsive?

Two additional terms—*directive* and *responsive*—also highlight contrasting methods to help children. With directive approaches, as outlined above, an adult takes the lead in instructing a child to learn a skill, step by step. The goal is to improve targeted behaviors through prompting and shaping children's responses (Cooper et al., 2020). In directive instruction, teachers and parents work to focus a child's attention on a specific adult-selected objective. Adults may frequently ask children questions to assess and measure abilities or knowledge learned.

Responsive interactions are more child led, and caregivers seek to recognize and flexibly adjust to child-initiated actions, interests, and speech. Adults are also encouraged to tune into children's nonverbal communication, facial expressions, body language, gestures, and eye gaze. Studies with parents and their young children on the autism spectrum have documented that a responsive parenting style supports greater levels of joint engagement and communication development (Shire et al., 2016). Related research also found that "when the children were the ones to initiate joint engagement with their parents (versus their parents being the ones to start the interaction), these interactions lasted longer and the children used more social skills while interacting" (Lowry, 2018, Recent Study section, para. 3). These skills included paying attention, using eye gaze to communicate messages, and imitating actions. Thus, being responsive involves adults focusing on what is catching the child's interests and joining in their play, while trying not to take over or lead the interaction, suggests Lauren Lowry from the Hanen Centre in Toronto, Canada.

In contrast with the emphasis on frequent assessment used in directive approaches, Lowry (2016) recommends that caregivers limit their reliance on repeated questions to measure children's gains in knowledge:

> Questions that aren't sincere or aren't based on a child's interests tend to be "testing questions." Testing questions are aimed at getting a child to show us whether he or she knows something or not, such as "What colour is it?" or "What's that?" Asking a lot of testing questions tends to discourage conversation. (Common Questions About Questions section, para. 6)

This may lessen young people's motivation to participate in shared social interactions. Therefore Lowry recommends tuning into—and adaptively participating in—activities that are attracting a child's attention in order to better promote shared exchanges between caregivers and children on the spectrum.

THE IMPACT OF RESPONSIVENESS AND RELATIONSHIP IN THERAPY

The concept of responsiveness is also being debated in wider discussions within the field of psychotherapy, in addition to the above perspectives from early childhood development and autism. For example, psychologists John Norcross and Bruce Wampold (2019) assert that flexible interpersonal responsiveness, and the ability to foster a strong therapeutic relationship between therapist and client, are the most important

factors in effective psychotherapy. Their findings clarify that the therapeutic relationship, and an adaptable responsiveness within it, are more
important than the particular treatment method used, the authors affirm. Tailoring therapy to the individual client—their preferences, their
race/ethnicity, and other factors—will demonstrably improve client
outcomes, according to meta-analyses of hundreds of studies reviewed.
Conversely, a focus on adhering to a standardized treatment method
with a specific sequence of directive steps can leave little room for variation, adjustment, and spontaneity by therapists, children, or caregivers. Norcross and Wampold contend that what is truly healing—the
therapeutic interpersonal connection—is de-emphasized when treatment guidelines become preoccupied with the method used rather than
with the relationship and responsiveness between the therapist/care-
giver and the client.

Emotions and Sharing Positive Affect

In related additional ways, exchanges of emotion and positive affect between children and caregivers are seen as crucial in relationship-based
models. These interchanges motivate and enable interaction, communication, and favorable states of self-regulation and mutual regulation of
arousal and mood. Behavioral skill-based models, in contrast, traditionally concentrate on changing a child's actions rather than closely considering a youngster's internal feelings or focusing on encouraging the
give-and-take of emotions between a caregiver and a child. When emotions are addressed in skill-based approaches, it may involve an adult
training a young person to identify and label feelings, and instructing a
child how to give appropriate responses to other people's emotions.

From a relationship-based perspective, however, therapeutic benefits come not only in "teaching" emotions. Growth comes from fostering shared emotional and social interplay and from the communication
of positive affect between caregivers and children. Daniel Stern's (2000)
child development research highlights the key influence of a mother's
attunement to an infant's feelings, which contributes to a fundamental
sense of being emotionally connected. When interacting with autistic
youngsters, caregiver attunement and responsiveness are also viewed
as vital in promoting joint engagement and child initiatives.

In the research of Patterson et al. (2014), the interactions between 85
toddlers on the autism spectrum and their caregiver partners were video-
taped and analyzed. Their study demonstrated that a caregiver's communication of positive emotions, and their ability to recognize and flexibly

respond to a child's activity choice led to higher rates of child-initiated joint engagement and increases in attention, interest, coordinated gaze and gestures, and signs of enjoyment through laughing, smiling, and vocalizations. The video analysis did not ignore the significant challenges involved: In this study, two-thirds of the interactions were spent in states of seeming disengagement or lower states of engagement, including wandering around the room or focusing on objects in apparently isolated ways.

Paralleling experiences reported in the research of Greenspan and Wieder (2006), the many instances of children's apparent disengagement may lead parents and caregivers of children on the spectrum to believe that gaining shared attention and emotional engagement can sometimes seem an almost impossible task. Yet research like that of Patterson et al. (2014), described above, sheds light on the possibilities that shared social interplay can develop when approached gradually through communication of emotional warmth and positive affect and through responsiveness to a child's initiatives.

In describing another related approach to enhancing the communication and interpersonal abilities of individuals on the spectrum, the SCERTS model, described earlier, includes the following quotation from Stephen Cope (as cited in Prizant et al., 2002, p. 11): "In order to feel real, we all need to be recognized and affirmed. We need to be accepted and appreciated. Most of all, we need to be seen with loving eyes, and reflected back with warmth and enthusiasm . . . as much as we need oxygen and food." To help children, I believe that it is crucial to focus on bringing this loving energetic attention into interactions, which we see emphasized in the SCERTS model and the research of Stern (2000) and Patterson et al. (2014).

Blending Contrasting Approaches

As I reflect back on my music sessions with the children, I realize that I have been attempting to interweave some of the differing autism goals and methods outlined above. I have been working with the belief that the interactions during music can promote skill building as well as relationship building—that is, can promote the development of abilities in communication and shared attention, and can foster engagement in relationships that are caring, emotionally positive, and interactive.

Attempting to respond to contrasting autism approaches is a necessity during the era in which I've been working. Along with many people throughout the United States, my experiences in a school have been fundamentally affected by larger policies—such as the No Child Left Behind Act (NCLB), the Every Student Succeeds Act (ESSA), the Individuals with Disabilities Education Act (IDEA), and the evidence-based practice (EBP) movement. In education, many of these national laws and medical-model approaches have given preference to, and pre-scribed the use of, scientific and behavioral methods to achieve improve-ments in children's skills that could be counted and tracked. Federal funds have often been limited to educational procedures intended to provide scientific evidence of measurable student outcomes. However, giving primacy to behaviorally focused and medical-model approaches as "best research evidence and practices," and placing an emphasis on a "narrow kind of test-based accountability" (Cochran-Smith et al., 2018, p. 6), has led to disregarding teachers' and therapists' practice-based knowledge and experiences. It has also discounted qualitative research studies that are not the large-scale randomized controlled trials (RCTs) that evidenced-based practice portrays as the truly reliable method of research.

With this national educational agenda of delivering measurable stu-dent outcomes, I became aware that many teachers and school-based therapists were under pressure to get children to perform concrete ac-tions to demonstrate progress. Yet sometimes this focus on prompting children's specific observable behaviors was not consonant with giving children the time and space to develop their own initiatives. This nation-al agenda does not support funding for programs that concentrate on developing interpersonal relationships. Nor do behavioral and evidence-based methods typically focus on the ways that skills and interplay can grow organically out of personal connections and supportive adaptations rather than through predetermined adult goals, drills, and prompts.

So, in my music sessions I was trying to demonstrate that students were meeting clear observable objectives, while also trying to create a group climate that was musical and playful, and an environment that drew upon the warmth and energy of the classroom teachers and the interests and spontaneity of the children. Sometimes my attempts to blend differing approaches worked, and sometimes they didn't. For example, it wasn't possible to be both directive and responsive or to offer interventions that were both consistently repeated and flexibly adapted. Or was it?

Actually, I think this is an area in which music therapy can make a useful contribution to the field of autism, because music can sometimes be both directing and responding, repeating and varying, in back-and-forth turn taking or simultaneous play. Kenneth Aigen (1996) highlights the words of music therapy innovator Clive Robbins:

> You've got to be half-inviting and half-directing, a mixture of the two, so that your direction at the same time is an invitation . . . The clinical inter-ventions through music can be simultaneously challenging and supporting, inviting and demanding, leading and following; they can simultaneously offer all of these things and thus support contact with the child's present functioning level while still providing an invitation to growth. (p. 18)

Clive Robbins' ideas about music's abilities to combine polarities do not, in my viewpoint, mean that we should ignore the divergences and even incompatibilities between differing autism treatment approaches. But it does draw attention to music therapy's potential to blend contrasting goals and methods. Songs and improvised music can include both rep-etitions and variations, and can provide participants with structure and direction as well as possibilities for freedom and initiative in playing instruments, vocalizing, and moving to the rhythms.

THE CONTRIBUTIONS OF MUSIC THERAPY

I'd like to focus further on the assistance that music can give, by dis-cussing evidence from a multinational study and also from experiences during our preschool February session.

In research that involved children from seven countries who were 4–7 years old and diagnosed with autism, Mossler et al. (2019) exam-ined the effects of music therapy. In particular, the researchers sought to determine whether the quality of the therapeutic relationship impacted changes in the communication and social interaction of 48 participants from Norway, Israel, Australia, the United States, Austria, Italy, and Korea. The method of treatment was improvisational music therapy, which focused on the therapist attuning with a child's movements, rhythms, emotions, vocalizations, and instrument playing. The duration of the study was 5 months and there were two frequencies of therapy studied. Participants attended either once-a-week, 30-minute music sessions, or they took part in three-times-a-week sessions. Mossler and colleagues analyzed randomly selected video sequences of 3 minutes in length from every second week. This totaled 10 music therapy se-quences for each participant. Along with video analysis, the researchers used three standardized tools to assess results: the Assessment of the Quality of Relationship (AQR), the Autism Diagnostic Observation Schedule (ADOS), and the Social Responsiveness Scale (SRS).

The research findings showed that musically synchronizing and attuning with a child's emotions, movements, instrument playing, and vocalizations—in a well-matched therapeutic relationship—contributed to a child's social interactions, and generated evidence of decreased limitations in social responsiveness and communication. The study's authors also raised questions about how capably the standardized assessment tools—which necessitate assigning numbers to represent complex intermixtures or alternating cycles of behaviors and emotions—are able to fully reflect the complicated realities.

There are many aspects of this research that I've found revealing and valuable. The study's focus on the quality of relationships, and the responsive tailoring of musical interactions to meet the needs of participants, offers an alternative perspective on what can promote mutual development and learning in therapy and education. This is important because, as mentioned earlier, many recent behavioral or biomedical research studies and professional guidelines give limited attention to relational and responsive dimensions and instead concentrate on demonstrating the effectiveness of consistently applied techniques or "best practices" in therapy or education (cf. Norcross & Wampold, 2019; Cochran-Smith, 2021). However, this prevailing focus on techniques often misses, or minimizes, interpersonal dimensions, which are crucial in supporting growth and learning.

Another noteworthy characteristic of the research of Mossler et al. (2019) is that it highlights the ways that music-making, and the relationships that develop during shared musical experiences, foster social and communicative interactions: Young children on the spectrum can become actively involved in music sessions through playing instruments; expressively moving; vocalizing; and inter-responding to emotions, facial expressions, body language, and sound making. Because talk-based treatments for autism continue to predominate, music therapy can provide additional avenues for engaging children and promoting their development. The research of Mossler and colleagues helps demonstrate music therapy's potential to expand current autism supports and therapies, and it does so using an interesting balance of depth of study (the microanalysis of short segments of music sessions) and breadth from multiple examples of music therapy with children from seven countries.

CONCLUDING THOUGHTS

To end this chapter, I'll underline several points about our experiences with the opening "Hello Song" and the closing chime instrument song at the preschool on February 25th, and I will highlight how these experiences corresponded to several of the broader concepts discussed above.

One of the main ideas to convey is that the chime enabled contact with the children by engaging their interests and motivation and by facilitating play and shared control rather than by attempting to directly instruct or modify their actions. Dylan, Emily, and Gabriel each became involved in interactive play with me and with the silver chime tone bar as they reached forward to take the offered wooden mallet for the chime and then tapped the chime as I sang, "Good job" or "Sounds good!" We also moved together, looked at each other, and responded to facial expressions, body language, emotions, and other signs of communicative expression.

Although these interactions involved a therapist and teachers introducing an appealing musical instrument and then attuning to a child's actions, this chime activity was also characterized by Emily's and Dylan's own initiatives in communication and social interaction. For example, Dylan immediately said, "Give it to me." He was not prompted to say this. The chime motivated him to verbally communicate these words on his own. Emily also clearly demonstrated her own curiosity and excitement by standing up and marching straight toward me and reaching for the chime in order to try to play it. Rather than an impassive or distant look, which we sometimes saw with Emily, she gave a clear smile, and she made happy-sounding vocalizations and movements after her turn with the chime. She also showed awareness that the chime song was our closing ritual for the music circle when, unsolicited, she chose to speak up to say "Bye" when I brought out the chime. Her verbal utterance encouraged Rowen's verbal approximation of "Bye" too.

To return to concepts discussed earlier, the closing chime song represented an emphasis on a more facilitative and mutually interactive musical approach to encouraging the development of social communication. By attempting to tap into children's interests and to spontaneously respond and co-participate in shared sound making and interactions, the music group was aligned with relationship-based and responsive approaches.

Our chime song also blended together directiveness and a repeated structure into the ritual of each child taking a turn to play the chime with the music therapist. It was not simply child-directed free play in a one-to-one setting but a turn-taking activity within a group. It combined opportunities for child-initiated and mutual play with an organized and familiar process. On this February morning, the chime song interactions were also actualizing a skill-based goal of promoting the children's verbal and nonverbal communication and interpersonal interaction, while simultaneously fostering the sharing of emotions and positive affect that are seen as crucial in relationship-based approaches.

In addition, I began to perceive that I was influenced by directive and behavioral approaches during the "Hello Song," as I attempted to encourage children to say their names as part of a greeting routine. I sought to draw on the motivation of music. Yet there were limitations encountered in my attempt to musically adapt a behavior-prompting approach: Children sometimes did not seem willing or able to verbally communicate their name. They may have experienced this as a "testing question." Even so, the children were beginning some welcome steps in communication during today's session, such as Emily's taking initiative to say her classmate Rowen's name, Rowen subsequently saying his own name, and both children interacting with lead teacher David. The children were visually seeking him out and connecting physically through David's playful energetic touch—his rapid congratulatory chest taps for Rowen, for example. Rowen also reached out to connect with me for a high five. So, while I was endeavoring to help children develop the social skill/behavior of saying their name during a greeting routine, I also tried to keep a spirit of musical play and caring in saying hello to each child while paying interested attention to each individually.

SUGGESTIONS FOR REFLECTION

- **The chime.** This tone bar chime made a sustained bell-like note when a child tapped it. Why did this sound and this instrument have such appeal for many class members? There are many other possible sounds in any environment, but what is it about some specific instruments and musical sounds that draws children's attention and inspires their engagement and communication? Assistant teacher Rachel earlier commented on the unusual motivating force that the chime had for Dylan, seeing his very high level of active interest "Only . . . only when this comes out."

- **Possible contributing influence of ritual and quiet meditative energy.** Was there something about the quiet calm feeling in the closing chime ritual that also contributed to the children's involvement? People often believe that activities need to be fast paced to be exciting and stimulating for children. Why might a slower and more hushed activity attract the attention and anticipation of children in a class, when combined with an appealing musical instrument and sound?
- **Peripheral awareness.** Emily synchronized saying her classmate's name with his turn although she had not appeared to be paying attention to him during the "Hello Song." In your own experiences with young learners, have you observed children engaging in indirect attention by almost-imperceptible sideways awareness, which may not show conventional attending behaviors like direct visual gaze or facing-forward body orientation? What might be some of the benefits, or possible problems, of expanding our understanding of shared attention to include the peripheral attention of young children on the autism spectrum?
- **Which approaches to treating autism have most influenced you**? Behavioral, developmental, skill-based, relationship-based, directive, responsive? Does your school primarily adhere to one model? If you've attempted to incorporate the methods of differing approaches, what have been some of the challenges and opportunities that have arisen?
- **Music-therapy group work supporting early steps in shared attention, engagement, and peer awareness**. To close this chapter, I am recommending that early childhood programs include music therapy as part of the services for young children on the spectrum. On February 25th, we saw examples of the ways that the music group helped encourage shared attention and peer awareness among children, as they watched each other's turns and said each other's names. We saw the preschoolers communicating and interacting with the teachers and therapist. Children were seeking teachers via eye gaze or reaching out for physical connection with a high five and were actively moving and playing the chime instrument. The music group not only supported one-to-one adult-child social communication during turns. It also led to chains of interactions. These were noticeable when Emily's

verbal communication prompted Rowen to speak up too. A ripple effect was also visible when the teachers' warmth and contact with students brought about increased participation by the class members. The group music activities made a network of multiple interactions possible among participating children and adults. Currently, however, many schools do not provide music therapy for students, either individually or in a group. I am urging local school leaders to make music therapy part of their budget and planning. I am also advocating that our nation's Congress and president more fully fund IDEA (Individuals with Disabilities Education Act) and more specifically identify music therapy as an included related service such as speech therapy, physical therapy, and occupational therapy.

CHAPTER 5

Rhythm, Entrainment, and Movement "Like This!"
March 24

I turn on a recording of a drum groove. I start playing my guitar along with the drum's strong backbeat and syncopation in a rhythm-and-blues style. It's the beginning of "Like This!," a song that I wrote after seeing a young man in Washington, DC, who was showing his peers a dance move while saying decisively: "This is how you do it . . . Like *this*!" I got energized by his vitality, and now I'm ready to share my newly created song with the children.

Today's classroom semi-circle includes seven students: Dylan, Gabriel, Emily, Carlos, James, Caleb, and Rowen. Five adult staff are present: lead teacher David; assistant teachers Rachel and Elizabeth; teaching intern Lisa; and Kristy, an aide assigned to James. We've come to the fourth activity of the session.

SMILING AND STANDING UP

When the drum groove starts, Lisa looks at Carlos, the student sitting next to her. She pantomimes a look of exaggerated surprise and starts bobbing her head to the music in a loopy, playful way. Carlos smiles.

I haven't yet noticed Gabriel moving in response to the music, but Elizabeth, maybe sensing something subtle from him, says, "Gabriel likes this." She places her hands on Gabriel's shoulders and urges him side to side to the beat. He doesn't join in but he doesn't resist either. He sits up tall in his chair, looking at me with apparent curiosity as I play guitar in sync with the recorded beats.

A smile slowly starts to come to his face. His eyes open wider. And his look of surprise and pleasure grows. Elizabeth draws others' attention to Gabriel, "Look at his face!"

Dylan's face is changing expression too. His jaw lowers and his mouth is slightly open as he listens to the up-tempo rhythms of the percussion and my playing guitar along with it.

Rachel says, "Can they get up?"

"Yeah," I say, "People can get up and dance if they want . . ."

"Wanna dance?" Elizabeth and Rachel both say to the children they are nearest. "Let's dance!"

Gabriel stands up and starts lifting his arms and hands up, marching, then stepping side to side with the music.

I get up too, and I start moving like Gabriel, joining him in stepping side to side.

"Go Gabriel!" says Kristy, admiringly.

"All right, Gabriel!" says David, also noticing Gabriel's movements and enjoying them.

I am singing the verse of the song: "Like a flashlight in the night . . . like a flashlight in the night . . ."

Dylan stands up. At first, he stands still. Then he starts bending his knees, down and up, fast, bouncing as he stands. He moves his arms out to his sides, and his body sways left and right.

Rachel is standing up dancing hand in hand with Rowen.

Carlos has stood up too, with Lisa kneeling in front of him, and they are holding hands and pushing and pulling their arms backward and forward like pistons.

Emily remains in her seat.

Rachel points to Gabriel's feet and says, "He's on the beat!"

I continue singing the lyrics, "Let your light shine! Let your light shine!"

"That's the way, Dylan!" says Kristy, "Dylan's doing it!"

Elizabeth points, "Look at James!" James turns around in a small circle, while stepping side to side to the music.

"All right, James!" says Kristy.

"Ja-ames!" says David, cheering. "Woo-hoo!"

"Look at this," says Elizabeth, pointing at Dylan. "Wow!"

I'm singing, "Your light will help someone . . . Your light will help someone . . . Like this!" I start the song's chorus, "Come on, yeah. Like this! . . . Here we go . . . Yeah . . . Like this!"

To borrow the words of early rock 'n' roller Jerry Lee Lewis, there is a whole lot of shaking going on in the group now: James circles, Gabriel steps, Dylan bounces, Rowen and Carlos shake and wave their arms with their partners.

Amidst his dancing, James reaches out his hand near me and then near Gabriel. I'm not sure if either of us fully noticed or reciprocated his outstretched hand. James is looking directly at Gabriel and sort of pointing to him.

Then Gabriel lifts his hands up a little higher and makes vocal sounds. Are Gabriel's vocalizations and movements in this moment just spontaneous free expressions? Or do his nonverbal vocalizations mean, "Don't bother me now, James, I'm busy"? Or, conversely, is he affirmatively responding to James's eye gaze, proximity, and possible pointing gesture?

"Here we go! Like this!" I sing. "Good job!" I say, appreciating people's moves.

James is really striding around with great energy and purpose, making a circle in three empathic swivels of his body.

"Come on, Caleb," I call out, wanting to recognize and cheer him too.

Elizabeth and David talk nearly simultaneously. Elizabeth says, "Look at this," pointing to James. David says, "All right, James!"

"I've never seen James do this," says Elizabeth.

"Wooo!" hoots someone. Elizabeth is dancing to the music. I am dancing and playing. The other adults are moving enthusiastically, and the children pick up on this too. Or is it the children's heightened responses to the music that are invigorating the adults? Both seem to be occurring simultaneously, and this energizes my playing and singing, creating a positive chain reaction.

David is now moving Rowen's hands in a dancing swimming-like motion.

I kneel on one knee, getting my body down nearer the children's height. I am rocking my head and upper body to the beat as I play guitar and sing, "Like this! Come on, yeah. Like this! Here we go . . ."

Elizabeth gestures both palms toward Dylan, ushering our attention toward his movements: "He's got rhythm!" she says.

"Dance it!" says David.

I hear a loud "Daaaah" from someone. I look up. It is coming from Emily or Caleb's direction. I start echoing a loud "Yeah," at the same pitch the child is using, incorporating it, and making it part of the song.

Dylan turns back to look in Caleb's direction and smiles. Both of Dylan's hands start tapping onto his hips simultaneously, along to the music.

As the song gradually moves toward its end, a lot of the class members are making noises—children clapping and vocalizing, adults saying "Yeah!" and "Good job!"

"Well, that felt good!" I say. "I wrote that one," I add, expressing my feeling of fulfillment, seeing the children and teachers respond positively to a song that I had composed.

"That's great!" says David. "James, you little dancing machine, come sit down." David hugs James and pulls him back toward his chair. "Nice dancin', buddy. Nice dancin'," David says with enthusiasm.

Elizabeth says, "So, that was fantastic!" as she leans forward to let me know.

"Yeah, that was good inspiration [to get up and dance]," I say.

David starts to say, "It was Gabriel who kept . . ."

And at nearly the same moment, Elizabeth interjects, "And it's nice and loud. It's just the beat, nice and loud."

Kristy agrees, "James was jammin' . . . Gabriel's got some good moves!"

Elizabeth says, "You see Dylan? Dylan had some good ones."

"Gabriel's cool," says Lisa, still thinking about him, and she smiles and bobs to the side one more time.

"He's still got it in his head," says Kristy, noticing Gabriel's continuing smile.

THREE ELEMENTS—RHYTHM, ENTRAINMENT, AND MOVEMENT

As I viewed the session video recording later, I was really encouraged to see the children's energetic and sustained involvement in this movement/dance activity. My initial goal had been to offer class members an appealing song that might stir them to sing, hum, sway, and interact with adults and peers while we were seated in the circle. But as we started, the teachers picked up cues that the preschoolers might be interested in standing up and dancing to the song. Tuning in to their responses and flexibly adjusting in the moment enabled larger and livelier expressions of involvement from the children than I'd anticipated. In the following sections I focus on three elements—rhythm, entrainment, and movement—that contributed to the children's level of engagement.

Rhythm

The drumbeat added a propulsive drive to the song. Combined with the guitar and singing, it got us—both children and adults—standing and moving to the music. Rhythm's power to move people has generated diverse traditions of dance, music, ritual, and other activities in cultures throughout history. The effects of rhythm and music have also been explored by neuroscientists like Patel et al. (2009). These authors have noted people's innate tendency to move in rhythmic synchrony with a beat—from subtle foot tapping or head nodding to expressive movement and dancing.

Music therapist Michael Thaut and colleagues (2007) have studied the human impulse to move to rhythm, and their research has endeavored to assess music's potential to assist patients in learning to walk again after a stroke. When a protocol of rhythmic cueing was introduced in rehabilitation sessions, patients with walking difficulties were able to gain increased evenness and stability in their gait after their stroke. The use of rhythm, Thaut found, stimulated the improvement of neurological processing and cortical reorganization in the injured brain. This technique proved to be more effective than conventional physical therapy in the research he conducted.

In different but related ways, the drum rhythms in our March music therapy session drew on the powers of rhythmic cues to evoke movement, and the percussion groove helped promote the participation and the dancing of the children and adults. All of the teachers and six of the seven children in the group stood up and began to move soon after the beat and the song began. The preschoolers were taking initiatives and joining in a shared activity—stepping side to side with the music, bouncing up and down, and turning circles—without adult verbal direction.

The children's simultaneous movements to the music and rhythm in a common activity in the classroom gave this collective dancing song a social dimension. Children were gazing at the motions of other children and adults, and class members appeared to start imitating other children's actions (i.e., James began to move in circles soon after Gabriel did).

Entrainment

Entrainment is "two or more rhythms synchronizing into one," writes musician Andrew Schulman (2016, p. 106). Musicologists and neuroscientists have studied the role of rhythm in prompting people to move in coordination together, not just separately and individually. *Entrainment* describes this process whereby people (or objects) rhythmically synchronize with each other; interacting in such a way that they adjust toward and eventually lock into a common phase and/or periodicity (Clayton et al., 2005).

In 1665, Dutch physicist Christiaan Huygens, inventor of the pendulum clock, identified the phenomenon of entrainment. He noticed that two clocks, when placed on a common support, would synchronize with each other. Even if the pendulums were deliberately placed into motion at different times, the clocks would soon re-synchronize into one shared rhythm. Entrainment can also manifest in people's everyday lives: tapping toes or nodding heads matching the beat of the music, footsteps becoming in sync when walking next to someone, or musicians coordinating to play in time together in a group.

The drum rhythms I introduced to the children, along with the song, contributed to an entrainment effect that resulted in children's and adults' simultaneous active involvement. In a classroom where I was trying to encourage shared attention and engagement in group activities, the beat of the recorded drum rhythms offered a welcome addition.

Movement

The opportunity to freely move and dance to the accompaniment of rhythmic music was another important aspect of the activity in the March session. Denac (2008) conducted research to determine the musical activity preferences of preschool children at school and at home. In that study, the children's three favorite activities at school were dancing and moving to music (42.7%), singing songs (29%), and playing instruments (16.5%). At home, the children's top three interests were listening to music, dancing and movement to music, and singing songs. Denac's research highlights movement and dance as one of the most preferred music activities at school and at home for many children.

As I have reviewed the vigorous responses of the seven children during the dancing in our March session, I have gained a new appreciation for movement as a means of encouraging children's attention and engagement in a group. Dance therapist Janet Adler (2007) documented her early work with children on the autism spectrum in the 1968 film, *Looking for Me*. Throughout her career, Adler explored the role of the *witness* in a dance/movement therapy approach called authentic movement. The witness is the one who watches and supports a mover's individual expressive movements, and this observer dialogues with the mover after their dancing experience. Thus, the authentic movement process was understood not simply as a solo dancer's venture but as the collaboration of a mover and a witness. Adler (1999) conceived that "the inner reality of the witness appears to be as vast, as complex—and as essential to the process—as the inner world of the mover" (p. 142). The amount of freedom, understanding, and play that are released in the mover may be directly related to the quality of the witness's presence and reactions.

I sensed that the excitement and enthusiastic praise voiced by the teachers and me—witnesses to the movements of Gabriel, Dylan, James, and other classmates—contributed to and helped sustain the children's participation, along with the beat, the music, and the chance to move. Attentive witnessing can become a form of social interaction. I believe that Gabriel, Dylan, and James were involved in implicit give-and-take interactions—not simply moving in individual self-expression. They were also perceiving and being influenced by peers' movements and teachers' verbal and emotional reactions. Norma Canner (1968) was another leader in dance/movement therapy, whom I found particularly inspiring. She captured some of the potential of movement and dance for children with developmental delays or disabilities when she wrote that movement is a way that young children *discover* their world, their bodies, and themselves.

I sometimes experienced insecurity about moving in front of others. But, at times, as in this March session, I could become encouraged by the energy of the children and teachers, and my worries and inhibitions would ebb. I would find myself freely moving to the music along with the preschoolers, surprisingly, modeling an enjoyment in moving and being enlivened by the dancing and expressions of the children and adults.

SUGGESTIONS FOR REFLECTION

I hope that the suggestions below may support you in exploring the following approaches:

- **Adding drum rhythms**. To add energy and drive to songs and to invite movement and dancing, you might experiment with combining live or recorded drum/percussion rhythms with playing guitar or other instruments. Sometimes a recorded percussion backing track can give the combination of syncopation and groove that helps people want to start moving and joining in the music. Or there may be participants in your group who can contribute improvised and interactive live percussion playing.

- **Including opportunities for free dancing in a group**. As a person who spends time with young children, you know what research confirms: that dancing is one of the most preferred musical activities for preschoolers. So movement and dancing can be effective catalysts for attracting shared attention and for promoting joint engagement. By allowing and encouraging free expression during the movement song in March, children on the spectrum were taking initiative and joining in the shared activity—stepping side to side with the music, bouncing up and down, and interacting with teachers and peers—without relying primarily on adult-directed verbal prompts.
- **Creating openings for simultaneous participation.** One of the benefits of this group-dancing song was that it enabled multiple children and teachers to be actively involved in social interactions and self-expression at the same time. All of us talking at once would have been chaotic and unintelligible, but all of us moving simultaneously gave a sense of togetherness. It prompted many moments of interpersonal, emotional, and social contact between the teachers and children. It caused some children to notice peers and to join in their movements.
- **Bringing your vitality into the group and getting influenced by the energy of the students and teachers.** You may find, as I did, that creating a new song and adding the drum rhythms and dancing garners active lively participation and decreases distress or lethargy.
- **Reflecting on how teachers can develop their abilities in leading an activity while also simultaneously improvising plans** in order to notice, adjust to, and incorporate the reactions of participants. Furthermore, it may prove useful to exchange ideas with a colleague about this question: What are some strategies to help music therapists grow in their skills in coordinating their guitar playing and singing—while also looking out at class members and picking up on the movements, emotions, and communications of the children and the adults?

CHAPTER 6

The "Beanbag Song"

Tactile and Visual Materials; Modeling and Mirroring Movements—April 13

There is a momentary pause before I begin the third song of our music session on April 13. Seven children—Carlos, Gabriel, Dylan, Jin Li, Emily, Rowen, and James—and four teaching staff look toward me.

I reach into my equipment bag and begin to lift something out of it, drawing inspiration from the way a magician might pull out an object from a hat.

"Ooo, what are these?" asks lead teacher David, building anticipation for the activity that is about to start. Dylan, Emily, and Carlos lean forward to watch from their semi-circle of yellow pine chairs. Gabriel wiggles, kicks up his feet, and vocalizes, "eee-yee-yee-yeee."

I lift up my orange-colored beanbag and quietly place it on the floor in front of the group. Four white dots, the numeral *4*, and the word *four* are printed on it.

"Four," announces Dylan, surprising me with his quick initiative to read and speak the number on the beanbag.

James cries out in an agitated voice, "Ah ma ma ma." Then he stops.

"A-fo," says another voice.

I then place several other brightly colored cloth beanbags next to the orange one.

CHOOSING, PASSING, AND MOVING DURING THE "BEANBAG SONG"

In the upcoming song, children can choose one of the beanbags that are lying in a row in front of them (e.g., a purple beanbag with the number *6*, a red one with the number *8*). The song's lyrics ask the child to pass the beanbag to the next child, who passes it on, person to person, around the circle. When we stop singing the verse, whoever is holding the beanbag will show us a motion. Then the teachers and preschoolers will join in the child's motion, repeating it for the number of times imprinted on the beanbag. So, when Carlos takes the number 4 beanbag that is passed to him, he chooses a motion of stretching out his legs, and then all of us join him, stretching out our legs four times with him.

Several primary goals of this activity include the following:

- Giving children a variety of opportunities for communicating choices through verbal/vocal expression or gestures
- Passing objects to each other
- Observing and imitating each other's body movements
- Engaging in social interactions in a shared musical game

Children want chances to move during class and to see and touch colorful materials with interesting textures. The "Beanbag Song" offers these possibilities and also supports learning about numbers and colors. As important as other goals, this music activity is meant to be fun, because children can often learn well during activities that tap into interests and foster enjoyment.

I reach again into my equipment bag and place an additional yellow beanbag on the floor, slowly and quietly as if engaging in a ceremony. The children and staff are watching. From their expressions, I sense that they are absorbing some of the sense of suspense and expectation.

"Three," says Dylan, reading the white printed number on the yellow beanbag.

"Three," says another child in a high-pitched voice. It is Rowen, who had earlier vocalized "A-fo," although I had not recognized that he was approximating the words "a four" at that moment.

I'm heartened as the class members speak up and initiate participation—children who can sometimes appear silent, or nonspeaking, or disconnected. Now, I'm seeing more of their abilities and interests as I try varied materials and activities.

I hold up another beanbag, a purple one, to show it to the children before I place it on the floor. Dylan is also noticing and communicating the colors, as we find out a few minutes later when we pass it to him and he spontaneously says, "Purple, purple."

Then Rowen speaks up. "Seeeks," he says, referring to the number printed on the purple beanbag.

"Six, that's right" says David, clarifying and confirming Rowen's verbalization.

"Good knowing, Rowen!" says Rachel, joining in the encouragement. I take one more beanbag, brown, with the number 7, out of my bag.

James begins crying loudly, insistently. The other six children are still quite focused, looking at the array of beanbags. But James punctuates the quiet with cries that continue for 10 seconds as we try to keep going with the activity. This periodically occurs within the group—one or more children start loudly expressing distress, side by side with other children who are content or enthusiastic, awaiting the continuation of the activity.

How best to respond? I don't have a fixed answer. One approach, however, is to rely on the teachers to respond to an individual child's distress, while I keep leading the activity for the group as a whole. When we try it this way, we're trusting that the activity and the music and the adults' interventions will eventually re-engage the child, or at least minimize the disruption.

Often that works tolerably well but today it proves difficult. For the next few minutes, James continues start-and-stop crying in cycles, and it seems to bring on unhappy noises from Gabriel too. Carlos slides to the floor. Noise and restlessness grow in the group. When one of the teachers tries to lift Carlos back into his seat, he yells and bucks in his chair like a bronco. "Sit down, sit down, no!" he yells. In the commotion, Emily starts to cry. Leaning back in her chair, hands raised, distress fills her face and open mouth. I usually don't see this kind of overt expression of emotion from Emily, nor do I typically witness her being so affected by the emotions of her classmates.

I'm still steadfastly (and almost comically in retrospect) trying to lead the activity as bedlam is breaking out. Somehow my persistence, and the galvanizing qualities of music, succeed in getting the children to settle back into the musical activity as I sing. I see that several of the children like Rowen and Dylan stay interested and focused. Dylan says, "Show it . . . Show it to me," as classmates and teachers pass the red beanbag to each other. When Carlos and James are each able to have a turn to hold and pass the beanbag, they, too, regain calm. In music therapy sessions, I am often inches from either chaos or cohesiveness within our group!

Gabriel—"He Knows!"

When we pass the beanbag to Gabriel, he initially does not reach for it. He is gazing into space. At this moment, he does not seem to be responding to the activity or relating to the people around him. Assistant teacher

Elizabeth takes his hand and puts the beanbag into it. He looks down at it and lightly taps it with his other hand: Pat, pat, pat.

"What number is this?" I ask him.

But he looks away and puts his hand over his forehead and cheeks. Covering his face and rubbing his eyes, I realize, may be signs that I'm asking him to attempt something that he either is not able to do yet or does not want to do. So I adjust and shift to offering him a chance to show us the next actions that we'll do in the song.

"It's eight! Number eight," I say. "Okay, we're going to do eight movements with Gabriel."

Gabriel slowly makes an upward stretching motion, raising both arms directly over his head. Is this an "I'm tired and don't want to be disturbed" stretching version of a yawn? Or is it the beginnings of an awakening response—someone starting to move after being roused from sleepiness or uninvolvement? I decide to react as if it's his first steps of waking up and getting into action. Maybe it's a hint of an opening for shared interaction. I mirror his motion, moving my hands up high to follow his. He looks toward me again and slowly changes his movement, bending his arms backward and down until his elbows are beside his ears, and his hands touch near the nape of his neck. Simultaneously, I do his same actions with him, and I add my voice to start counting out slowly and rhythmically, "One—two—three . . . ," in order to recognize and affirm his motions as part of our activity. My chanting the ascending numbers gives a common pulse for our movements that the whole class can hear and join in with.

At the count of three, a classmate, Carlos, begins imitating our motions and taking part in our shared arm movements.

Gabriel now seems to know that the class adults and some peers are following his motions, and he continues his movements in ways that start to almost resemble an exercise leader at a gym. He varies his movements once more and stretches his arms wide and high—like someone gathering an armful of sunlight—and I join him. He makes direct eye contact with me now and starts moving both arms forward, steadily bringing his hands closer together like he's going to do a giant slow-motion hand clap. He seems to adjust and momentarily pauses to give me a chance to catch up with his actions.

On the count of six, Dylan joins us in slowly bringing his outstretched hands toward a clap too.

Gabriel brings his hands closer together in front of his chest until they are about 10 inches apart. I do the same. Gabriel smiles.

With her own smile of wonder, Elizabeth says, "He knows!"—spontaneously pointing to Gabriel and glancing toward David, as if to share the moment of Gabriel seeming so aware and involved in the interpersonal connection between us.

During such shared attention and enjoyment, the distinction between leading and following becomes eclipsed by both of us adjusting to each other's motions. Gabriel looks energized, and just before I proclaim the last number on the beanbag, he opens his mouth wide in an expression that I am quite certain reveals both pleasure and anticipation.

We move together in sync as we bring our own right and left hands closer toward a simultaneous parallel hand clap, mirroring each other, each of us arriving at a clear audible "Clap!" at the exact moment that I count, "And . . . eight!"

"Yeah——!!" I cheer and so do several of the teachers.

Gabriel laughs, vocalizes, and wiggles happily.

Carlos is also clapping. Jin Li and Dylan are smiling too.

Elizabeth leans over to David. "That's something to do with him [Gabriel], right? We could do this, really . . . He likes it!" As I've later looked back on this moment from the video recording of the music session, I've thought that this is another small example of the potential benefits of collaboration. Teachers and therapist can learn from each other about varying approaches to help the students. The teachers see the ways that Gabriel becomes interested and interactive when we begin mirroring his movements during the beanbag song. They believe that they may be able to add this approach to other classroom activities.

Emily—"The Orange Four"

After a few moments I say, "All right, we have time for one more turn . . . Who wants a turn?" A brief pause ensues.

"Oh, good job," says David, "Emily said, 'I do.'"

I'm thankful that David has heard her reply. She had spoken softly and in a high pitch, and I did not hear it at that moment, although I hear it after reviewing the video later. I would have missed it, amid the other noises, unless David had brought it to the group's attention.

Emily then gets up from her chair, walks forward a few steps, bends down and scoops up two of the four remaining beanbags from the floor, taking one in each hand.

"Just one, Emily . . . ," I say. "Pick which one . . ."

Instead, Emily moves closer to me, and seems to have her own project in mind. She places the two beanbags beside me on the carpeted block where I am sitting. She is leaning into me and making sing-song sounds. In retrospect, I wonder if she thought this activity was like a previous class routine that involved returning an object back into a bag. Or is she interested in proximity with me, while grasping and carrying a couple of the beanbags, rather than following the steps for choosing one and passing it around the circle?

Soon, she makes a big arching reach and brings the orange beanbag next to me. And she allows me to get the yellow one from her other hand. I decide to welcome her big outstretching motion as an approximation of a choice of the orange beanbag. I begin to sing, "The orange *four* . . . goes round and round," and we ask Emily to sit back down and begin the process of passing the beanbag.

Dylan readily receives it and excitedly starts to shake it. David urges him to keep passing it on to Jin Li, and he does, although she does not hold out her hand to receive it as Dylan had. Jin Li doesn't seem to register much involvement in the passing, and Elizabeth ends up fully guiding her hand. When the orange beanbag comes toward Carlos, he reaches out to receive it, and then he independently passes it to Rowen. And we conclude the song by following Rowen's body movements four times. I'm pleasantly surprised to see Jin Li and Dylan imitating Rowen's movements and joining in these actions toward the end of the song without verbal prompting.

THE VALUE OF BRINGING TACTILE AND VISUAL MATERIALS INTO ACTIVITIES

Adding tactile materials such as the beanbags into music therapy sessions is an extension of the strategy of using visual aids (pictures and written cues) to support learning and communication with children on the autism spectrum. One characteristic of spoken communication is its transience—once voiced, the message is no longer directly present for participants. The beanbags, however, were appealing visual aids and tactile objects that the children *could continue to see and touch* in order to help extend their attention and interactions.

In fact, we saw several instances of the children reaching fundamental goals during today's beanbag song. We noticed the shared attention, social interactions, and synchronized movements with Gabriel and other children. We observed the verbal communication of naming the numbers by Dylan and Rowen. We also saw communication via gestures, facial expressions, and eye gaze by other classmates. At the same time, there was considerable disruption, too, especially during the middle of the activity. James's cycles of crying were followed by vehement expressions of unhappiness from several peers. This seemed an example of the contagiousness of emotion within a group.

It was surprising that out of these moments of distress and apparent disunity came subsequent moments of togetherness, cooperative movement, and happiness shown by Gabriel and others in the group. It was through movement that Gabriel began interacting with me. Shared physical action was the key ingredient that enabled our give and take during the "Beanbag Song." He smiled, and he increased and varied his movements when I joined him in his motions. He led and I followed and then we both moved in synchrony, clapping and laughing together at the same time. Researchers have been investigating the ways that imitating and joining in the actions or vocalizations of children on the spectrum can elicit responsiveness and social interaction between adults and children. Psychologists Daniel Stern (2000) and Edward Tronick (2007) have also raised awareness about the important role of mirroring, empathic responsiveness, and building upon a child's actions and emotions in nurturing children's development.

However, research has also found that preschoolers on the spectrum often display notably fewer acts of imitation and social and emotional reciprocity than typically developing peers. Therefore, Gabriel's and my capacity to find shared ways to interact through imitation and simultaneous movement during this song was something that I was grateful for. What happened between us seemed to demonstrate the benefits of balancing child-led initiatives and adult-directed elements within activities. During this song, it was my following Gabriel's body movements that led to his more enhanced level of interest and coactivity.

I was also struck by music's role in providing a flexible consistent song structure that helped us synchronize with one another and enjoy the playfulness of it. Songs that involved mirroring, movement, individual attention, and improvised exchanges gave the children increased opportunities to become engaged in reciprocal interactions. In the midst of the music, the preschoolers had openings to learn through observing others and through having others attune to and follow their lead.

My thinking has been challenged by those who assert that children on the autism spectrum do not learn through observation and imitation. Psychologist Ennio Cipani (2008) has written, "One of the primary characteristics of children with autism is their inability to learn observationally" (p. 148). He has stated that the language deficits and joint-attention impairments of autistic children prevent this. I understand his emphasis on the potentially formidable challenges with language and attention for some children. But as a result of my work in this classroom, I do not agree with the assertion that children on the autism spectrum do not learn observationally. Gabriel, Dylan, Jin Li, Carlos, and Rowen *were* learning observationally. They watched adult leaders and peers and began joining in shared movements, and they were participating in social interactions though passing beanbags, smiling, clapping, and communicating with words. The children's abilities were emerging when given the additional supports of music, the playful and consistent routines of the song, the visual and tactile materials, and the responsive adjustments of adults in the group.

Emily's Verbal Communication

Saying, "I do," Emily verbally requested a turn to pick one of the beanbags. This was a welcome development that reflected an increasing communicative responsiveness on her part. It also reflected David's crucial role in recognizing and encouraging Emily's utterance. The advantages of teamwork within a group were clear in this moment: Working together, the teaching staff and I could become more aware of, and collectively support, the children's early steps toward communication, which were sometimes small or easy to overlook. When Emily did get her chance to choose a beanbag, she picked up two beanbags simultaneously instead of selecting one—similar to her previous attempts to get two instruments at the same time. It was possible that she was still learning the process of choice making itself. Perhaps she did not quite understand the assumption that choosing meant selecting just one object among several. And, it's also possible that she was instinctively wanting to rewrite the rules so that she could choose to have both beanbags!

Dylan's Increasing Participation

As I review Dylan's participation in the song, I see his spontaneous and repeated use of expressive language. He named numbers and colors, and requested a chance to hold or see one of the beanbags, saying, "Show it . . . Show it to me." He joined in the group activity by imitating the actions of his peers who were involved in the song. He smiled and clapped as we cheered Gabriel. In earlier months, I had experienced how he sometimes shut down by putting his head in his lap or evading certain tasks or interactions. More recently, I was becoming aware of how often he *was* participating and interacting.

The children, teachers, and I had been involved in the weekly music therapy group for 7 months at this point. Now, in my research, I've looked back to describe and consider in particular the participation of Dylan, Gabriel, and Emily. Amidst the continuing challenges, I've found encouragement in Gabriel's synchronous movements and play during this class session, and I have been heartened to see and hear Dylan's and Emily's emerging abilities in verbal communication and shared interpersonal interactions.

SUGGESTIONS FOR REFLECTION

In today's "Beanbag Song," class members participated in synchronized movements and communication through speaking words and joining in motions together. Ideas for your future consideration include the following:

- **Bringing tactile and visual materials into activities (e.g., beanbags, scarves, parachutes).** As indicated above, the beanbags can give children chances to see and touch appealing visual and tactile objects during the song. This helps to extend their attention, interaction, and communication.
- **Creating motivating consistent routines and structures with songs.** An enjoyable melody and lyrics repeated in a song provide clear structure and establish predictable routines that can inspire and guide the children's next steps of participation in an activity.
- **Inviting and responding to a child's initiatives to offer shared control** and back-and-forth opportunities during adult-facilitated songs and activities. Children's active involvement often happens when adults are able to make flexible changes during activities to adjust to the varying abilities and needs of the children in a classroom group.
- **Seeing and affirming physical movements as key openings into communication and interpersonal connection**. For Gabriel and for other children like him, the opportunity to move as a form of self-expression—while having one's movements noticed, validated, and responded to by another person—can lead from isolation and lack of

involvement into active participation and communication during shared play.

- **Sparking children's emerging abilities in verbal communication and interpersonal interaction.** The combination of colorful tactile objects and music and movement can help stimulate children's use of expressive language (e.g., Dylan asking, "Show it to me," and Rowen and Dylan speaking the names of the colors and numbers). These combined factors can galvanize class members to take an interest in interpersonal exchanges during the musical game and to move in sync with classmates.

- **Working in collaboration within the classroom group.** Cooperating together we can become more aware of, and collectively support, the children's early communicative actions which were sometimes faintly discernible or easy to miss. For example, it was David's hearing of Emily's, "I do," that let the class know that she was quietly requesting a turn. This enabled me to follow through and give attention and encouragement to Emily as she joined in the activity and communicated with spoken language.

CHAPTER 7

"Three for Three"
May 26

In late May, nearly at the end of the first year in our preschool music group, I'm beginning to sing the "Hello Song." I turn toward 4-year-old Carlos. Though he's sitting in a chair, he has bent down low, stretching his arm toward the floor to touch it with his left hand. Yet his right hand is raised, reaching up.

Lead teacher David grasps Carlos's extended right hand and pulls him upward, and for a moment it somehow reminds me of pulling on a rope to bring up a bucket of water from an old-fashioned well. Then David gives Carlos a hug around the shoulder until he's sitting upright in his chair. Carlos rests his arm familiarly on David's knee. In these acts of physical contact, I see the affectionate trust that the teachers and students have developed over time in this class.

"WHAT'S YOUR NAME?"

Five boys and two girls are seated in the circle now: Gabriel, James, Dylan, Rowen, Carlos, Emily, and Jin Li. Three adult staff are with them: David; assistant teacher Elizabeth; and Kristy, the personal aide for James.

Carlos—"Give Me Five!"

I play the guitar once, stop the rhythmic strumming and sing, "And . . . what's your name?" I move closer to Carlos and gesture.

David leans in toward him and also whispers, "What's your name?"

Carlos looks up at me and says decisively, "Car-los!"

David gives him a fast chest rub and responds, "Good job, buddy!"

"Carlos! Nice job!" I say. Then I sing "Carlos!" boisterously.

David pats Carlos's hand vigorously; the multiple fast pats sounding like applause. "Good job!" David says again quietly. Understanding the background is important here: Carlos could sometimes become dysregulated with frustration and anger that would boil over at times. So it is hopeful to have these alternative moments of harmony and greeting and affirmation.

I lean back, sway in my seat, play the guitar, bend forward, and gesture my open palm toward Carlos, inviting a high five.

He tilts his chin up and says "Ji," or "G," looking at me steadily. I take this as an approximation of "Geoff," or the "G" sound that starts my name. Carlos's expression, his direct eye contact with me, and his smile seem contented and playful too.

"Geoff! That's right!" I say, feeling happy and energized. "Give me five!"

Carlos then slaps my open palm with strength and purpose.

Kristy laughs softly.

"Yeah!" I say, then turn to invite the rest of the group, singing, "Let's wave hello to Carlos!"

Carlos looks out toward the teachers and children. After a pause, he raises his hand, as if starting to wave to classmates. Then his fingers find something interesting on the bulletin board behind his head, and he starts to explore it while still looking out at the group.

There was one child's response to Carlos that I had already missed, I realized in hindsight, after reviewing the video recording of this session. When I had asked him, "What's your name?" Emily had said a soft quick sharp-pitched "Cah," and then "Cah-oh!" As I relisten to the video recording, Emily's "Cah-oh," sounds like an approximation of "Car-los." She looks toward him and seems to attempt to communicate this.

Now I'll return to my account of the session as it's unfolding. I'm singing the chorus again. "Hello everybody, yes indeed . . . yes indeed . . . It's good to see you." The teachers are singing with me and their involvement helps create a supportive spirit in the group.

Dylan's Name and Wave

Turning toward Dylan, I then sing, "And . . . what's your name?" and I pause.

He looks in my direction, his head tilted slightly off to the side. He doesn't say anything for 2 seconds. Then he softly says two sing-song, nearly-inaudible syllables; the last one sounds like "sox."

David leans toward Dylan, points, and whispers the beginning sound of his name. David's prompts—his whispered voice and gesture—have an intimate rather than coercive quality.

Dylan turns to look at David, then he turns back to face me with a smile, and he says loudly, "Good job!" He gyrates excitedly in his chair as if he's already received praise for saying his name.

Leaning in closer, David puts one arm around Dylan's shoulder and guides his other hand in position to tap his chest.

David prompts him, "Say 'my name is . . .'"

"Dylan!" says Dylan in a raspy, excited, forceful voice. He says this at the same moment as David directs Dylan's open hand to tap his chest.

Various congratulatory noises and motions erupt simultaneously.

"Dylan!" I call out, "Good job, Dylan!" I play along hard on the guitar with percussive beats on the chords.

"Dyl—an," Kristy sings.

David pats him on the back fast, along with a few circle rubs.

Dylan smiles with his mouth open, tilts his head back, and seems to soak up the praises that are filling the room.

"Dyyyyy-lan!" calls out his classmate Carlos, joining in the commotion. And it's exciting to hear Carlos using his words to acknowledge and pay attention to his peer Dylan.

Then I sing, "Let's wave hello to Dylan."

"Say 'Hi, Dylan,'" Elizabeth invites the other children.

Carlos extends his hand in Dylan's direction, and David energetically takes Carlos's hand and shakes it with him toward Dylan, saying, "Hi, Dylan!"

Dylan's face goes expressionless, a pause for a moment.

Then Dylan smiles and raises his left hand and swipes it in the air, right to left, in what seems an idiosyncratic approximation of waving hello. His jaunty rhythm and raised index finger remind me of a person making an emphatic gesture during a debate.

"Hi, buddy!" says David. Dylan looks into David's eyes, smiling.

From across the room, Jin Li, who very rarely speaks, turns to Elizabeth and says, "Elizabeth." Jin Li's unexpected foray into talking and directly initiating contact with a teacher is a major surprise. Is her verbal communication inspired by Elizabeth's waving and friendly response to Dylan?

"Elizabeth, that's right!" confirms Elizabeth warmly, as she turns her attention to Jin Li.

It seems that when excitement and happiness get generated during the greeting and naming in the "Hello Song," peers like Carlos and Jin

Li are drawn into the process. This is especially remarkable for Jin Li, who until then was one of the most silent and seemingly withdrawn members of the class.

"Hello, everybody. Yes indeed," I sing, reintroducing the chorus again and signaling that we are moving on to greet the next classmate.

"Em-lee" and "Ga"

Facing toward Emily, I sing, "And . . . what's your name?"

Emily, who has been looking directly at me during most of the "Hello Song," then starts to look away, to her right, as if saying with her body language, "Who, me?"

David moves toward Emily.

I say "Yeah," and nod to Emily, to confirm it is her turn.

David begins to reach for Emily's left hand to cue her to tap near her heart and say her name.

But immediately Emily taps her own chest, saying "Em-lee."

She looks to David's face and then to me. I sense such interpersonal awareness in this, as if Emily is communicating, "Did you see and hear what I just did?"

Overlapping praises start.

"Yay——" says Kristy with a long call.

"Yea-hey!" I interject enthusiastically, "All right!"

Gabriel says, "Aayyyee" in a sustained oscillating sound, like the ending vowel of "Yay!" or "Hey!"

"Emily!" cheers Elizabeth.

David claps his hands together several times, saying, "Yaaaayyy!" in a deep carrying voice, like a playful imitation of a loud fan at a sports event.

David says, "Three for three!" He looks at Carlos, Dylan, and Emily with appreciation. David's words also help me realize and enjoy the three children's willingness and ability to each say their own name during today's "Hello Song." Taking these steps in social and verbal communication within the music group is an encouraging development!

Emily looks up steadily, alertly, and yet without much expression as we loudly celebrate her.

Then she covers her face with her hands and rubs her eyes.

She removes her hands from her face. And a brief hint of a smile appears and then is replaced by a neutral look. She arches her back, stretching in her chair. I start singing, "Let's wave hello to Emily." She sits quietly, facing forward, and doesn't turn to look at the adults or children as we wave.

Dylan, however, jumps and pivots in his chair, turning left. He breaks into a smile and starts covering his face with his hands while saying "Hello" into his hands.

David reaches for Dylan's hand to guide him to wave hello to Emily.

"No! Hi! Hemmie!" Dylan loudly proclaims. Actually, even upon review, I can't tell if Dylan said, "Hemmie," or something approximating "Emily" or another word. He is grinning widely, bouncing in his chair, bringing his hands together and apart, and eventually touching his forehead and mouth with both hands cupped together.

In this moment, Dylan and Emily present a great contrast. He becomes excited and loud, and she becomes quiet and still. His emotions and energy seem to burst forth, and her emotions and energy seem contained and enigmatic, with her alert eye gaze and slight smile hinting at awareness and possible reactions under the surface.

Emily keeps her gaze up but doesn't direct it to one person. This makes me feel, as it often has, that she is still watching our reactions, checking out what is happening while also keeping a distance.

When I move on to the next child's turn, Emily's body seems to relax and become more animated. She stretches upward, makes a squished-up face, and then clearly smiles and makes noises. It is as if a careful watchfulness shifts into a childlike funny facial expression, stretch, squirm, and brief vocalization.

When it is Gabriel's turn, I sing "What's your name?" He makes a breathy expelling "Ga" sound that might be an approximation of the beginning of his name. This would be an exciting development. Or it might be some other expressive sound—it is hard for me to tell. His classmate Carlos says, "Gabriel," in the kind of loud stage whisper that adults sometimes use to prompt children. Then Gabriel rubs both eyes and opens his mouth wide, but no more sounds come out. He twists, stretches in his chair, and yawns. He doesn't look upset, but he doesn't appear to focus on the waving greeting of a classmate or the teachers' attempts to draw him further into communication at this moment. Two familiar questions arise for me: How do I best recognize and affirm Gabriel's vocalizations or interactions, even when I'm not quite sure what I'm hearing and what he's conveying? And how can I create new activities, or refine current ones, to help Gabriel further his communication with the adults and children in their classroom?

DEVELOPMENTS DURING THE FIRST SCHOOL YEAR

In addition to describing the children's actions during this morning's "Hello Song," as I've done in this chapter, I'd like to delineate some of the positive developments with several of the children during the span of the first school year. And I'll attempt to summarize some of the continuing challenges.

Earlier in the year, Dylan often hadn't said his name, even when we tried our best to facilitate this. Sometimes he had looked slightly at a loss, and often he had turned away from us. In the preceding excerpt we see traces of Dylan's earlier difficulties or elusiveness—initially hesitating and uttering some not-quite intelligible sounds. However, he also showed fundamental differences from earlier class sessions. In the May session, he engaged in the "Hello Song," gave his name, showed his pleasure, and interacted through smiles, eye contact, a waving gesture, and verbal expression. These were substantial developments. He was showing an increased ability and willingness to relate with us

Similarly, early in the year, Emily had often responded with averted gaze, withdrawal of attention, blank expression, and no vocalization or verbalization during her turn in the "Hello Song." Here at the end of the school year she was attentive, and she said her own name, looked at adults and peers, and seemed to approximate a peer's name, Carlos. In these and other moments during the music therapy sessions, she was demonstrating a developing engagement with people, objects, and activities. Emily's responses still contained moments of seeming remoteness or absent facial expression. Nevertheless, like Dylan, it was becoming evident that at times she was clearly interacting with us rather than turning away.

Partnerships Involving Teachers, Music Therapist, and Children

To understand key factors that were contributing to the children's increasing communication and interaction, I think that it is important to reflect on the decisive influence of the teachers. Throughout the school year, David, Elizabeth, and Rachel encouraged the children's engagement and communication, which helped lead to steps like Carlos, Dylan, and Emily saying their names in the "Hello Song." For example, David's actions of moving closer to each preschooler during their turn, whispering encouragement, and offering positive physical contact helped activate the children's interest and involvement. His enthusiasm and humor also had an impact. Rather than a drill instructor pushing children to complete work, his approach was intimate, friendly, and playful. During the whole semester, the teachers had a pivotal influence, in combination with the attracting forces of the music and the participation rituals that I was leading with my guitar and voice, in helping to enable and inspire the class members during the group.

Our experience in the preschool music group has been that a team approach of teachers, therapists, and children cooperating together is vital to making class activities helpful in promoting development with children on the spectrum. What a contrast this is from the popular idea of the individual hero (whether a charismatic principal, teacher, or therapist) whose exceptional personality and skills almost single-handedly bring about the needed changes for a school, class, or child. A more-group-centered understanding of the causes of change, however, is also emphasized in approaches to education and therapeutic support like the SCERTS model introduced earlier. "Learning is a partnership" the SCERTS founders assert, in which all the involved school participants—children and their adult partners—share the responsibilities "for making interactions work and for growing and adapting over time" (Prizant et al., 2006, p. 79). This approach urges adults to regularly adjust and improve to meet the children's needs (rather than focusing solely on getting the children to change). The partnerships also involve cultivating in-class collaboration between teachers, assistants, music therapists or other service providers, and the children. And although family members were not usually able to attend the classroom music group because of their work and life commitments, I share the SCERTS model's recognition of the crucial irreplaceable role of parents, siblings, and extended family in the broader learning partnership.

The distinction between individual effort and collaboratively working together is also a key issue because the factors that promote children's development, I believe, are often too narrowly defined. Researchers frequently seek an independent variable or an individual intervention that causes change. This can distort the reality that change is often precipitated by multiple *inter*dependent variables. Developments result from the combined influences of several different interacting adults, peers, and interventions.

Constraints That Can Limit Cooperation

By emphasizing the value of collaboration among teachers, music therapist, and children, I do not mean to minimize the challenges involved. There are many factors that can limit or prevent cooperation. School leaders may officially recognize the benefits of collaboration, yet also structure teachers' meetings or teachers' preparation during hours that conflict with the music session times. When a teacher is working in another part of the room or attending to other responsibilities or preparing for future activities, that can prevent actual teacher-therapist teamwork during a classroom music group. Hayes (2016) outlines additional possibilities of envy and differing agendas that may arise as varied school professionals each strive in their own ways to help children. Or it may not be clear to teachers how they can best contribute to the group when the music therapist temporarily leads the class. Thus, teaching staff may sometimes over-direct the children in an attempt to help them get involved. Conversely, teachers may sometimes become disengaged because the music activities do not seem stimulating or useful. Staff shortages and frequent staff turnover, rising class sizes and caseloads, limited or nonexistent time for shared planning and meeting together, differences in teaching philosophies and practices, and "turf wars" are some of the challenges to collaboration also discussed by Prizant et al. (2006).

Collaborative Relationships and Group Cohesiveness

When I think of all the possible hindrances to cooperation outlined above, I gain a new appreciation for the harmonious partnerships that we experienced during the first year in the preschool music group. Teachers David, Rachel, and Elizabeth created a classroom environment that was not only welcoming for the children; it was also welcoming for me as the music therapist and for related services professionals, internship students, and others. The teachers were very actively involved during the music group in supporting and playing with the children. The dynamics of collaborative leadership were remarkably free of envy or disagreements about methods. Our interactions were more characterized by valuing each other's contributions as we combined a range of educational and therapeutic expertise. I am reminded of psychiatrists and educators Irvin Yalom and Molyn Leszcz's (2005) description that "members of a cohesive group feel warmth and comfort in the group and a sense of belongingness; they value the group and feel in turn that they are valued, accepted, and supported by other members" (p. 55). I appreciated the cohesiveness of the classroom group and the warmth and sense of belonging shared during the music sessions. We were able to find enjoyment in the songs and in the caring attention among the teachers and children.

In summary, I believe that the classroom dynamics of learning as a partnership—in which collaboration contributed to group cohesiveness—were important factors in supporting the children's increasing communication and interaction within the music group.

Ongoing Uncertainties and Possible Idiosyncratic Approximations

With some children, however, it was more difficult to perceive developments in communication. For example, since Gabriel did not seem able to articulate his name yet, the invitation to verbal expression offered by the "Hello Song" may not have been well-matched for him. Yet in this session, he responded to "What's your name?" with a vocalized "Ga" that might have been an approximation of the beginning of his name. Or it might have been sound making unrelated to his name. Even after reviewing the video recording multiple times, I am not clear about his intention or the meaning of his vocalization and the subsequent way he opened his mouth without emitting sounds. It was noteworthy that Gabriel responded with a vocalization directly after I sang him the question. His timing suggested some form of communicative response. If so, such beginning proto-verbal communication would have been a positive step.

However, his body movements and attention, as in this excerpt, often did not appear recognizably focused and purposeful during his turn, and this made it harder for me to gauge the intention of his vocalizing. In hindsight, because Gabriel had greater intellectual and language challenges than classmates Emily and Dylan, I wonder if I should have more vigorously supported and praised what he *might* have been doing, even if I was unsure. It was difficult, because my offering genuine acknowledgment and praise was usually dependent on my ability to understand a specific child's response. Yet my understanding of Gabriel's response was often incomplete or uncertain. My aspiration was to continue to discover ways to authentically affirm his current efforts while still encouraging him toward further developments.

MY CONTINUING LEARNING AND QUESTIONS ABOUT APPROXIMATE STEPS

In this session, there were also other more recognizable moments when children were approximating words or gestures, in addition to giving more-fully-realized versions. Emily had said "Cah-oh" in reference to her classmate, Carlos. Dylan and Carlos each gave what seemed to be idiosyncratic versions of waving hello. Growing in awareness of these approximations—and building upon them—was complicated by current professional pressures to provide concrete measurements of "successful outcomes." The children's not-fully-formed steps toward conventional communication were less noticed and valued when preschoolers' achievements of adult-defined predetermined educational goals were the only behaviors that "counted" and were being measured. The risk, I thought, was that we were being directed to focus so much on getting the end result, that we could miss the actual small signs of progress that were emerging because they didn't yet demonstrate narrower preconceived ideas of success.

As I reviewed my first year with the preschool class, I saw more clearly the importance of actively watching for, and responding to, the small early steps of approximation, intention, or communication with children like Gabriel, James, and Jin Li. I also recognized, with appreciation, the children's increasing engagement in interpersonal interaction and verbal communication: Dylan, Emily, and Carlos each speaking their names and, in prior sessions, requesting and playing instruments; dancing, following, and initiating movements during action songs; attending to visual images; and reaching forward to choose and pass tactile materials.

SUGGESTIONS FOR REFLECTION

- **What led to several of the children saying their own names and showing signs of developing social interaction and communication** during the "Hello Song" toward the end of this school year?
- **How much of a role did the classroom teachers play in promoting participation and group cohesiveness in the music therapy group**? What nurtures, or hinders, cooperative appreciative interactions among children, teachers, and music therapist in a classroom group? How much are broader systemic factors—local school practices and current national education policies—impacting classroom cohesiveness?
- **What is the optimum balance of familiarity and adjustment?** How do group leaders decide when to stick with a familiar social routine/ritual in order to give children time to gradually know it and join in? And when do leaders choose to

revise routines and activities to try to better match the abilities of the class members?

- **What could help adults grow in recognizing and responding to children's idiosyncratic approximations,** early possible small steps of communication or interpersonal contact, which may differ from familiar demonstrated acts of conventional communication or social interaction?

- **How can researchers account for the possibilities of *multiple* causes and *interdependent* variables?** Studies often seek to isolate one independent variable as the cause of change, based on a binary paradigm of independent variables or dependent variables. In our preschool classroom, however, it seemed that there were multiple interdependent causes of change: It was the music and the familiar structure of the "Hello Song," the warmth and physical contact and positive emotions of the teachers, and the therapist's and children's developing connections with teachers and peers, all of which were resulting in steps in shared attention, communication, and social interaction.

Part II

THE SECOND SCHOOL YEAR OF MUSIC THERAPY WITH THE CHILDREN

CHAPTER 8

Beginning the Second Year

Changes and Challenges—October 20 to December 8

There were significant changes at the preschool during my second year with the music group. The local school system expanded its program of applied behavior analysis, intending to enhance its services for preschoolers on the spectrum. As previously mentioned in Chapter 4, ABA is a systematic instruction program based on carefully repeated drills, rewards, and consequences. By expanding its own ABA services, the school could save the costs of paying to send autistic children to an out-of-district ABA school or program. In the preschool's new plans, lead teacher David and assistant teachers Elizabeth and Rachel would be replaced next year with a group of new ABA staff.

During the year that I will portray in the upcoming chapters, neither David, Rachel, nor Elizabeth knew where they would be teaching next year. They would not be able to continue their current jobs, and they would no longer be part of the close-knit teaching team that they had formed. Their future assignments within the school system had not been decided yet. As the year progressed, the addition of several new children into the class brought further complexity and challenges to the group environment. David was tasked with coordinating the children's schedules with the new ABA director, while continuing to provide and oversee each of the previously scheduled educational and therapeutic services.

These changes introduced increased pressures and tensions. David did not attend as many of the music therapy sessions during this second year. I would see him at his desk near the doorway, working on student reports, parent communication, and coordination with the ABA program; the school administration; and the speech, occupational, and physical therapy services. Since I had been coming to share music with the preschool for 2 years before undertaking my practitioner research study,

I had worked together for 3 years with David, Rachel, and Elizabeth, and they were close colleagues. The school's decision to replace them next year very much saddened and troubled me.

I continued to work weekly with Rachel and Elizabeth during the upcoming year, but we often missed David's presence and his energy, strength, and spirit. He helped make music therapy sessions an effective partnership: He was gifted at discovering specific ways to encourage the children's participation and communication during the activities that I introduced into the classroom. Thankfully Rachel and Elizabeth's knowledge of the children and abilities in teaching remained powerfully in effect during the course of the second year. We appreciated those days when David was able to join us and again help motivate participation, enjoyment, and interconnections within the group.

FIELD NOTES FROM EARLY IN THE SECOND YEAR

Since the beginning of my work at the school, I had written field notes after each music therapy session. I described interactions with the children and the difficulties and questions that were arising within the group. To give a few specific examples, I will share several observations and concerns from my field notes during the autumn of my second year of research in the class.

"Gabriel said a word!" I celebrated on October 20th. "[He said:] 'apple' . . . as I showed a picture of an apple for 'The Sharing Song.'" This was one of the rare moments that I'd heard Gabriel speak a word. It was exciting to hear him use verbal communication when we introduced this picture as part of the song.

"Elina's mother brought her in late," I wrote in my field notes from October 27. "She cried loudly for the remainder of the session." The children's crying was a periodic reality within the class, but the difficulty was greater in this year's group than in last year's. Elina's incidences of crying were more frequent than her classmates, but she was not alone. Talan, Gabriel, and Jonathan also had bouts of crying, which ranged from brief to lengthy. During these times, it was challenging to keep the class focused and constructively engaged in the music.

"Chaos early but attention late," I wrote about the session on November 3. "Getting the group to settle was hard. I got to the class early, which was good. [It] took time to galvanize the group . . . I need one more activity for this month's plan. Need more movement, and visuals. How to promote speech better in the 'Hello Song'? Also, social interaction . . . How?"

My subsequent field notes from November 10 showed me attempting to formulate answers to some of these questions. I wrote, "Incorporate [asking the students]: Who wants a turn? Incorporate: Choosing from pictures and objects." Thus, in the early months of my second year of research, I was urging myself to ask the class members additional questions to elicit speech, and I was trying to figure out how to incorporate new choice-making opportunities. I wanted to bring in more pictures and objects to enable verbal and nonverbal communication, and I sought to create more chances for children to move to music with their classmates.

AN EXCERPT FROM THE SESSION ON DECEMBER 8

By the December 8th session I'd been working with the new class for 2 months. As I walked into the room, Rachel and Elizabeth were getting the children ready, bringing them to the circle of chairs. Emily, Gabriel, and Dylan were there, along with new classmates Talan and Jonathan.

"So we're still missing . . . ," said Elizabeth, scanning the children.

"Nicolas and Elina," said Rachel, naming two additional children who were part of this year's class.

Elizabeth brought the weighted vest and started to put it on Gabriel. Gabriel lifted his legs, waved his arms, made a loud continuing "eee" sound, and rapidly pitter-pattered his feet on the floor. "Stop!" Elizabeth said to him. He stopped. "Thank you," she said. She leaned over to give him a kiss on the forehead while continuing to put on his vest. Putting it on and adjusting it actually took a while on that day, 31 seconds to fully complete.

So while we were waiting, I started playing the guitar, softly introducing background music, without talking or singing. Children's voices from the hallway outside mixed with the children's in the classroom, and the teachers' instructions, and the chairs scraping into position. I was hoping that the sounds of the guitar would reach the children through the hubbub.

Gradually, the melody and rhythm and my gaze began to attract the attention of some of the children. Dylan, Emily, Gabriel, and Talan turned their bodies and eye gaze toward me.

Talan waved his hand and said "Hiiiiiii" to me, stretching out the word in a way that sounded like singing. This elicited a big smile from me. "Hi," I whispered back. I was keeping quiet because Elizabeth had just said a loud "Stop" to Gabriel. I also wanted that quiet shared listening to last a little longer.

I was moving as I played guitar—nodding my head, rocking side to side easily. Though it was a gray midwinter day, I was smiling and plucking the guitar strings.

Over time, the other sounds in the room temporarily subsided.

For 20 seconds, four of the five children sat quietly, leaned slightly toward me, and listened. They were attentive in a more focused way than usual. Perhaps I was also listening and paying attention to the children in a new way while simply playing nonverbal instrumental music. When I started singing the "Hello Song," all five of the children remained focused for another 22 seconds. I was looking to their faces, moving my gaze from child to child, then to the circle as a whole, trying to meet and encourage each sign of interest and each moment of shared attention.

I turned to Emily and started singing, "And, what's your name?" It was as if the spell of quiet attention was broken. Lots of motion ensued. Several children seemed to withdraw their attention and shift to a closed posture. Dylan lowered his head right down into his lap. Gabriel twisted in his chair to look behind him. Jonathan looked toward Emily, watching what would happen. Talan, on the other hand, said "Hiiiii" again and waved his hand in greeting, and he kept doing this repeatedly.

Emily made no sound, gave no response, when I asked her name. She looked at me with an alert unchanging expression. She wasn't slumped over, lethargic, or turning away. She was unmoving but attentive, hands resting in her lap, one on each leg.

"What's your name?" reiterated teaching intern Natalie, leaning her face right next to Emily's. I was wishing Natalie had allowed Emily a little more time before prompting her again. Emily remained silent. Natalie leaned close to Emily and physically steered Emily's face to look at her. "What's your name?" Natalie asked again.

"Aya name," said Emily, barely audible.

Natalie pivoted so that she was again facing Emily: "Say, my name is . . . ," Natalie's hand directed the side of Emily's face—like a large blinker steering a horse—to look only forward. "Say Em-i-ly."

Emily emitted a muffled sound like "Eh-guy" that sounded somewhat like the initial sound of her name.

But it felt forced and uncomfortable.

Why the use of hands like horse blinkers to direct her gaze? In the opening of the "Hello Song" Emily had been giving her direct eye gaze without this.

I felt troubled about Natalie's almost-domineering methods. My preference would have been to find ways to attract Emily's response rather than compel it. Yet David had sometimes been initially physically directive with the children. Over time, he cultivated an affectionate and cooperative rapport with the preschoolers which often resulted in their voluntary participation. What made the difference between Natalie's approach, which felt more forced to me, and David's, which felt strong but encouraging and intimate? How do teachers and therapists find a balance between assertive goal-directed methods and patient open-ended facilitation?

In this moment, however, my thoughts returned to the reality that Emily remained quiet and more withdrawn this morning. For whatever reason, she was not as willing or able to say her name as she had been at the end of the last year.

Subsequent turns with the other children did not fare well either. Gabriel remained relatively passive during his turn and made little apparent effort to interact with me or other people in the group. Dylan quietly said his name into his shirt—but he did say it! After a protracted turn of asking and waiting with Talan, we weren't able to enable him to say his name or greet the other children.

Jonathan began a loud outburst, refusing Rachel's attempts to prompt him. He reached out as if to hit her face or push her away, grabbed her arm, and threw part of his picture schedule across the room. It was quite unfamiliar to see this open conflict between one of the children and Rachel, who typically fostered warm and harmonious relationships with the children.

Today's "Hello Song" reminded me of a verse from William Butler Yeats's (1921) poem, "The Second Coming": "Things fall apart; the centre cannot hold."

ANALYZING THE RECURRENT AND ADDITIONAL DIFFICULTIES IN MUSIC SESSIONS

What was causing the difficulties during the "Hello Song" this morning? At the end of the previous school year, Dylan and Emily had said their names as part of this greeting routine, and Gabriel had vocalized the initial sound of his name. But in this December session (and during the fall months of the second year), we were witnessing problems similar to those we had encountered in the first year. Emily's social interactions in the autumn seemed delayed and not as clear or complete as they had been at the end of the first year. Dylan's communication seemed to combine elements of both completion and reclusiveness (saying his name into his shirt). Gabriel's response suggested a kind of detached disengagement. In addition, their new classmates, Jonathan and Talan, experienced their own challenges. Jonathan was sometimes explosive and unpredictable, with bursts of restlessness and conflict alternating with more-focused demonstrations of skills in speaking words or imitating actions. Talan said the word "Hi" many times, which was a clear social greeting, though seemingly inflexibly repeated. He did not say his own name or greet the other children.

In the upcoming paragraphs, as I review the "Hello Song" on December 8, I will focus on three factors that played a role in the difficulties that we were facing: my continuing commitment to requesting specific forms of conventional verbal communication, the changes in the school environment and class membership, and the need to redevelop or newly cultivate cohesiveness in this second-year group.

My Continuing Commitment to Spoken Names and My Eventual Adaptation

My consistent efforts to invite children to say their names as part of the hello routine was one aspect of my approach that may have contributed to the difficulties. I could have earlier shifted the goal toward more enthusiastically celebrating *all* forms of response during our opening song—nonverbal actions (handshake or high five), or child-directed verbal communication (like Talan's "Hi"), or other means. During all the prior sessions, I had really wanted to help the children be able to say their own names in the "Hello Song." Yet, over time, I became more aware that there might be an ongoing need for alternative options for children who were communicating preverbally. Could I become more varied or creative in the types of communicative responses that I "counted" and affirmed?

One step that I attempted, in the coming months, was to begin to hold out a drum or my guitar to each child during the "Hello Song" in order to expand the ways that the children could join in. I invited the children to "play and say" their names. This provided a musical means for instrumental communication for those who were less verbal. It also continued to encourage verbal communication for those who were able. I hoped that offering the guitar or drum might give additional motivation to each of the children to become involved in self-expression during the "Hello Song." In Chapter 14, I will continue further describing my experiments with this "play and say" approach.

Changes in the School Environment and Class Membership

A second set of factors contributed to upheavals and difficulties in the preschool music group during the early parts of this year. These included changes in the class environment such as the impending switch to ABA staff and programming, the entry of several additional children, and the fundamental change of David's less-frequent presence during music sessions. The not-yet-determined job placements for the next school year for Rachel, Elizabeth, and David added underlying uncertainties to the sense of community in the classroom. In upcoming paragraphs, I will turn attention to the interconnected topics of the mistaken minimizing of the impact of therapeutic relationships, and the misguided view of teachers as interchangeable widgets.

What could help explain why this second cluster of school environment changes might cause some of the disjointed experiences in the preschool music group? Why had it been hard to "pick up where we left off" last year and make further progress with the children? Contemporary child development models offered me ways to understand the problems that we were now encountering. In the bioecological model of Bronfenbrenner and Evans (2000) and the dynamic systems perspective of Smith and Thelen (2003), a child's social world, mind, and body constitute an interconnected system. Changes in any part of the system—like the key adults and peers in a child's classroom—will disrupt the current child-environment relationship and necessitate reorganization in order for the components of the system to work together again.

According to this view, the reductions in lead teacher David's participation in the music group, the increased number of children in the classroom, and the uncertainties about the larger school reorganization would inextricably unsettle the existing interactions and relationships in the class. This would require adaptation from children and adults in order to move toward new ways of interplaying and learning. The music therapy sessions in the early part of the second year of my research, therefore, might be more accurately conceived of as a process of the teachers and me working to integrate multiple new changes rather than simply "picking up where we left off" and building upon past performance.

As I reflect back on the autumn sessions, it is clear that the teachers, children, and I were experiencing challenges within the music group without David present. My self-suggestions in my field notes to offer children alternative ways to participate, Natalie's forceful and difficult attempt to get Emily to say her name, and Rachel's uncharacteristic conflict with Jonathan could each be viewed, in part, as examples of our ongoing efforts to provide some of the encouragements, authority, and limit-setting that David had provided in the group.

Our early results in these efforts were mixed, and this was understandable given the importance of specific significant adult leaders like David to a child's development. His contributions (and by extension, the contributions of other significant people in the children's lives) consisted of more than just skills put into action. David's impact also came, in large measure, from the relationships that he had developed with each of the children over many hours and months together.

The New ABA Program Displacing the Current Teacher-Student Relationships

Indeed, the crucial role of personal relationships in learning and development, I felt, was often not sufficiently emphasized and promoted in the ABA program—nor in the contemporary medical model or evidence-based approaches that had become nationally prevalent in education and therapy. Changing the preschool class to a primarily ABA model appeared to be based on two foundational assumptions: (1) an ABA approach for children on the spectrum was superior to other educational and therapeutic practices; and (2) establishing the ABA classroom was the paramount priority, and its crucial methods were more important than which particular staff members implemented them. These notions seemed to reflect a belief that it mattered less who provided the therapeutic treatment or educational plan—because if the method was valid, it should work, and the results should be the same regardless of the specific staff person involved.

This idea did not correspond with my experience. I had witnessed specific teachers decisively influencing children's learning and development in the classroom. In terms of both process and outcomes, it did matter greatly *who* was teaching and interacting with the children. The children's behaviors could be powerfully impacted by the particular individual who was their interaction partner, either teacher or peer. Teachers David, Rachel, and Elizabeth, for example, helped spark the children's communication and person-to-person interactions because of the supportive nurturing relationships they had built with the children over time. I did not think that bringing in replacement staff and a primarily ABA-centered curriculum would better help the children's development. And for those of us continuing to work with the children this year in the music group, often without David's crucial involvement, it was unlikely that we could simply replicate his connections with the children even if we tried to implement the techniques that he used. In the second year we had to *develop and deepen our own relationships with the children* if we hoped to reach new goals and work together effectively.

In a critique of the increasing dominance of behavioral and medical therapeutic approaches, clinical psychologist John Norcross (2001) remarked on the "oddly person-less" quality of current evidence-based practice, which shares some common philosophical ideas with behavioral models like ABA. Evidence-based practice has focused on the identification of effective treatments or techniques, using randomized controlled trials "as the principal, if not only, means of assessing the effectiveness of a particular intervention . . . RCT's were designed with drugs and surgical procedures in mind: clear problems arise when trying to adapt this methodology to music therapy" (Ansdell et al., 2004, p. 11). Evidence-based practice guidelines have sometimes seemed to depict disembodied therapists performing the same consistent intervention for anonymous clients with standard diagnoses. Norcross (2001) asserted, "This stands in marked contrast to the clinician's experience of psychotherapy as an intensely interpersonal and deeply emotional experience" (p. 346), more characterized by individuality and diversity than uniformity and homogeneity. Summarizing 30 years of therapy research, the American Psychological Association (APA) task force, headed by Norcross, found that when essential relational aspects were cultivated—therapeutic alliance, cohesion in group therapy, empathy, goal consensus, and collaboration—then positive outcomes were demonstrated across a range of differing therapeutic treatments and techniques.

"Missing" and the "Widget Effect" in the School's Decision to Replace the Current Teachers

The need to focus on facilitating personal relationships involving children on the spectrum and teachers and caregivers has also been spotlighted in the Early Start Denver Model (Rogers & Dawson, 2010). This autism treatment approach has sought to meld teaching practices from three intervention traditions: ABA, pivotal response treatment, and the Denver model. In describing the distinctive differences of their hybrid model, the authors wrote that in the Denver approach, "There is an explicit focus on the quality of relationships, affect, and adult sensitivity and responsivity, a feature that is often missing in many ABA programs" (p. xiii). This characterization of the "missing" focus on the qualities of relationships in ABA programs is notable for its candor and for the fact that it comes from clinicians grounded in behavioral teaching procedures and principles.

The importance of the teaching relationship in fostering children's learning has been further asserted in a publication from the New Teacher Project (Weisberg et al., 2009). This report criticized a phenomenon that it termed the *widget effect*: "This decades-old fallacy fosters an environment in which teachers cease to be understood as individual professionals, but rather as interchangeable parts. In its denial of individual strengths and weaknesses, it is deeply disrespectful to teachers" (p. 4). Educator Marilyn Cochran-Smith (2006) has also critiqued the tendency to view teaching as a "technical transmission activity" (p. 9) rather than as as an interpersonal process involving students and teachers in shared learning and adjustments. Cochran-Smith stated that the methods of evidenced-based medicine often did not fit well in certain educational contexts or areas of specialization such as teacher education: "Hospital medicine deals with single individuals, and the point is usually to get rid of something (pain, disease, broken bones) . . . education in contrast deals with groups and the idea is to instill or provide something (knowledge, strategies, problem-solving skills)" (p. 9). Yes, for me the idea of education and therapy as nurturing participants' abilities, more than a process of eradicating disease, has very much resonated. I had firsthand experience that the preschool teachers David, Elizabeth, and Rachel were providing effective strategies for connecting with the students and nurturing their abilities. I knew that the teachers were not replaceable widgets simply carrying out the technical transmission of information. In order to help the children continue to take steps in interpersonal engagement and communication, I wished that the preschool administration had placed more value on the current teachers and their relationship-based developmental approaches. A balanced incorporation of ABA might have served the children better than the complete replacement of the current staff and program.

The Need to Newly Cultivate Cohesiveness in the Changed Preschool Class

A third and final factor affected the participation of Dylan, Emily, Gabriel, and others early in the second year of the music group: the group's cohesiveness (or lack thereof). In the "Hello Song" at the end of the previous year, Carlos's and Dylan's successful articulation of their names, and the subsequent praise and excitement had seemed to contribute to a chain reaction in which Emily, Gabriel, and other peers communicated or approximated their names more fully and quickly than previously. Perhaps the reverse effect was happening in the second year's December "Hello Song": Natalie and Emily's difficult and forced interaction was followed by Gabriel's uncertain and inaudible response, Dylan's audible but muffled speech, and protracted and frustrated turns from Talan and Jonathan.

Group climate has been defined as the degree of engagement, avoidance, and conflict in a group, and it has been identified as closely related to group cohesiveness (Yalom & Leszcz, 2005): "Cohesiveness is not fixed—once achieved, forever held—but instead fluctuates greatly during the course of the group. Early cohesion and engagement is essential for the group to encompass the more challenging work that comes later in the group's development, as more conflict and discomfort emerges" (pp. 55–56). This description of challenges and conflicts following cohesion and engagement in a group has been helpful, as I have reflected on difficulties that emerged or returned in the early months of the second year with the preschool music group.

In closing my remarks on this chapter, the image of the up-and-down pedaling that propels a bicycle seems a more applicable metaphor for the process of learning and therapy in our current music group than the idea of continuous steps of progress up a staircase. In his studies of child development, Jean Piaget (1964) wrote of learning as *cycles* of equilibrium and disequilibrium. Yalom and Elkin (1974) have written that "psychotherapy is *cyclotherapy*" (p. 219), a process of returning to similar issues—but from a different perspective—each time in varying depths.

In the music group during the first few months of the second year, we found ourselves dealing with up-and-down cycles of problems arising, as well as some continuing positive participation. We were experiencing a mixture of recurring challenges with previous students and new difficulties with children who had recently joined the class. We also faced the impending dismantlement of the current class curriculum and teaching team in favor of an ABA program. Often, the classroom staff and I had to adjust to leading the class music sessions without David's helpful participation.

SUGGESTIONS FOR REFLECTION

- **If you have faced major changes in your class environment, what did you do to try to cope with the changes?** The differences in your classroom may have come from decisions made by the leadership in your school, from the changing number and needs of students in your class, or from state and national influences that have been shaping education and services.
- **Who were the colleagues, and what were the activities, ideas, or resources that were supportive** to you and the children during these times of change?
- **How would you describe the ways that your colleagues foster their personal relationships with the children** in the class in order to help support the learning and engagement of the new students as well as the previous class members during a new school year?
- **How have you pictured the path of children's development?** Like steps on a staircase that steadily rise? Like a curving road with valleys and hilltops along the way? In addition to new challenges, have you found yourself facing previous predicaments again, in a process resembling cyclotherapy or a notion of spiral development?

CHAPTER 9

Visual Supports, Movement, and Alternative Communication Aids

December 15

I'm starting a song called "At the Store" to share with the class. I've written new verses to add to a tune that was popular 100 years ago. The narrator in this comic song has forgotten to wear eyeglasses to the food store and begins to see increasingly strange and imaginary sights: "There were grapes, grapes, painting the number *8*, at the store, at the store"; "There were french fries, fries, marching down the aisles." To add pictures for this song, I've brought colorful drawings by my wife of grapes, the number *8*, french fries marching down the store aisles, and so forth. Corresponding key words are printed underneath each drawing, and I show these images and words to the children during the song. I also invite the class members to join me in accompanying movements such as pantomiming painting, marching our feet, and other actions.

"AT THE STORE": JOINING IN MOVEMENT

By introducing the visual images, the movements, and the playful spirit of the song, I'll team up with the teachers to encourage the children to take part. Our goals are (a) to promote attention and interactions through class members' moving together in coordination and (b) to support opportunities for the children to communicate verbally and nonverbally in response to the pictures, words, music, and body movements.

Emily's Interactions

In the early part of the song, Emily is attentive but subdued. She watches without expression or movement. I sing, "My eyes are dim, what can I see?" while I act out a peek-a-boo-like motion of cupping my hands in front of my face and trying to peer through my slightly open fingers to see. Then one of the teaching interns, Natalie, takes this motion further and places her hands fully over Emily's eyes, and tilts her head back until Emily's posture resembles a child leaning far back to receive teeth cleaning at the dentist. It looks truly odd, seeing Emily reclined backward, both arms remaining limp at her sides, and I feel initially bothered. Why is Natalie rough-handling Emily like this? But when Natalie slowly pulls her hands away from Emily's eyes, Emily sits up again, and her previous serious-looking face breaks into a smile. She scrunches up her shoulders and shows a happy facial expression. She whirls around in her chair to look back at Natalie. They share a moment of directly looking at each other. This makes me remember other classroom moments when roughhouse physical contact seems to be experienced by some preschoolers as playful and engaging; whereas at other times, or with other children, physical touch from a teacher or classmate can be unwanted or distressing. In this moment, Emily responds favorably to Natalie's physical "horseplay."

"I have not brought my specs with me," I sing while I gesture my hands out to the side, both palms open and empty, as if to say, "Look . . . I don't have any."

Then Emily faces forward to watch me. Her mouth is slightly open with the corners of her mouth upturned in a smile. Emily continues to appear overtly pleased, which is unusual. Her expression can often appear serious even in moments when she is actively engaged.

Next, I begin depicting specs by circling my fingers in front of my eyes to suggest a pair of eyeglasses. Emily begins to vocalize a nonverbal warbly sound for a few seconds. She sounds like a child dipping her toes into the water's edge and feeling surprised by the experience.

Jonathan's reaction to my specs motion is to make a high-pitched, sing-song sound like "I—see you." It is not entirely clear if he is communicating in English or Chinese, which is also spoken in his home, or in a nonverbal vocalization. Jonathan's intonation sounds like part of the childhood game: "Peek-a-boo . . . I—see you!" Perhaps Jonathan is making a connection between my hands-over-my-eyes motion in this song and the peek-a-boo game in which a partner hides their face behind their hands and then pops back into view. Previously, he hasn't seemed to be giving much attention to the song, but his vocalization now makes me wonder if he has been following along more than I realized.

I continue the song: "There were french fries, fries, marching down the aisles, at the store, at the store."

Natalie tries to get Emily to march her feet, by modeling it and by giving a touch prompt to her legs. Emily doesn't respond to this.

I start the chorus again, and I turn my face toward Emily, bringing my hands over my eyes like peek-a-boo. Emily suddenly raises her own hands up to her face and covers her eyes too, joining me in making this motion.

"Good, Emily!" I say loudly, happy to see her moving in unison with me. I sing, "What can I see?" With my elbows at my sides, I gesture my arms out wide, palms open.

Emily again joins me and imitates this next movement; her two small bent elbows and open palms looking slightly like a winged angel from a school play.

I sing, "I have not brought my specs with me." And I pantomime specs again, and Emily approximates this action too!

Emily is attending and moving in sync with me and the teachers, and I am encouraged and delighted by her interactions with Natalie and me!

How Will Dylan React?

When I turn toward Dylan, I notice that he is bent over at the waist. Sometimes, when he puts his head down, he's avoiding what is being presented. Is he turning away from the activity now?

No. After reviewing the video, I see that this time he is leaning down and peering at the picture-board that I have propped up on the floor near me so that the children can view the pictures representing the song's different fruits, vegetables, and accompanying actions. Dylan is anticipating that the next verse of the song is about to start, and he is searching for the pair of pictures that will be featured in the next verse.

So, I lift the picture board up and hold the images closer to all the children. "There was fruit, fruit," I sing, pointing to the pictures, "blowing on a flute . . ."

Dylan lifts his head up and looks at the pictures at eye level, intently. He laughs in three shorts bursts, bounces forward in his seat and immediately back, like a pinball shooting out and rebounding back. His mouth is open in a smile at the incongruous suggestions of fruit blowing on a flute. He vocalizes sounds that are a mixture of laughter and verbalization.

I start laughing too, in the middle of singing "at the store, at the store."

"There was fruit, fruit, blowing on a flute," I sing, playing an imaginary flute with my two hands to the side of my mouth, my fingers wiggling rapidly. I mimic the high-pitched flute sound "twee-dilly-tweet!"

"Flute!" says Dylan.

"Flute!" I say, "That's right!"

We are both leaning forward, looking directly at one another, and are nearly speaking at the same time.

"Flute," says Dylan once more, laughing and moving.

After Dylan's participation (looking, smiling, laughing, speaking), assistant teacher Elizabeth leans over and whispers to her colleague Rachel: "I really wish Sarah could see this!" Sarah was the director of the ABA program. Elizabeth wants Sarah to see Dylan showing pleasure in social interactions during the music therapy sessions and initiating verbal communication without being directly asked.

"SWITCH" SONG: "THE KIDS COME MARCHING"

Next, I reach into my music bag and take out a switch, a small recording and playback device. Switches have been used to offer augmentative and alternative communication (AAC) to people who do not use speech as their sole or principal means of communication (American Speech-Language-Hearing Association, 2021). Many forms of alternate communication exist. Individuals use gestures, facial expressions, body language, and sign language. In addition, people who have difficulty speaking may use speech-generating devices, voice-output communication aids (VOCAs), and visual aids such as language boards, pictures, drawings, letters, and written words.

During "The Kids Come Marching" song in the December session, I'm going to introduce the children to a VOCA switch. The children can reach forward and press a large blue button on top of this switch, and this will activate a short segment of the song's melody and words that we've recorded: "Hurrah! Hurrah!"

I'll also use a musical-fill-in-the-blank technique—singing my newly created verses to the song's familiar melody, and then I'll playfully stop, wait, and leave an open space. Children are often instinctively drawn to speak or sing out the "missing" part of the song, filling in the blank. For class members who have difficulty speaking, the VOCA switch will offer an additional way to communicate and participate. As I sing, and leave an open pause, the children can reach out to press the voice-output switch and activate the next part of the song's tune and words. The open pause also gives additional time, and a clear cue, for children's responses, which can be helpful for preschoolers with cognitive or social challenges. Moreover, the sounds, color, and tactile option of pressing the switch can motivate children.

I strum the guitar and pick up the switch, with its curved rounded shape similar to a miniature VW Beetle car. I'm ready to sing and record "Hurrah! Hurrah!" onto the switch for the class members.

However, at this moment, many of the teachers and children are talking and moving. Rachel, Elizabeth, and Natalie are conversing, and Talan and Jonathan are turning backward to glimpse them. Jonathan is making rapid agitated noises, and Gabriel is also emitting a series of increasingly loud sounds, like a car engine trying to start on a cold day—"Ee-ee-yee-ee-yee-ee."

Transitions between class activities often lead to this kind of diffusion of attention and expansion of noise. Official or unofficial breaks follow periods of joint focus. But I still wonder if we'll be able to shift from this noisy hubbub to a shared group involvement in the song.

Starting to Use the Switch

Into the classroom mixture of competing sounds, I record "Hurrah! Hurrah!" onto the switch. Several members of the class hear this and slow down their sound making or talking. Then I show everyone how to activate the switch: I move my index finger toward the blue center button of the switch. I press it. "Hurrah! Hurrah!" the recorded words and melody play.

"Cool . . . ," says Rachel, stretching out the "oooo."

"That's—" Elizabeth starts to say.

"That is really cool," says Rachel. "Okay, you've got my interest!"

Jonathan turns his head forward toward the sound. The five children and three staff members start looking at the switch.

I look up and laugh spontaneously. Rachel and Elizabeth's enthusiasm helps to create an atmosphere of fun in the group and often encourages the children's attention and involvement.

Dylan and Talan start to smile, and Jonathan makes sounds. Gabriel shifts in his seat, keeping his gaze toward me. Emily watches with no expression.

I wait for a brief opening in Jonathan's vocalizing, and then I sing, "The kids come marching one by one. . . ." I pause. I hold the switch in front of me, and I look out toward each child. Nonverbally, I'm trying to communicate with eyes and body language, "Here. Look. Watch what happens."

With a bit of dramatic presentation, I raise my index finger high in the air to show what I'm about to do. I press/click down onto the switch: "Hurrah! Hurrah!" plays out into the room.

Dylan Takes Initiative

Dylan scoots to the front of this chair and leans his head forward with his eyes really near to the blue switch, studying it. I demonstrate the process one more time. I pause in my singing, show the children the switch, and press the switch: "Hurrah! Hurrah!"

I start the third line of the song, but this time, taking his own initiative, Dylan darts his arm forward to tap the switch. "Hurrah! Hurrah!"

He pushes back in his chair, and he lowers his eyes down toward his lap. It seems that he is not sure if it's okay to take a self-initiated reach for the switch before the teachers or I have prompted him.

From my perspective, it is great to see him decisively move forward into the activity, showing clear interest. "Good!" I say, and I rock my head side to side and start singing again, "And they all come marching . . ."

Dylan's eyes rise up to meet mine and he smiles.

In a few moments I sing, "The kids come marching two by two . . ." I reach out to invite him to press the switch at a specific moment in the song. This time, he unhurriedly reaches his hand forward, presses down on the switch, and lets his hand linger there for a moment: "Hurrah! Hurrah!"

"Good!" I say again, very happy that he is responding to my outreached invitation to play. I'm glad for the switch's part in facilitating our interaction. Dylan leans his head back, smiling, like someone basking in the sun. Rachel laughs appreciatively.

What's happening in the group thus far? The first significance of these early moments is that the colorful sound-making switch is attracting the attention of the children and adults; it is giving a common focus to a potentially disparate group. It is also the teachers' expression of enthusiasm ("That is really cool," and "Okay, you've got my interest!") that helps galvanize the children's attention. As the teachers show interest, the children also focus. Part of my role as a group leader is to try to inspire the engagement of both these two constituencies within the classroom. It is a synergistic process. When I bring activities that catch the class members' attention, the teachers then play a key role in adding life to the group by joining in and enriching the sessions with their energy and extensive knowledge about the children. As a result, we are able to better motivate the children to progress toward goals. A classroom music therapy group can function if the teachers are less involved. But music therapy groups more fully realize their potential when the therapist and teachers and children are functioning as engaged co-participants.

What do Dylan's initial reactions tell us? His posture—leaning in to look intently at the switch—distinctly contrasts other moments in class when he looks away, or when he drops his head onto his lap to shut out an activity or request. This is one positive development. It's gladdening to see Dylan expressing interest by reaching forward in a mixture of impulse, comprehension, and anticipation of a coming opportunity.

But he takes additional developmental steps in his next turn by accepting an invitation to tap the switch at the specific fill-in-the-blank moment in the song. He connects with me by reaching out to meet my outstretched hand to press the switch. In such steps of cooperation, therapists attempt to establish a therapeutic alliance (Brewe et al., 2021), and educators strive to develop a learning partnership (Burgess et al., 2013). Instead of remaining stuck in a cycle of adult approach and Dylan's withdrawal, Dylan and the teachers and I are able to establish and sustain shared attention, turn taking, and reciprocal responding to each other's actions within the sequence of the song. Dylan's eye contact and smile also express a welcome degree of direct interaction and communication.

Gabriel Suddenly Smiles

Before his turn, Gabriel has watched, sitting upright, almost motionless. The expressions on his face have been altering during my demonstration of the switch—his initial open-eyed curiosity shifting toward tensed-eyebrow concern.

Then, when Dylan presses the switch, Gabriel suddenly smiles. His eyes open wide, he raises his body up so he is sitting taller in his chair, waves his right arm, and makes excited vocal sounds.

I face Gabriel and hold the switch toward him as I sing, "The kids come marching three by three . . ."

Elizabeth begins to move her arm to physically prompt him to touch the switch. But it is quickly evident that this is not necessary. Gabriel is already reaching forward to grasp and press the switch firmly.

The sound of the recorded hurrahs come! And so do the praises from Rachel and me: "Good job, Gabriel!"

Gabriel looks directly at my eyes, just as he had looked directly at the switch. I'm smiling and so is he. I had leaned forward to offer the blue switch, and he had reached out toward me to press it. We looked like two sides of an A-frame, our outstretched hands completing it.

I usually offer each child a few different opportunities to fill in the blank. So, I offer Gabriel another chance as I sing again, "The kids come marching three by three . . ."

Again Gabriel reaches out, right on time, and activates the recording of the next phrase in the song, and I join in singing the words too.

I smile, nod, and turn my attention back to the whole group, singing, "And they all come marching . . ."

But what I had not realized—until I later reviewed the video—was that, soon after his two turns, Gabriel had extended his arm and used his right index finger to point at the switch. He appeared to use a conventional pointing gesture to ask for more.

This could have been a great chance to affirm and encourage Gabriel's use of a pointing finger to make a request. But I and the other teachers had shifted our focus toward other children who were waiting for a turn. Quickly giving turns to waiting children was part of how we kept the whole group's attention. But, in retrospect, Gabriel's clear pointing was such a potentially important communicative step for him that I wish I had noticed it and rewarded his gesture.

When Gabriel communicated, it was usually through smiles, wiggles, or crying or distressed facial expressions. There were also many times, perhaps the majority of times during the group sessions, when I was not quite sure what he meant by his sound making and body language. He did not often tell his feelings or preferences to teachers or peers with words, signs, or other conventional means of communication. This is why Gabriel's use of an intentional communicative gesture today—pointing his index finger toward the switch in an apparent request—seems like an important step, though, regretfully, a step that the teachers and I don't catch or capitalize on in that moment.

It is likely that I am missing other embryonic attempts by Gabriel to communicate during the sessions. Repeatedly reviewing tapes for this research project helps increase my familiarity with the sounds and motions that represent his budding attempts at communication. My work outside of the preschool with children with a range of disabilities has also heightened my awareness that the first steps of progress for children often come in these easy-to-miss partial responses and approximations.

Fortunately, during this activity Gabriel takes other valuable steps that we do recognize and celebrate. He reaches forward and responds to two different opportunities to press the switch. The switch that Gabriel uses in the December session offers him a way to expand his avenues for communication. It can enable him to activate music or a variety of recorded spoken messages. It can be customized to deliver messages as simple as a single sound, or as complex as several sentences. AAC communication can potentially help adults in Gabriel's life pay increased attention to his new efforts to communicate. In addition, as Gabriel causes the recorded words and sounds to play out loud, and hears them in interacting with others, he might gain more chances to understand and use language.

Emily Stretches Forward

For most of the song, Emily has been a quiet unmoving watcher. I periodically try to make eye contact with her, but I can't gauge what she is feeling or thinking.

When it comes time for her turn, I hold out the blue switch toward her and she stretches her arm forward without hesitation to press it. The quickness of her response indicates her attention to the turn-taking process, even though her subdued demeanor hadn't made that apparent.

"Good!" I say. She keeps her hand on the switch for a second after activating it, perhaps getting a feel for how it works.

I offer the switch to her again, singing, "The kids come marching five by five . . ." Emily moves forward again to press the switch, activating "Hurrah, Hurrah!" This time, she glances up at me, making eye contact.

"Good!" I say again in affirmation.

Her facial expression remains placid, seemingly without emotion. Then she starts to stretch her arm back as if waking up from a sleep. At the very top of her stretch, I see her lips purse slightly, a hint of a smile.

Scientist and autism spokesperson Temple Grandin (2006) discusses how her early teachers introduced activities that could draw her into interaction with objects and people outside of her usual favored pursuits or preoccupations. With Emily, and with the other children, the small blue switch for recording and playback likewise seems to awaken interest and a willingness to interact. One potential challenge, as mentioned before, is that an "insistence on sameness" (Black et al., 2017) could lead some individuals to respond to new experiences or objects as if their security or well-being are being jeopardized. For those seeking to help children on the spectrum, a fundamental question is: How can new information and materials be introduced in ways that are tolerable or even appealing?

One answer is to blend newness and familiarity, a synthesis that music often delivers. Songs can be created or chosen during music therapy to offer the familiarity and security of repeated routines, choruses, words, and melodies, along with new features like the switch, introduced above. Other changes can be incorporated, such as different verses, vocabulary, and varying instruments, objects, visual supports, and movements.

When the song is over, Rachel says, "That is the handiest thing—that little tape recorder!"

"Yeah," I say, "This one is called a Step-by-Step. I also use it at the other school where I work."

As Rachel is talking to me, Emily stands up and walks toward me, vocalizing a sound like "see," and gestures toward the switch with her outstretched arm. It seems that Gabriel's earlier pointing gesture isn't the only example of a child expressing a preference for continued participation in this activity. Here Emily has stood up, come closer, gestured, and vocalized to communicate that she wants to continue activating the switch. Though I have regretted it later, at the time I said that the song was over, and therefore the adults began to get ready to start the stretch band song, which was a favorite of many of the children. So, Natalie pulled Emily back to her seat, amidst Emily's high-pitched protests.

"Okay, we'll do this again next time," I start to reassure Emily, but I don't get to complete the sentence because Elizabeth and Natalie start talking about possible messages that they would like to convey if they had access to this switch at home or on the job.

In reviewing this moment, I really wish that I had more overtly acknowledged and praised Emily's use of vocalization and gesture after the song was finished—clear communicative actions—even if I had completed the song and the other children were ready to begin the next activity. In the future, when I am faced with a similar moment again, I'll consider taking the time to give her another turn, to clearly reward her for using her voice and pointing gesture. I might also use it as a teaching moment with other children by saying, "Wow, Emily used her voice and a gesture to let me know she wants more. Those are great ways to ask for another turn during music time!" Even Emily's subsequent high-pitched protest is appropriate communication, given the circumstances. Hopefully, my reviewing of the video recordings from these class sessions will help me refine my responses to children's communications over time.

Balancing Newness and Routine

Later, Rachel and Elizabeth talked about the overall impact of including the blue VOCA switch during "The Kids Come Marching."

"That was fabulous," says Rachel.

"Excellent. They loved that!" says Elizabeth.

I pause from speaking. I'm thinking that it might take too long to express the idea I have, so I don't finish the sentence. But I am thinking that although children on the spectrum can exhibit an insistence on sameness, all five children in this song responded favorably and actively to a new object and the new fill-in-the-blank musical game. This was evidenced by their reaching out toward the switch and their smiles and attention.

Two ideas have often been expressed in autism literature—that children's abilities are best developed through "systematic instruction," and that people on the autism spectrum need routine and structure. The children's responses in the preschool today suggest an alternative perspective that I want to touch upon again as I close this chapter: Systematic repeated routines may be *part of* an effective approach to support children's emerging abilities. However, in moments like those represented above, it seems that a balance of newness and routine can also be important and effective in facilitating children's participation.

SUGGESTIONS FOR REFLECTION

How can new information and materials be introduced in appealing ways to children who may be attached to repeated behaviors or a restricted number of activities? Here are some suggestions:

- **Adding visual images and body movements to songs** can offer children multiple paths for joint engagement in a shared activity.
- **Combining a musical game with a colorful sound-making VOCA switch** may increase the participation of the children and adults and give a potentially disparate group a common focus.
- **Introducing songs that tell a story—with pictures, humor, and playfulness—**can promote children's shared attention and interaction in ways that vary from systematically repeated instruction.
- **Utilizing a musical-fill-in-the-blank technique—**playfully pausing, waiting, and leaving an open space—may motivate and enable preschoolers' participation. Children are often instinctively drawn to respond by speaking, singing, or reaching forward to activate a switch in order to fill in the blank or missing part of the song.

CHAPTER 10

Observing the Children During Classroom Play and Morning Circle

December 22

What is it like in the class on the days when I'm not coming to lead a music session? I think it would be useful to find out, so I schedule a visit to observe during the preschool's activities one December morning. I watch a period of child-directed play and a "morning circle" with the entire class. Since I have an ongoing relationship with the children, I don't pretend to be an uninvolved onlooker. I still aim to respond to them in friendly ways, but I also try to nonverbally communicate my desire to quietly look, listen, and follow what they are doing this morning.

EARLY MORNING CHILD-DIRECTED PLAY

I begin my visit by sitting down near Gabriel. He is playing with a plastic gray elephant on a tabletop, while making "eee" and "ouu" sounds. Also on the table are a giraffe; a yellow plastic picket fence; a round-faced, 2-inch girl; and other toys.

Dylan—Comes Close, Jogs Away

Dylan comes up near me with a big smile, his face very close. For a moment, practically all I can see are his facial features, inches from mine.

"Huh," he laughs, his brown eyes looking intently at me for an instant.

Then, just as quickly, he turns away.

"Dylan?" I say.

But he is jogging away to the opposite side of the room, making a 90-degree turn, and heading into a far corner where he ducks behind a bookshelf.

"What have you got over there, Dyl?" says David, striding over to find out where Dylan has gone and what he is doing.

Emily and Her Father

Meanwhile, Emily has arrived, and she comes near the table where Gabriel and I are sitting.

"Hello," I say.

Emily says nothing, stands close by me, with her back turned, and picks up a toy palm tree. She brings it with her as she walks back to the other side of the room. Her dad is standing there. He has brought her to school, and now he is ready to leave and go to his work. Before he goes, he bends closer to Emily and says to her, "Look at me."

"Bye" says Emily. She doesn't look at him or at the nearby teaching intern Natalie.

Emily's father seems to want to share a moment of goodbye with his daughter that includes her clearly gazing toward him before he goes. "Look at me . . . Look at me," he asks, taking Emily by the arm, while he kneels down so that his face is level with hers.

But Emily looks down toward her hands. Natalie reaches over and removes the toy palm tree from Emily's fingers, probably attempting to get her to focus on her dad.

"Right here," says her father.

Emily, still not looking at him, swivels her head away and appears to continue to look for the little palm tree. But at the same time, she says, "Buh-bye," in a loud sing-song voice. Yet her gaze is directed toward Natalie's torso. Her father takes both of Emily's hands and places them on his face.

"Buh-bye," says Emily again, not looking at him, but allowing him to keep her hands resting on his cheeks.

Her father then reaches out and briefly touches Emily's cheeks with both his hands.

"Buh-bye," says Emily one more time.

And her dad holds up his palms for a "high ten."

Emily makes contact with his hands. But she does not look at him. Then she quickly walks across the room, to the table with the toys, where Gabriel and I are sitting.

As Emily's father leaves the classroom, I'm thinking about the ways that he asks for, but doesn't receive, a look from his daughter. Emily says goodbye verbally several times. But she appears somehow detached or distracted, even amidst the physical closeness (touching faces, touching hands) that her father creates and that Emily eventually joins (patting his hands for a "high ten"). I think about what it might be like for Emily's father. In my personal experiences, I've felt hurt when my attempts to connect feel unfulfilled. I've also seen people's hunger to be looked at with loving eyes in family relationships, and I feel that I am witnessing a moment like that. But I also realize that from other perspectives, Emily's momentary interactions with her dad could be viewed as a variation of a common dynamic at a school drop-off time: Sometimes parents are largely ignored as a child quickly goes into a classroom, while at other times parents are clung to.

As I look back at the interactions between Emily and her father, two impressions have stuck with me: first, the memory of Emily appearing half-remote and half-involved even in one of her most significant relationships and, second, a realization that her contact with her father came in the forms of proximity (coming near to him), verbalizing, accepting his touch and tapping palms rather than through eye contact, in this moment.

"WHO'S IN SCHOOL": PICTURES, MOVEMENT, AND READING FROM A SENTENCE/PICTURE SIGN

After a period of child-directed play, the teachers—David, Rachel, Elizabeth, and Natalie—gather the six children together: "It's time for circle!" For the next half hour, David leads the class and introduces songs, books, numbers, days of the week, and other activities in a fast-moving varied program. I notice how David incorporates singing and recorded music into many of these segments.

Midway through circle time, David announces, "It's time to see 'Who's in School' today." David shows the children a visual symbol for this activity, and he begins to place photographs of each of the children and teachers on a portable display board resting on his lap.

Soon, David is going to hold the display board in front of the class members. Each child gets a turn to choose a photograph of a classmate or teacher. Children will reach out and take someone's picture off the board. Velcro strips on the back of the photographs will enable children to pull off the photographs from the display board and later stick them back on.

Nicolas Chooses

"Nicolas, pick a picture," says David.

Nicolas touches a picture. It is David's picture.

"Who'd you pick?" asks David, giving a sharp intake of breath, as if surprised, while helping Nicolas pull the picture off the board. "Who is it?"

"David," says Nicolas very quietly, looking up at David, and holding his photograph.

"Can you give it to me?" asks David. His quick, energetic, friendly voice communicates a sense of pace, purpose, and play.

"David, David," says Nicolas standing up but not yet relinquishing the picture.

"Give it to *me*," David reiterates.

Nicolas bends down and almost puts the photo on the floor. Then he straightens up and gives it David. David does not intervene or redirect Nicolas but waits expectantly.

"Thaaaanks," says David happily, when Nicolas places the picture in his hand, "Look, this is *my* picture" he announces to the group.

Behind him, on a black cloth bulletin board, is a circle of crayon-colored symbols representing upcoming holidays: a menorah, a bell, a dreidel, a star, a gingerbread man, and others.

David puts his photograph on the bulletin board, near a picture of a menorah.

Then he holds up a sign with one sentence, which reads, "I put my picture on the _____." He announces to the group, "I put my picture on . . . the menorah," while pointing to the corresponding words and picture.

David swiftly puts down the sentence-and-symbols sign, grabs the board with the children's and teacher's photographs, and prepares to offer Gabriel a turn.

Gabriel Protests

"Gabriel, . . . pick one," says David.

Gabriel vocalizes one short sound, like "bee" or "pee." Is this an arbitrary sound or an approximation of the starting "p" sound of "pick?"

Then Gabriel simultaneously reaches down his pointer fingers from both hands: left pointer finger near Dylan's photograph, right pointer finger on the empty space where David's photo had been. Is Gabriel placing his hands down by chance, or is he indicating some intention, although idiosyncratically using both hands to point?

David takes Gabriel's right finger, directs it over to Dylan's photograph, pulls the photo off the display board, and gets Gabriel to hold onto the photo.

"Who is it, Gabriel? It's 'D' . . . . 'Dylan,'" says David, enunciating the starting sound of Dylan's name. Gabriel silently looks down at the photo and doesn't move. David then pulls Gabriel up out of his seat toward Dylan while saying, "Let's give it to 'D' . . . 'Dylan.'"

Gabriel starts emitting a series of loud sharp protesting sounds, "Wah . . . boo . . . dye-eeah," after being pulled up out of his seat. Whether he is startled, not comprehending, or simply not willing, Gabriel doesn't seem to want to go toward Dylan and has to be pushed by David, who also directs Gabriel's hand to pass the photograph to Dylan.

Dylan Reads and Speaks

Quickly, Dylan takes his photograph, stands up, and walks toward the bulletin board. He stops when he gets near the board.

I wonder if this will be one of those moments when Dylan comes tantalizingly close, only to halt on the brink of completing a task?

"Put your picture up, Dylan," says David.

And in a moment, Dylan places his photograph on the black bulletin board, almost touching a yellow star and a brown gingerbread man.

"Oh, good job, Dylan!" says David. He moves Dylan's photograph over slightly so that it rests more clearly on top of the gingerbread man.

"Come here, tell the kids," David says. He brings the sentence/symbols sign in front of Dylan. David points his finger toward the first word in the sentence.

"I . . . ," starts David, "put . . ." Then he waits for Dylan to start speaking with him.

But Dylan is not making a sound, although he is peering intently at the sentence sign. He seems content to look, and to just stand near David.

David puts his arm around Dylan, pulls him closer, takes his hand again, and together they point and look at each word as David reads, "I . . . put . . ." Dylan's soft voice also joins in to say, "put."

David continues, "My picture . . . on the . . ."

"Gin-ger . . . ," says Dylan, slowly articulating and sounding out the first part of the printed word.

"Gingerbread man! Good job, Dylan, nice reading!" says David.

One of the things that stands out for me in this interaction is the level of physical contact and comfort between Dylan and David. I also notice what seems to me a process of mutual adjustment based on familiarity with each other. Dylan accepts David's closeness and hands-on direction and remains willing to participate in the routine. David insists that Dylan do more than "look on," but David accepts and praises Dylan's partial completion of the reading and speaking portion of the routine. David affirms Dylan's timely placement of his photograph on the bulletin board and his overall cooperation in giving his attention to the words and pictures.

Consistent Approach, Varied Results

The "Who's in School" activity often gives children two turns—one when they choose a photograph, and another when their photograph is chosen by a classmate and delivered to them.

Without portraying each of the remaining sequential turns, I want to briefly make two additional observations. First, when David asks Dylan, "Who'd you pick?" Dylan says the name of his classmate "Gabriel." This is another occasion when a child in the group directly communicates peer awareness verbally. Second, when it is Gabriel's turn to put his picture on the bulletin board and articulate the sentence, Gabriel is very squirmy and evasive. I have not often seen such active resistance from Gabriel, wriggling his head and ducking out from underneath David's attempts to physically prompt him to look at the words/symbols of the sentence.

These moments are a reminder of the individual differences in response and ability among children with the same diagnosis. David's intimate and assertive approach seems to help facilitate Dylan's participation, but the same approach with Gabriel evokes wriggling unhappy responses, possibly affected by Gabriel's greater expressive-language difficulties or differing cognitive understandings of some of the steps in this activity.

Emily—"Nice Big Sentence"

After a few other children have taken turns, David pivots toward Emily. "All—right," says David, "Emily, pick one!" He presents her with the photographs of her classmates and teachers.

Emily chooses a picture, pulls it off the board, and stands up, all in one motion.

"Who is it, Emily?" asks David.

"Ema-me," says Emily, tapping her chest with one hand. She walks quickly toward the bulletin board.

"Oh!" says David, "Good job!"

I chuckle, not quite hearing what Emily has said but enjoying her speed and energy and the way she rushes to the bulletin board to put up the picture she's chosen.

"Emily, me," says Elizabeth, clarifying Emily's words for me, which I later confirm during video review: Emily has chosen her own picture and vocally approximates, "Emily, me," while using a "me" gesture by tapping her chest.

Then, without direct prompting, she comes and stands close to David, facing out toward her peers in the circle and looking at the sentence sign that he holds in front of her.

She is already saying "I" before David has a chance to point to the opening word of the sentence.

"I . . . ," joins in David too, but then he listens and follows Emily's pointing and speaking, rather than telling her what to do.

Emily is already continuing, quite quickly, "I . . . put my . . . eecher . . . on . . . bah."

"On the *bell*," David affirms and clarifies. "Very good, Emily, nice big sentence!"

"Hmmm," I murmur. I recognize her intention and ability in approximating the sentence, "I put my picture on [the] bell." I have not heard Emily communicate like this before! Not only is she verbally communicating, she is using a full sentence and a pointing gesture. With David's help, and the help of other teachers and speech therapists at the school, Emily is developing in her communication abilities. I am happy and excited to see this!

"Chatty girl!" says Elizabeth, both teasing and praising Emily as she returns to her chair.

"Love that!" says David, reiterating his praise for her participation. "All right . . . ," he says, and reaches to get the photo display board for the next child's turn.

David's energetic and close interactions with the children—involving pictures, words, movements, and choice making with peer photographs—are inspiring to witness. In retrospect, I have realized how much I could have gained from more opportunities to view how the teachers and other school specialists were working with the children (e.g., the speech, occupational, and physical therapists). I saw new possibilities with the children, and I admired how choosing and passing peer photographs had been incorporated into an activity that was motivating and effective with many of the children.

However, the observation day described above, and other efforts like it, were not included in my work at the school and remained self-generated unpaid initiatives that I took. My work schedule consisted almost exclusively of giving direct services with the children. I had no built-in time to meet with other specialists or teachers, nor any designated hours for joining them for other activities during their classroom days. As I looked to the future, I took two principal lessons from this:

1. At times, in order to make classroom observations possible or to initiate other meetings to exchange information with teachers, I might want to give such unpaid time anyway, even if the school system had not yet incorporated such opportunities.
2. In the future, I wanted to learn how to effectively advocate to the school that the children and staff would benefit if we built in time for me to join other class sessions. I could meet and discuss strategies with classroom teachers and related-services therapists, in addition to leading my class music sessions.

In fact, in subsequent years, I was able to persuade the school to take one step to incorporate a before-school information-sharing meeting with individual teachers with whom I worked in four classrooms at the school.

OUTBURST

Near the end of my visit during that December day, after several other circle activities, a difficult and thought-provoking episode occurs.

One of the children, Talan, becomes upset and begins an extensive period of yelling and crying. It happens as the children are being called one by one to go to the sink to wash their hands and begin snack. Jonathan, Nicolas, Dylan, and Talan all try, at various times, to get up and walk to the snack table without waiting to wash their hands. David, Rachel, and Elizabeth redirect them to their chairs to wait until the previous child finishes handwashing at the sink before having a snack.

Talan tolerates being redirected back into his chair a few times and then begins to complain loudly with nonverbal vocalizations. The other children remain relatively quiet while they wait, and David asks Talan to wait his turn quietly too. But Talan becomes louder and more urgent. He is eventually yelling and crying, although he had been happy and participating in the morning circle.

His yelling escalates to a continuous screeching. Even David, with his skills, experience, and even temperament, is having great difficulty with Talan. David and the other teachers don't want to take Talan over to snack until he settles down and realizes that there are situations when he has to wait for his turn. The daunting fact is that, according to Elizabeth, when these episodes of crying and frustration begin, they can go on for a long duration. Several times, David tries to bring Talan to the snack table when he has momentarily calmed. But each time, bafflingly, as David approaches the table, Talan begins wailing again, punctuated by intense, guttural vocal outbursts. It is an unexpected and troubling event that follows what has been a positive participative morning.

IMPRESSIONS FROM MY DECEMBER OBSERVATION

As I look back on the events in class this morning, I'd like to highlight a few of my observations. Early in my visit, Dylan runs directly up to me and then rushes away—an apt metaphor, I feel, for the mixture of approach and withdrawal that I sometimes experience with him. I am then very affected by Emily's interaction with her father, and its complicated combination of compliance, communication ("Buh-bye" and "high ten"), and qualities of remoteness and disengagement as Emily does not look at her father although he repeatedly asks her to. With Gabriel, I notice a surprising level of resistance to passing a photograph to a peer. Yet in back-and-forth exchanges between David and the children, I'm able to see the engagement of many of the class members with peer photographs, picture symbols, and printed words that promote the children's communication and peer social awareness.

During the "Who's in School" activity, I witness Nicholas, Dylan, Emily, and other class members developing their abilities in social contact with peers and teachers, as they choose photographs of classmates and adult staff and pass pictures to them. I learn that several of the children can engage in verbal communication at higher levels than I have previously seen or heard! And I continue to notice the supports and affirmations that fellow teachers Elizabeth and Rachel are providing for each of the children. For me, this is another primary theme from my observation—seeing anew the teachers' skills as well as the children's abilities during this morning! Finally, with Talan's outburst, I also regain an awareness of the formidable challenges faced by the teachers and students in this class.

SUGGESTIONS FOR REFLECTION

- **What might be the benefits and the difficulties of creating time to observe the children when a classroom colleague or another service provider is leading the class group?** Would it help you gain different perspectives and see the children's interactions with other teachers and peers in new ways?
- **What about issues of fairness?** Is it right to advise helping professionals to come to class for additional unpaid hours for observations as a form of practical continuing education and supporting the children's learning? In your circumstances, what could be one or two effective steps to advocate that time for class observations and teacher/specialist collaboration be included in professionals' paid working hours? Who would be the person or persons to whom you would need to talk to propose change?
- **In what ways did lead teacher David's "Who's in School" activity promote the children's communication, peer awareness, and steps in interacting with each other?** As a music therapist, are there ways to musically adapt his approach and provide these additional opportunities for choice making with peer photographs, picture symbols, and printed words while also creating chances for students to reach out, walk, pass a photograph to a peer, and place a symbol on a display board?

CHAPTER 11

Before the Sessions
Shared Guitar Playing and Vocalizing—February 9 and 16

On the morning of February 9th, before the other children have come to the music group, Emily walks from another part of the classroom and takes a seat in a chair across from me. I have just started unpacking my music bag. Emily and I are currently the only two people in the circle of chairs.

From the left side of the room, assistant teacher Elizabeth asks, "Emily, do you want to look at this one?" and brings her a large picture book to view while she waits for the rest of her classmates to arrive.

Emily opens the big book and begins to leaf through its pages, while I take my guitar out of its case and watch her sitting quietly near me. I smile and she glances up toward me. Then we both go back to what we're doing. She flips the book's pages. I zip open a side pocket to the guitar case. She examines the pictures. I take out a black-and-yellow-striped guitar cable. For 60 seconds, we each focus on our separate but adjacent activities.

COLLABORATIVE GUITAR PLAYING

Then Emily closes the book and looks directly toward me. I haven't realized that yet, because I've turned sideways to plug the guitar cable into the amplifier. I play a single note on the guitar. I play a couple more. I turn back to Emily. She is already heading directly toward me, hand outstretched, reaching for the guitar strings, which she strums once.

I move my hand where hers had been. I'm trying to finger a chord for her to play, but Emily seems to take this as a signal that I'm asking her to stop. It is true that during the music group, it is an unwritten rule that the children should ask first, and then take turns. But with Emily and I the only ones in the circle of chairs, I'm happy that Emily has communicated that she wants to play. So, without a word, I reach out the guitar toward her, making a clear offer: She can play if she wants.

She does. With her right hand, she sweeps her fingers over the guitar strings, and the sounds ring out. I have pressed down the strings on the guitar's neck, so her strum creates a harmonized chord, not just a clang of adjacent notes.

She pauses. She plays again, leaning forward, extending her right hand, just barely remaining seated on her chair, and still holding onto her book with her other hand. She tries playing the guitar with her thumb, then with her other fingers.

I make a new chord, pressing my fingers onto the guitar's neck in different shapes. She strums the new chord. Then she plucks individual strings, and the single notes echo in the room.

"Oh—Emily . . . this is *your* lucky day!" says assistant teacher Rachel, laughing and calling from across the room, as she sees and hears Emily getting her own personal time to play the guitar before the others have arrived. Elizabeth, her fellow teacher, also says, "Aww," and joins in her appreciative response.

I smile but otherwise don't turn toward the teachers to talk further and acknowledge their good spirits because I don't want to break the spell of Emily's concentration and our shared focus. Emily keeps playing—intent, involved, exploring. She switches hands, places the book in her right, strums the guitar with her left, stands up, strums more, and then walks over near my music bag.

"Good, Emily, that's great!" I say. "Sounds good!"

The other students begin to arrive, and Emily walks back to her chair and sits back down, as we prepare to start the group session.

Reflections About Parallel and Cooperative Play

When Emily comes to sit near me before the music session, we focus on our own actions. But we are aware of each other, and glance at each other, during our initial parallel activities while we wait and prepare for the other children to arrive in the circle. Parallel play has been defined as people playing beside each other rather than directly with one another (Hännikäinen & Munter, 2018). Early on that February morning, however, I sense that Emily and I are both beside *and* with each other, indirectly relating through peripheral attention and proximity. Our parallel activity then leads to overt cooperative play when Emily comes forward, reaches out to strum the guitar, and I hold it out toward her and finger the chords.

Spending time together, spontaneously relating to each other, without my asking for something, allows these interactions to take place between Emily and me. To foster the social interaction of children on the autism spectrum, it seems important to nurture such moments of indirect parallel play and child-initiated cooperative activity, in addition to facilitating adult-led opportunities to practice conventional social skills.

British educators Dave Sherratt and Melanie Peter (2002) express a similar point of view when they write about the capacity of play and drama to enable children on the spectrum to further understand and explore interpersonal interactions:

> Something has always puzzled us during our 20 years in special education: Why is it that educationalists know that children learn through play, yet seem to lose sight of this when it comes to children with special needs? This becomes even more of a paradox with children with autism, to the extent that "work" and "play" become totally separated in their perception . . . [However,] children learn best when they are enjoying themselves, and teaching, too, becomes so much more pleasurable! (p. vii).

I agree with the authors' viewpoint that shared play—and not only systematic didactic work—can help children on the autism spectrum learn and develop. Through musical interplay with me this morning, Emily is moving toward the goals of increased social interaction and attending skills. In our collaborative guitar playing, there is growing interpersonal familiarity, initiative, and enjoyment.

Co-playing a Musical Instrument as a Gateway Toward Shared Engagement

Instrument playing is one of the four fundamental ways that people participate and interact during music, along with singing/vocalizing, movement, and listening (Goodman, 2007; McLaughlin & Adler, 2015). Partner play with an instrument gives two people chances to touch the instrument, make sounds, and engage in back and forth or simultaneous play. While co-exploring a piano, guitar, or hand percussion at the preschool, spontaneous contact between adults and children can be fostered. An adult can match, build on, and introduce variations of a child's sounds, body movements, facial expressions, moods, and communications. And musical instrument play can also promote a child's learning of new abilities. Psychologist Lev Vygotsky (1987) writes about the zone of proximal development (ZPD) to highlight a child's learning of new capabilities. With the guidance and collaboration of a knowledgeable adult or peer, a child starts to gain skills that are beyond what the child can currently do alone. Is Emily expanding her abilities by strumming the guitar with me at the preschool this morning? I believe that both she and I are developing new capacities in interpersonal interaction and musical collaboration. My skills in fingering the guitar chords complement her strumming to create varying melodic sounds rather than dissonant clanging. And she is expanding her interest and willingness in social interactions and shared engagement while discovering the different sounds and rhythms that she can play on the guitar.

The possibilities for developing children's capacities through instrument play and other musical means are also primary themes in the writings of music therapists Paul Nordoff and Clive Robbins (2007). When caregivers and helping professionals inspire and complement a child's instrumental, vocal, or movement expressions, it enables participants' potentials to emerge and grow: "You increase what's already there," says Clive Robbins (as cited in Aigen, 1996, p. 28) as he suggests how music interactions can bring out latent abilities. Through cooperative play with the guitar, Emily and I are increasing and enhancing our contact with each other, and we are also sowing seeds for musical engagement in the future.

To encourage reflection about these interactions with Emily and about the music experiences that you offer your students, I want to share the following questions and observations:

- *What attracts children's attention and opens doors to interpersonal interaction?* Touching and playing a musical instrument, and trying out its sounds during shared activity, represents one of the main musical approaches to encouraging interpersonal contact and joint involvement. This current chapter focuses on one-to-one partner play of a guitar. As you consider how to foster cooperative instrumental play in your own environment, it will often involve more than simply passing out an instrument for a child to manipulate separately, alone. In addition, a relevant question is: How can you find ways to collaboratively interact to make music with a shared instrument? In this February 9th session, both Emily and I are actively creating the sounds and rhythms that come forth from the guitar. As Emily strums with varying rhythms and speeds, and I responsively change the guitar chords, we can simultaneously adjust to each other's actions.

- *What differences do you notice when working individually with one child in comparison to facilitating the class group?* Individual attention can allow for closely tuning in to the moment-to-moment reactions of a single child. Thus, it's possible to solely focus on building connections with one person. Group work involves the wider focus of promoting the engagement of the whole group, in addition to giving attention to an individual. Class group activities can also help foster group belonging and peer influences.

VOCALIZING AND MUTUAL SIMULTANEOUS SHAPING

A week later on February 16th, both Gabriel and Emily have taken their seats in the circle of chairs before the start of music group. I am setting up my equipment and getting ready for the session. The rest of the preschool class members haven't arrived yet.

Assistant teacher Rachel says, "[You have] an audience of two so far, Geoff."

"That's good," I say.

Emily and Gabriel sit quite quietly as I bend down to take some pictures out of my music bag.

A familiar faint droning sound begins, "Eeeee." It is Gabriel. This is a repetitive vocal sound that I've often heard Gabriel make. Then I hear a child's voice making an unusual high sing-song patter of sounds, "Dey-poh-dee-aht."

I look up, and Gabriel is vocalizing in a new way, looking at me, smiling, and I smile and laugh. He softly continues.

Emily then starts making percussive blowing vocal sounds.

Gabriel restarts his vocal sounds too, as if continuing a chant or a conversation, but in tones that seem different than usual.

Emily utters a high-pitched "oooo," which doesn't sound familiar to me either.

"Those are new sounds," I say, smiling and looking up at Emily and Gabriel again momentarily.

I peer back down into the black bag of music supplies on my lap.

A quiet pause.

Then both Gabriel and Emily resume making more sounds.

Gabriel makes a low "B'oing."

Emily chirps a high "Ribbit, ribbit" sound.

Gabriel interjects a forceful "Eh pwoi tee."

It is like a chorus of vocalizations. I am reminded of the mingled sounds of the birds that I hear in the woods in the morning.

Emily Calling Out

I start to wonder if Gabriel and Emily are spurring each other on with their vocalizations? Are they also using sounds to get my attention, to get me to look up and interact?

Apparently, that inkling hasn't quite settled in yet, or I haven't found what I need in my bag, because I continue to look down, sorting through a group of pictures and instruments.

Then Emily says a long musical "aaaaaaa" (lengthening the vowel sound that is present in the words "bat" or "hat").

There is something in this sound that I instinctively know is Emily calling out to me to be seen and heard. I look up. She is looking directly at me. I look into her eyes. I raise my eyebrows. I begin to put away the bag, and I glance down once again to zip it shut. At the same time I vocalize a quiet echo of her sound, "Aaaaaa."

Then, Emily vocalizes again, "Aaaaaaa," still looking at me, intently, and using slightly more volume. She opens her mouth wider this time.

I am interested and happy to hear her repeat the sound. It was possible that her initial vocalization could have been disconnected sound making, not intended as an attempt to communicate with me (though my instincts had told me that it was). But the timing of her second vocalization is coordinated and interrelated to my response. I feel her intention to interact with me through sounds, which she is originating on her own with no verbal prompts, no printed script to read.

"Aaaaaa," I vocalize, again mirroring her sound, this time with an animated expression on my face, and I open my mouth wide to vocalize like her. Then I shut it quickly, looking for her response.

Quiet. No discernable response.

Instead, Gabriel rumbles a lower pitched "mmnn-nah-nay-nay." It sounds more like a conversational "um" rather than a "statement." So, I wait and listen for further cues, but nothing more comes.

After a while, I return to looking back down, this time unpacking the picture schedule board that I use to indicate the sequence of activities in the coming session. Am I really studying the schedule in order to place a new picture on it? Or am I unconsciously withdrawing from the children because Emily and Gabriel don't seem to be responding further, as I was hoping? Probably it is a combination of things. In any case, I place the picture schedule on the floor in front of the chairs, where the children will be able to view it when the session begins.

"Be right back," I say quietly to Emily and Gabriel. I walk to the other side of the room.

Triangle and the Small Purple Maraca

While I am gone, Gabriel and Emily don't turn to look at each other. But Gabriel has a small purple maraca shaker in his hand, and he runs it along the armrest of Emily's chair. They both are quiet.

From across the room, I say, "Here comes . . . Nicolas," acknowledging their classmate's arrival.

Emily stretches, looks backward across the room where I've gone and says, "Eh-choo . . . juh-gee-gah." On reviewing the videotape, I notice that although Emily's vocalizations initially sounded random, the rhythm of her sounds mirror the pattern of the words that I have spoken: "Here comes . . . Ni-co-las." Then Emily rocks in her chair.

Gabriel softly shakes the purple maraca.

As I come back to the circle, Gabriel makes another vocal sound.

Emily also exclaims, "Tri-an-goh," as I reach down to the floor and place a new picture symbol—the triangular-shaped roof of a house—in preparation for a song called "The Snow Is on the Roof," which we are going to do later in the session.

Emily is approximating the word "triangle"! She is referring to the shape of the roof of the house that I have just placed on the picture schedule. But I don't realize it at the time. However, as I have later re-listened to the video recording and watched her look and speak just as I show them the picture of a triangular roof, I understand. Thank goodness she proves persistent in her subsequent attempts to communicate in the coming minutes because it had been easy to miss her initial verbal approximation of "triangle."

In the meantime, Gabriel continues to move the small purple maraca up and down on the armrest of Emily's chair. Then he reaches farther and touches the back of her hand with the maraca. She rotates her hand so the maraca shaker is in her palm. Then Gabriel releases it, and she takes it, as if they have agreed to pass the shaker. Many times in the past I had tried to prompt the children to pass instruments, and it often seemed that the adults essentially had to make it happen for the children. Now in an unscripted moment, the children seem to pass the shaker, taking their own initiative. Neither Gabriel nor Emily seems surprised by this transaction. But I am! It looks like, especially on Gabriel's part, a move toward peer interaction. But it is subtle and unconventional.

For some reason, I am glancing down again. In hindsight I wonder: Why? Do I simply need this time before the session to prepare materials for classes that day? Or am I partially aware, on this day, that when I appear to be looking down and engaging in my own project, the children are making more attempts to interact and communicate with me?

Tag With Sing-Song Sounds

Though my gaze is downward, Emily looks directly at me, and she makes another clear call for my attention. She makes a series of sing-song sounds, "Ah-a'-ahh-a" that resembles the cadence and pitches of the children's song, "Ring Around the Rosie."

I look up at Emily as she continues to repeat this theme four times, as I laugh and watch her with my mouth open in both playful and genuine wonder.

Emily stops briefly, and I respond by starting to echo her sing-song sounds.

As soon as I join her, she adds her own voice again, this time louder, and with a higher pitch.

I sing in reply with some variations of my own. I'm changing some notes and rhythms, but still using the "a" sound that she has introduced.

We pause.

She vocalizes a new one—a quick two-syllable "eh-eh" that she pronounces abruptly. Then she looks at me, as if waiting to see how I'll respond.

I give her an "eh-eh" right back, and I stop to see what she'll do.

She follows that up with an "eh-eh" to me.

I pass the "eh-eh" back to her, this time very fast, like a game of tag.

She starts another "eh-eh," and then we both break into a simultaneous sound-making free-for-all. For 15 seconds, we both vocalize in a fast-paced improvised mix of rhythms and pitches, alternating and overlapping our voices.

Then Rachel, approaching us from a nearby part of the classroom, welcomes Nicholas as he walks forward to take a seat in the circle of chairs: "Hey, Nicolas, look, Geoff is here for music this morning!"

Emily and I stop making sounds together, as if we realize that the coming arrival of the rest of the class meant that this "before session" time is soon ending.

While we were vocalizing together for about 30 seconds, we also continued our direct gaze toward each other for more than 10 seconds. This was much longer eye contact than I usually experienced with Emily or, for that matter, with most people.

It was a surprising contrast to those times when she would not look directly at adults. Previously witnessing her absence of eye contact with her father at the morning drop-off time had revealed that vividly. So too, I had many experiences within the group in the past when she had looked away from us when we had tried to interact with her.

VOCALIZATIONS AND ATTUNEMENT

Now, I am reviewing the video recording from the beginning of the music group that morning and attempting to summarize and discuss what happened. My focus is drawn to the moments when Gabriel and Emily started vocalizing some unusual sounds, attracting my attention. Their sounds seemed communicative, and I looked up and listened. I responded by echoing and varying their sounds with my voice. And I reacted through my body movements and facial expressions. In addition, Emily verbalized the word *triangle* in response to a picture of a triangular-shaped roof, and Gabriel had reached out to touch Emily's chair and hand with a purple shaker. Emily had taken the shaker into her hand, with no protests, just an unspoken coordination. Then, as the children began to vocalize again, Emily uttered sustained and varied sounds, resulting in 30 seconds of back-and-forth exchanges and simultaneous improvised vocal play with me.

When young children coordinate attention with another person, or focus on shared experiences or objects, these actions have been described in terms of joint engagement or joint attention (Adamson et al., 2019). Early communication and social development depend on this kind of shared focus. Children learn language and the back and forth of social exchange during joint interactions with objects, adults, and peers. Research indicates, however, that children on the spectrum often have particular difficulty in *initiating* joint attention—that is, using gestures or eye contact to direct others' attention to themselves, to events, and to objects (Bottema-Beutel et al., 2014).

Yet on this February morning, Emily and Gabriel initiated a variety of vocalizations to ask for my attention, to begin vocal expression and interplay, or to communicate recognition of the triangular-shaped roof in the picture I had introduced ("tri-an-goh"). Gabriel exhibited a happier affect and more variety during his sound making than I had noticed before. Emily voiced a range of tones and rhythms, and she inaugurated and continued eye contact and back-and-forth vocal play with me. Gabriel also used a shaker to reach toward Emily and facilitate a passing interaction with her.

What was bringing about their joint engagement, interactions, and communicative vocalizations? It was noteworthy that Emily and Gabriel started vocalizing before today's planned activities and that our interactions developed as I responded to (and reflected and varied) their sound making in spontaneous interplay. Responding to and building upon the interests, sounds, and actions of children on the autism spectrum similarly resulted in increased communication, interaction, and shared attention in research by Koegel and Koegel (2019) and Greenspan and Wieder (2006).

This process has also been referred to as attunement, which Daniel Stern (2000) and other parent-infant researchers have identified as crucial in the development of interpersonal relationships. Attunement has been defined as the capacity of a caregiver to synchronize with a child's motions and emotions (Mossler et al., 2019). However, psychologists Ed Tronick and Marjorie Beeghly (2011) have refined this concept to emphasize attunement as mutually discovered. Attunement not only occurs through an adult's sensitive responsiveness to a child. It is also co-created by children and caregivers finding ways of feeling and moving in harmony, along with experiencing subsequent moments of disconnection and reconnection. From this perspective, there are cycles of attunement, mis-attunement, and re-attunement. It is during ongoing successions of developing, pausing, and re-establishing contact that qualities of intimacy and understanding are nourished.

Stern (2000) reports that interactions earlier in children's development often have a mirroring and imitative quality in which a mother closely approximates the child's behavior. For example, when a child makes a notable facial expression, the mother mirrors it. When a child vocalizes, the mother vocalizes back. "However, the dialogue does not remain a stereotypic boring sequence of repeats . . . because the mother is constantly introducing modifying imitations . . . or providing a theme-and-variation format with slight changes in her contribution at each dialogic turn" (p. 139).

In "affect attunement" (Stern, 2000, p. 138), therefore, behaviors between partners are not simply copied but are reflected back in different modes than originally expressed. Stern gives the example of a 9-month-old girl who excitedly grabs a toy and lets out an exuberant "aaaah!" and looks at her mother. Her mother looks back, raises up her shoulders, and shakes her upper body like a dancer, about the same length of time as her daughter's "aaaah!" In response to the intensity, duration, and delight of her daughter's vocal expression, the mother creates cross-modal expressions in her own enthusiastic body movements.

In the vocal exchange with Emily in the preschool, she soon began to introduce changes in her vocalizations. She was not simply relying on me, as the adult, to introduce modifications. The variations that she launched into were an encouraging development, one that opened up possibilities for a more complex simultaneous singing/vocalizing together. In this sense, it felt like another moment of meeting in which we entered a new cooperative shared form of play. The process, in my view, was an example of "mutual simultaneous shaping" (Aigen, 1997, p. 34) in which influence flows in both directions between communicating partners, or in multiple directions within a group.

Music therapists Kim, Wigram, and Gold (2008) have described some of the contours of a specifically musical attunement: "The term 'musical attunement' implies a moment-by-moment, responsive use of improvised music which is sensitive and attentive to the child's music and non-musical expression. This often involves matching the child's pulse, rhythmic patterns of movement or musical play" (p. 1759). The ability to tune in and musically respond to a client is envisioned as creating the conditions for the development of abilities and shared relationships. Musical improvisation enables the therapist to create and alter music to meet the varying individual needs of clients. Yet I have also experienced that people can attune with each other through shared familiar music too. The connecting power of familiar preferred music has been corroborated by the research of Israeli music therapist Cochavit Elefant (2002). She studied the process of enhancing communication with girls with Rett syndrome through songs in music therapy. She found that four out of the five most preferred songs for the girls were familiar ones: "Further findings by researchers and clinicians support the present one that girls with Rett syndrome who selected familiar songs became more animated and generated greater communication and responsiveness when songs are heard" (p. 203). In a related way, in my career I have found that playing songs that participants know and like and that they can join in with—through singing, instrument playing, dancing, moving, and listening—can also help us establish rapport and attune to each other in shared interest and involvement in the music. So, musical attunement may be fostered in multiple ways—through existing songs and games, flexibly adapted and adjusted to the individuals in a group, and through original and improvised music. A balance of freedom and structure, familiarity and newness often seems helpful to the groups and individuals with whom I have worked.

Psychiatrist Bruce Perry (2021) wrote that "the core of good teaching is attunement . . . Throughout our lives, attunement helps us build and maintain our relationships" (para. 2–7). I was thankful for the recent moments of attunement and improvisation with the children—the shared collaborative guitar playing with Emily depicted in the previous episode, the spontaneous sound making involving Gabriel and Emily before this session, and the playful vocal exchanges of pitch and rhythm in our alternating and overlapping voices with Emily.

SUGGESTIONS FOR REFLECTION

- **How can music therapists and teachers include opportunities for children to explore strumming and playing a guitar?** In the February 9th session portrayed earlier in this chapter, it was through spontaneously responding to a child's interest. Emily's initiative in playing guitar, before the beginning of a group session, created this opening for interpersonal contact and musical experimentation with her.
- **How can teachers and therapists nurture their abilities to be responsive to spontaneous child-initiated vocalizations** with children who may appear to rarely take initiatives or display their reactions in social relations?
- **What are actions that schools can take to foster teachers' efforts to promote shared engagement and attunement** with young students on the spectrum?
- **What are some of the distinctive or essential features of "musical attunement"** in encouraging early forms of shared attention, vocal expression, and interactions through movements, facial expressions, and emotions?

CHAPTER 12

The "Microphone Song" and Goodbye to Dylan
March 30

Before I had started working at the early childhood program, I had witnessed that children were often motivated by the chance to speak or sing into a microphone. So, I composed a simple "Microphone Song" this year for the children in the preschool class. I had begun introducing it to them in the previous month. Seeing and touching the microphone, and hearing their own voices amplified, had appealed to many of them. The words and structure of the "Microphone Song" created a consistent pattern of individual turns followed by a chorus. The song also offered children freedom and support in whatever sound making, singing, or talking they chose to express during their turns.

Today there are nine children taking part in this March 30th session, one of the larger groups of children in this classroom in the past 2 years. The class was initially designed to accommodate six preschoolers on the autism spectrum, who would receive the school's highest level of support and services. The presence of nine children this morning reflects the growing number of autistic children receiving extended school hours and therapeutic services.

This session includes lead teacher David, assistant teachers Rachel and Elizabeth, and the children: Emily, Dylan, Gabriel, Jonathan, Carlos, Elina, Nicolas, Talan, and Shen.

DYLAN'S "HURRAH"

I had not seen Dylan for a number of weeks. But today he is here, and it is great to see him again. I have missed him. I do not know the reasons why he has not been present in class for several weeks when I have come. Earlier this morning, the coordinator of the Applied Behavior Analysis program talked with David about taking Dylan to a separate room for an ABA session. In the preceding weeks, Dylan may have been scheduled for an ABA session on the same morning that I came, thus causing him to miss the music therapy group. Or, perhaps, since David's classroom has gained more children during the course of the year, Dylan is spending parts of the day in one of the other classrooms at the school.

Additional one-to-one ABA sessions and visits to other preschool classrooms would offer Dylan different opportunities. But I only wished that things could be coordinated so that he could still attend our music therapy group too!

As this morning's session gets underway, Dylan speaks up early on, and his words reveal that the music activities continue to motivate his social interactions and self-generated communications.

"Hu-rrah, hu-rraaaah," he says, stretching out the sounds, looking up toward me, smiling, as I am taking the microphone out of the bag.

"Hurrah, hurrah!" I say, looking up, smiling. I nod my head. "Yes! We used to do that song!" I acknowledge and laugh. "That's right!" I continue, "We used to do 'The Kids Come Marching.'"

I'm surprised that even after weeks away from the group, Dylan is referring to a song that we had included in the music sessions before, which had involved another electronic device that I had taken out of my bag—a voice-output communication aid.

"Hurrah, hurrah," says Dylan again.

Several of the teachers join in smiling in appreciation of his spontaneous recall and communication.

But looking back later, I question myself. Should I have begun singing "The Kids Come Marching" song right then to give Dylan a chance to build on his response? Why didn't I? Was I concerned that other children in the group were looking forward to the "Microphone Song," and might be thrown off balance if I changed our planned schedule unexpectedly? Yes, but in hindsight, I think I may have missed an opening to follow up with Dylan and reward his communication about a past shared experience.

PARTICIPATION IN THE "MICROPHONE SONG"

In the moment, I choose to jump into our microphone song, with its usual start of asking the class as a whole, "Who wants a turn?" Jonathan, Talan, and Elina each respond, "I do." It's pleasure to see their interest and to hear them meet one of their goals by using spoken language to make a request. Shen also reaches out and tries to intercept the microphone when I hold it toward Elina. This is surprising, since Shen often appears physically passive during activities. But in this moment he assertively stretches forward to try to grasp the microphone. Emily also reaches for it with energy and makes forceful sounds during her turn.

Talan's Infectious Enjoyment

Before continuing with more descriptions, I want to share some background information about the large role that 4-year-old Talan plays in creating the atmosphere during the "Microphone Song." Both the teachers and children have been influenced by his actions. Early on, last month, when I introduced the song, he seemed surprised and happy at the children's amplified sounds and the lively encouragement from the adults. He became the most animated cheerleader in the group, clapping, bouncing up and down, and often saying "woo-woo!" after children's turns, each week during the "Microphone Song." He did this with great enthusiasm and, thereafter, his happiness was contagious to the other children and adults. His classmates would sometimes join him in clapping. In other circumstances, when we had tried prompting the children to clap along, it had seemed more artificial and coaxed. But Talan's delighted clapping and distinctive sing-song "woo-woo" cheering seemed to naturally inspire peers to join him in clapping, moving, and making sounds. During the semester, I sometimes questioned if much peer interaction was occurring in the group. In retrospect, I see that Talan's excitement during the song was generating peer imitation and interaction in ways that I had only partially recognized. Because his cheering was coming from his own self-directed responses, rather than from adult plans or requests, it has taken a while for me to perceive its actual effectiveness. I now realize that Talan's energy played a big role in sparking children's and teachers' interest and participation during the "Microphone Song." He helped shape a more-positive, joyful mood than we adults could have done on our own. His happiness was also quite a big contrast with Talan's crying at other times of the day.

Dylan With the Microphone

After several other children have made sounds with the microphone today, I ask, "Who else wants a turn?"

Dylan says, "I do."

I sing, "What do you want to say—Dylan?"

He soon says into the microphone in a deep breathy voice, "Hi——"

The teachers in the group voice their appreciation: "Good job, Dyl," says Rachel. "That's great!" I say. Not only had Dylan requested a turn, he began to participate quickly during his turn (rather than becoming evasive or stuck). He had also chosen to give a social greeting as his sound—a form of communication that we were glad to support. Would he say more now, or would he withdraw, when we gave him another opportunity to make sounds with the microphone?

"What do you want to say?" I sing again, to offer him his second chance to vocalize with the mic.

Dylan says again in a deep breathy voice, "Hi——" and then, "Too-wah too-wah too-wah!"

I'm a little quieter in response to this, and so are the teachers. I think we aren't quite sure what he means by "too-wah, too-wah, too-wah," though we're still glad to see and hear his participation. Talan looks intently across the room at Dylan and claps his hands twice.

I hold the microphone toward Dylan for the third and final part of his turn, singing, "Please tell us right away . . . What do you want to say?"

Dylan leans forward and says, "Hi——" and "too-wah too-wah too-wah" again.

This time I echo and affirm Dylan's "hi" and "too-wah too-wah too-wah." Other teachers support him by saying "Yay!" and I join them. Pointing to Carlos, who has stood up and is clapping, Rachel says, "A standing ovation from the balcony." "Good job, Dyl," says Elizabeth. I add, "Wow. Never heard that before!"

But perhaps we had, in fact, heard his sound before. When later reviewing the session video recording, it starts to dawn on me that Dylan might be approximating another song that we had done previously in our music group: "Toombah!" which begins, "Toom-bah, toom-bah, toom-bah." This was very close to the "too-wah, too-wah, too-wah," that Dylan vocalizes today, though I did not realize it in the moment. Now I believe that he was recalling and vocalizing part of the "Toombah" song, just as earlier he had remembered and repeated the "Hurrah, hurrah!" of "The Kids Come Marching" song.

Over time, I have continued to view, with appreciation, Dylan's growing abilities in communicating using personal language ("I do"), in articulating a social greeting ("Hi"), and in recalling and communicating songs from previous sessions ("Hurrah, hurrah" and "Too-wah, too-wah, too-wah"). Perhaps most encouraging, he is showing his increasing interests and capacities in joining in social interactions within the group activities, and this contrasts with his past experiences of shutting down or avoiding some previous opportunities for interpersonal contact.

Gabriel Says, "My Turn!"

"Who else wants a turn?" I ask. For a few moments no one makes a sound, and we wait. Some of the children point to themselves again, even though they have already had a turn.

"Say, 'My turn,'" Rachel suggests to one or two of the children who have not yet asked for the microphone.

I'm looking in the other direction when I hear a commotion. Teachers are saying that Gabriel has asked for a turn.

Did Gabriel use words? Did he use a gesture?

As I review the video now, I can distinctly hear him say, "My turn." This is terrific. Now, even more than at the time, I appreciate his welcome moment of verbal communication. I'm glad for the teachers' sensitive attention, which helps me detect Gabriel's verbal request.

When I sing to him, asking him what he wants to say, he replies, "Yah! yah!" These sounds certainly seem to fit with the "Yay!" that we've been cheering when other children have taken turns.

Three times Gabriel takes his turn, each time vigorously saying, "Yah!" while adding more of this sound each time and creating new rhythms with his vocalizations.

David joins in and sings a familiar song that goes, "Yeah, yeah, yeah," and there are a number of smiles in the class group to hear this.

THE "GOODBYE SONG"

After the microphone song is over and we have completed two other activities, it's near the end of today's music session. I lean down to pick up a picture for the "Goodbye Song." I say, "It's time for . . ."

"By'bye," says someone in two song-like high notes. I look up. Whose voice is that? I look around the circle, but I am not sure. Only later, in reviewing the video, I realize it had been Emily!

She has spoken the words that complete the meaning of my sentence. She inserts her voice in well-synchronized timing, anticipating the coming words and instigating her own verbal communication.

The ongoing challenges of autism are now coexisting with her evident abilities (in shared attention, anticipation, self-initiation, verbal communication) that seem to be gradually and often quietly developing and being demonstrated during sessions.

Dylan then speaks up too, saying, "B'bye, Dyl-an."

"That's right," I say, "Goodbye to Dylan . . . and everybody!" I hold out the goodbye picture symbol for each of the classmates in the circle to see. I add "everybody" to include all of the children.

However, I also feel a particular sense of joy hearing Dylan say his own name while saying goodbye. I thought back to the early sessions last year when he had been unable to, or averse to, saying his name. Today he readily initiates saying his name as he says goodbye.

But I did not realize that this March 30th session was actually the last time I would see Dylan in the music group. In the remaining months of the year, he was no longer there on Wednesday mornings when I came. Each week, for a time, I kept hoping to see him again, but that did not happen. One of the hardest parts was that I never found out why he was no longer there during our music therapy group. I still have a keen sense of loss about it, while I also remind myself to be thankful for the months and years that he was in the music therapy group—loveable, surprising, perplexing, endearing, intelligent, and energetic.

I missed Dylan very much. Unfortunately, the children's schedules were not something that I had the authority to alter. David, Elizabeth, and Rachel themselves were sometimes troubled by decisions that other staff members and administrators were making about the children's schedules and services. The school administration and the growing ABA program were gradually shaping the present and future direction of this class. The remaining months of this year were a time when the teachers and I were working to accept and adapt to a number of upcoming changes. But even so, in retrospect, I regret that I didn't have a chance to request (to whom, I wasn't even sure) that Dylan's schedule be arranged so that he could continue to participate in the music therapy group.

PROGRESS IN SOCIAL AND COMMUNICATION DEVELOPMENT

I wished that Dylan could have remained in the group because of what he was giving: zest, surprise, perceptivity, and nonverbal and verbal expressiveness in music activities as a peer on the autism spectrum. I also wished that he could have stayed in the group because of what he was receiving: inspiration from peers, support from trusted familiar teachers, and encouragement from a music therapist who helped motivate him to develop his abilities. I noticed that Dylan said "B'bye, Dylan" soon after Emily spoke up to say "By'bye." It has made me think about the ways Dylan was influenced by his peers in the group and the ways he influenced them. I will further consider this topic, group dynamics, later in this section.

First, I will take a few moments to highlight one of the distinguishing features from the March session described above—the increase in verbal communication by the children (Dylan's "Hurrah," "Hi," and "B'bye, Dylan"; Gabriel's "My turn"; Emily's "By'bye"; and Jonathan's, Talan's, and Elina's "I do."). Partly, their active participation indicated that the "Microphone Song" was providing a motivating musical/social routine as well as multiple clear individual opportunities for vocal and verbal expression. The specific activity, and the mic, and the balance of structure and freedom were helping to engender more communication. In addition, I believe that the results were indicators of the relationships and cohesion that we had developed in the group during the year. Earlier in the year we had wondered if we could find a new cohesiveness with the reduced attendance of David in the group, the addition of new children, and the uncertainties and ongoing programmatic and staff changes at the preschool. The moments portrayed during the "Microphone Song" represented, from my perspective, how the group had begun to coalesce over time. This happened not only because of the activities and objects. The class also became cohesive because of the reliable supportive ongoing relationships involving Elizabeth, Rachel, and the children, which helped make the music group an enjoyable stimulating learning environment.

Assessments of the Children's Development

I felt that the children's spoken language, the interactions in the group, and the shared positive affect during joint activities were signs that the children were developing their social and communicative expressiveness over time. Yet how was it possible to accurately gauge progress in social and communication development with children evaluated to be in the more intensive ranges of the autism spectrum, like those in this preschool class? A number of different assessments have been created to evaluate the developments, and document the needs, of autistic children. But measuring gains and assessing the efficacy of interventions has remained a continuing challenge.

Two resources that I have found helpful in understanding more about the developments of children on the autism spectrum are the Early Social

Communication Scales (ESCS) (Mundy et al., 2003) and the SCERTS Assessment Process-Observation (SAP-O) (Prizant et. al., 2006).

The ESCS has focused on joint attention as a central variable affecting the early development of children diagnosed with autism. Specific behaviors are assessed over time—for example, frequency of eye contact, gestures, turn taking, reaching, giving, pointing to elicit aid in obtaining an object, clapping, following someone else's focus of attention, and other behaviors. Many examples of shared attention were in evidence during the March music therapy group: eye contact, turn taking, reaching for the microphone, clapping, and class members' paying attention to peers' vocalizations and actions. The ESCS has also underlined distinctions between child-initiated behaviors and child-responsive behaviors, observing the relative infrequency of some children's initiatives in interactions. Therefore, it was notable that Dylan, Emily, Gabriel, and the other children were instigating bids for joint attention, as well as responding to them, while engaging in social interactions and language use during the music group.

The SCERTS Assessment Process-Observation (Prizant et al., 2006) was formulated to identify the needs and treatment goals for young children on the spectrum in three developmental areas: social communication (SC), emotional regulation (ER), and transactional support (TS). The authors believed that these were the primary dimensions to be prioritized in supporting children and their families. In addition, three stages of development were outlined: social partner stage, language partner stage, and conversational partner stage. These could be characterized as the beginning, intermediate, and more advanced stages in children's communication and social development.

SCERTS descriptions of the social partner stage have helped clarify the beginning steps and the challenges often exhibited by young children on the spectrum. And these descriptions have also helped me realize that the children in the music group were developing abilities that were going beyond some of these restricted actions:

> Children with ASD at the Social Partner stage typically show difficulties with . . . shared attention, as evidenced by limited ability to orient to (i.e., turn to and focus on) people, to follow their focus of attention, to use gaze shifts, to share emotion, and/or to follow what others are pointing to or looking at (i.e., gaze/point following). (Prizant et al., 2006, p. 174)

In prior experiences in our music therapy group, we had encountered challenges similar to those observed by Prizant and colleagues—class members appearing to be remote or not responsive to attempts to begin shared social interactions. But in the video excerpts from March of my second year working with the preschoolers, the class members were giving their attention to peers and adults in the group, sharing positive affect, and increasing the length of interactions. Children like Emily and Dylan were also showing signs of taking an important developmental step that signaled a transition to the next stage of development, according to the SCERTS model: They were acquiring and using conventional gestures and vocalizations/verbalizations in reciprocal social communicative exchanges. Engagement in music was leading to enhanced communication, an outcome that was similar to the research findings of neuroscientist Megha Sharda and colleagues (2018). Their study demonstrated that 8–12 weeks of a music intervention could improve the social communication and functional brain connectivity in school-aged children on the spectrum in Montreal, Canada. The next chapter of this book will further explore ways that shared attention during music activities can support the emergence of social interactions and verbal communication.

The Influence of Group Dynamics

Solely focusing on the actions of individual children cannot give the full picture of what was happening in the music therapy group. It is important to also consider how group dynamics affected the participants.

Groups alter the individual behavior of their constituents—this is a fundamental tenet of group dynamics (Lewin, 1947). But some autism experts are skeptical about the potential of group process with children on the spectrum. Autistic children's multiple social, communicative, and attentional difficulties make many group interventions misguided and inadequate, according to this view. Psychologist and special educator Ennio Cipani (2008) has asserted that the efficacy of groups like "the morning circle" with young children on the autism spectrum "is minimal at best" (p. 177). The author questions the wisdom of using approaches whose prerequisite for success is good attending skills on the part of the child. "Does that make sense for children like Artie, whose attending skills are minimal to nil? Here is a hypothetical example of looking good but smelling bad," Capani continued:

> It is the start of class time . . . the instructional aides, whose job is to help keep the children in their seat (no small feat), are seated behind the children. The music comes on:

The itsy-bitsy spider went up the water spout . . .

Any observer to this class sees the following. Of the five students in the class, four at any one time are engaged in some other distracting activity such as hand weaving, turning around, tantruming, or getting out of their seat . . . The aides are in rhythm and sing their hearts out, following the lead of the teacher. But what also is apparent is the lack of vocal responding from the five students. (pp. 177–178)

However, in our March 30th music group, a number of the students *were* vocally responding and *were* reaching out and getting involved in the "Microphone Song" and the "Goodbye Song." The children were not simply "hand weaving, turning around, tantruming, or getting out of their seat" as the above quotation characterized. Instead, there were many moments of class members actively paying attention to peers' vocalizations and actions. And many of the children were engaging and in vocal and verbal communication. Talan watched and listened to classmates' turns with the microphone and then enthusiastically celebrated peers' turns by clapping and cheering. Carlos clearly followed Talan's lead in clapping. In fact, Carlos seemed to make an effort to show Talan that he was clapping by bringing his hands close to Talan's line of sight (showing/sharing a gesture). Dylan's abilities to recall activities and to jumpstart verbal communication about songs that we had previously done in the music sessions ("Hurrah, hurrah" and "Too-wah") showed attending skills during groups that were much more than "minimal at best." My experiences in our preschool class taught me that, yes, the difficulties and disintegration that Cipani (2008) pictured could be present as we attempted to facilitate a music group for children on the autism spectrum. But the group was also capable of fostering cohesion, enjoyment, shared attention, peer and adult social interaction, and communication. Looking back at our session, I see multiple instances of active participation and beneficial reciprocal influences occurring within the music group.

SUGGESTIONS FOR REFLECTION

- **What can help evoke increasing verbal communication by the children?** (e.g., Dylan's "Hurrah," "Hi," and "B'bye, Dylan"; Gabriel's "My turn"; Emily's "By'bye"; and Jonathan's, Talan's, and Elina's "I do."). Consider introducing a microphone and sound-making games and songs with children on the spectrum to motivate preverbal vocalizations and verbal communication and back-and-forth interpersonal interactions.

- **What might have been effective ways to advocate for Dylan's continuing participation in the weekly music group?** In your work, do you have regularly scheduled chances to talk with other school service providers in order to coordinate children's daily and weekly schedules?
- **What are some of the benefits, and the limitations, in group activities** that have most impacted the young children on the autism spectrum with whom you work and play?

CHAPTER 13

An Impasse and a Duet
May 18

Half way through our music group on May 18th, we've just completed a fill-in-the-blank game. During this activity I sing one of the preschoolers' favorite songs like "Old MacDonald had a farm . . ." and then I quickly stop in the middle of the verse, playfully leaving a wide-open space. This invites the children to vocalize the missing parts of the words and melody (such as "E . . . I . . . E . . . I . . . O"). During today's "Old MacDonald" fill-in-the-blank song, Gabriel twice vocalizes "E . . . I . . ." in time with the rhythm of the chorus. His vocalizing these two vowel sounds is a good step, and we clap and celebrate in our circle of five children—Emily, Gabriel, Carlos, Rowen, and Nicolas—and three teachers—David, Rachel, and Elizabeth.

TODAY'S TURNS DURING THE "MICROPHONE SONG"

Now, as we transition to the next part of our music class, I'm hopeful and curious: Will Gabriel vocalize any additional speech-like sounds during the upcoming "Microphone Song"? As I introduced in the previous chapter, this was a song that I'd written to use the appeal of the microphone to encourage sound making, singing, communication, and personal interaction.

Before describing today's events, I want to ask one key question about the purpose of this activity: Why am I so focused on whether Gabriel makes beginning vocal or verbal sounds? My answer is that I believe that each small step in his vocal and verbal communication may become a pathway toward more connection and understanding with his teachers, peers in this group, and family members at home. So, I embark upon today's activity to encourage the use of spoken or sung syllables and words.

At the Start of Gabriel's Turn

Gabriel gives a smile and reaches forward with both hands to grasp the microphone. I'm happy too, seeing his eagerness. He taps his front teeth onto it, and a scratchy click sound gets amplified into the classroom. An accidental bump on the mic, or is he trying to do this? He then starts tapping his teeth on the microphone repeatedly, creating a chittering repetitive sound. This has me wondering if our "Microphone Song" for promoting the development of vocal and verbal communication may turn into a series of tooth scrapings on the mic that other children may copy.

"Try using your voice, Gabriel!" I say, urging him to explore vocalizations of syllables or melodies.

Gabriel moves forward and forcefully says, "Yeh, yeh, yeh!"

Lead teacher David builds on Gabriel's response by calling out "Yeah, yeah, yeah!" like an enthusiastic fan at a sports event. Assistant teachers Rachel and Elizabeth and several of the children smile.

To hear Gabriel's voice, and to see his focused interest in the microphone and the song this morning, contributes a lively energy to our musical game. I try to capitalize on the momentum by offering him another chance to try some additional sounds or words.

I sing, "What do you want to say? . . . Can you say, GAH-bri-el?" I offer the microphone toward him, encouraging him to vocalize the "Gah" sound at the beginning of his name, as pronounced by his family members.

"Say Gah-bri-el!" urges Rachel.

Gabriel is silent, though. He holds onto the top of the microphone and begins to shift back and forth in his chair.

"GAH-bri-el," I enunciate again.

Gabriel gives a sustained difficult-to-comprehend vocalization that I would have a hard time writing out here phonetically.

Rachel tries offering him another option: "You can say, '1-2-3!'" she suggests.

But he has become quiet now, looking fidgety and unsettled. He eventually moves his head side to side several times when we try to prompt him again.

Reflecting back later on these interactions with Gabriel, I remember thinking that we'd reached an impasse. Now I think that these moments could also be envisioned as reaching the edge—of his current verbal abilities or my current capacities to help him add to these. In the past I had witnessed his classmate Dylan have considerable verbal skills but sometimes puzzlingly withdraw from using them. Yet with Gabriel, the issue seems different: He is facing the fundamental challenge of learning to develop the early beginnings of verbal communication. The microphone is arousing his interest in sound making, but it still remains difficult to expand from a small repertoire of current sounds into spoken words.

Emily's Vocalizations and Verbal Expressions

To continue our "Microphone Song," I begin singing its chorus again, signaling that soon it will be time for the next classmate's turn. "What do you want to say?" I sing. "What do you want to say? Please tell us right away—what do you want to say?"

I ask, "Emily, would you like a turn?"

I gesture the microphone toward her, but I don't wordlessly pass it yet. Earlier she's made nonverbal requesting behaviors of reaching out and moving toward the microphone. Now, to encourage verbal communication, I pause for a second to ask her, "Would you like a turn?" I'm trusting that her interest in the microphone may give her the extra impetus to communicate in words to ask for it.

Emily says a low sound like "na'nun."

"Yes?" I say, unsure of her meaning.

Rachel reaches forward, touches Emily's shoulder, and urges her, "Say, 'My turn!'"

Simultaneously, Emily says, "Na'nah," more loudly and looks expectantly at me.

"Say 'My turn,'" I encourage her, echoing Rachel's cue.

Emily then says, "My turn," in a surprisingly deep voice.

"Gooood!" I say in a deep voice too! I'm delighted that Emily is verbally requesting this! I also wonder if she has instinctively used a deeper voice to more closely mirror the pitch of mine.

I begin to sing the melody into the microphone, "What you want to say, Emily!" I kneel down in front of her to bring the microphone nearer. To support many forms of participation in this diverse class group, I'm ready to welcome simple phonetic sounds, babbles, and funny vocal intonations as well as recognizable spoken words and singing. Many of the students this semester are producing preverbal sounds if they are vocalizing at all.

As I reach the microphone toward her, Emily is already moving toward me and stretching out her hand to grasp it. And she rapidly and vigorously says, "Yo-nah-nah-nah. Yo-yo-yo!"

I vocalize her "yo-yo-yo" back to her as a way of playing with the sounds, rhythm, and tones that she's just uttered.

Emily then makes several additional kinds of vocalizations and I reply and elaborate on them with similar sounds. Emily's tones and rhythms are new to me—I have not heard her make these particular syllables and rhythmic patterns before.

She starts roaming her fingernails around the top of the microphone, making small amplified scratching sounds, which, as Gabriel had explored, might become a sound effect that several other children were going to be interested in.

Then I start to sing one more time, "Emily, what do . . ."

She anticipates this and pulls the microphone close to her mouth again and says, "Yo-mi, yo-mi. Nye-nye-nah-nah." She shifts her gaze from the microphone directly back to me. I feel that she is communicating that it is my turn to vocalize again. She is awaiting my response, anticipating turn taking.

I smile and answer her by singing back the last parts of her vocalization again.

Once more, Emily reaches toward the microphone for another turn.

"You should get her to sing a song," suggests Elizabeth. "What's her favorite . . ."

"How about . . ." I start to say.

But Rachel and Elizabeth spontaneously sing, "She'll be coming' 'round the mountain when she comes!"

Emily swivels around in her chair to look back toward Elizabeth and Rachel.

I join in singing, "She'll be comin' 'round the mountain when she comes!"

Then I hold out the microphone for Emily again.

Emily says, "Sh'way coming 'round the mountain when . . ."

Rachel smiles and nods her head.

"Good!" I say, "Good, Emily!" and Rachel and Elizabeth glance at each other and laugh in appreciation.

Emily pushes the microphone back toward me. She and I both look at each other.

"How about . . . Row, row, row your boat . . . ," I start singing and then bring the microphone in front of her.

"Gent-y down t'strea," says Emily softly and rapidly.

"Gently down the stream," Elizabeth clarifies for me, and this helps me understand Emily's soft quick response.

"Merrily, merrily, merrily, merrily," I sing into the microphone, then hold it back toward her.

"Life's like . . . a Dream," says Emily, emphasizing the word *dream*.

I smile and laugh! "Yes, life is but a dream!" I say.

One of Emily's peers, Jonathan, exhales a big breath and tilts his head backward with a smile on his face. Peers Gabriel and Nicolas are also smiling. Emily's classmates' listening and interest during her turn also helped make it possible for her to hear and closely focus in our back-and-forth exchanges.

"Good job, Emily!" says David.

"Yay, Emily!" says Rachel, clapping her hands. "A duet!"

REFLECTING ON THE INTERACTIONS WITHIN THIS WEEK'S MUSIC GROUP

As I review what happened during the music session, I'd like to focus first on Gabriel's response during the "Microphone Song" and then on Emily's.

The Challenge of Recognizing and Building Upon Gabriel's Communication

Gabriel's turn with the microphone led me to look further into research about the communication development of young children. My attention was drawn to an assertion made by a group of experts in language acquisition in young children on the autism spectrum: "There are no clear guidelines available for how to measure nonspoken language skills that are comparable to those available for spoken language" (Tager-Flusberg et al., 2009, p. 644). When experts within the field do not find clear guidelines for measuring *preverbal* communication development, this sheds light on the difficulties that we were encountering in the music group in nurturing communication with children who were currently nonspeaking or with limited speech like Gabriel.

Researchers Helen Tager-Flusberg and Connie Kasari (2013) have written that approximately "30% of children with autism spectrum disorder remain minimally verbal, even after receiving years of interventions and a range of educational opportunities" (p. 468). If so, what actions can support the communication development of children on the spectrum who are nonspeaking or preverbal? One approach that has been influential for me is the Communication Matrix (Rowland & Fried-Oken, 2010), which is an assessment for individuals at the earliest stages of communication. It advises that a child should be encouraged to use current abilities while being progressively urged toward the next level of competence. Seven levels in early communication development are envisioned: preintentional behavior, intentional behavior, unconventional communication, conventional communication, concrete symbols, abstract symbols, and language.

What was Gabriel's current level? He often exhibited what Rowland and Fried-Oken classify as "pre-intentional behavior." This reflected changes in Gabriel's comfort/discomfort and mood states but did not clearly communicate his interests or choices. However, his vocalizing "E . . . I . . ." and "yeh, yeh, yeh" in response to specific invitations within the songs, and his shaking his head from side to side in a refusal-like gesture, represented steps of intentional communication using conventionally recognizable sounds and a gesture.

With an approach similar to that advocated in the Communication Matrix, I had started today's "Microphone Song" by encouraging Gabriel to use his abilities at his current communication level. Then I suggested options for expanding his repertoire of sounds—beginning with the sounds in his own name. With chagrin, I am becoming more aware of my own tenacity when it came to this goal of prompting the children to voice their own names! Rachel offered Gabriel another option: "You can say, '1-2-3!'" However, Gabriel would not or could not say these sounds in that moment. Perhaps it would have helped if we had asked him to vocalize a simpler beginning sound, a phoneme, the smallest unit of sound. Or would it have been beneficial to follow his lead more closely and try to build upon his "yeh" sound? Should I have invited him to vocalize incremental variations like "yo" or "yee"?

My experiences with Gabriel during this session made me reflect about better recognizing and building upon whatever preverbal means of communication children like Gabriel were showing, in addition to helping them develop the sounds of speech. Many students on the autism spectrum may benefit as school staff introduce augmentative and alternative opportunities for communication—pictures, voice-output systems, sign language, and object symbols. Affirming and responding to nonverbal gestures, body movements, eye gaze, sounds, and facial expressions can further nourish the expressiveness of children.

Signs of Emily's Communication Development

With Emily, there were a number of positive signs of her emerging communication development during this session with the "Microphone

Song." She communicated interest through eye contact and posture shifts such as leaning forward and reaching out. She used words ("my turn") to request the microphone, and she quickly initiated vocalizing a variety of sounds and patterns. Then, as teachers suggested a specific song ("She'll Be Comin' 'Round the Mountain"), Emily spoke the words of the song, and she and I were able to take turns singing/speaking the lyrics into the microphone—an alternating back-and-forth "duet." We did this also with "Row, Row, Row Your Boat."

Emily's new steps in using spoken language were invigorating, particularly since last year she had sometimes appeared nonspeaking or withdrawn. Her participation in this duet involved coordinated timing and attuned social cooperation, which are often challenging for children on the spectrum. During the music, however, Emily was able to speak in synchronized alternating turns with me in several different exchanges. Increasingly, she was participating in, and appeared to be enjoying, the interplay and activities within the group. The songs and relationships in our music group were creating bridges to language use and personal interaction that were important and hopeful steps in her development.

Drawing upon the SCERTS model of social communication assessment (Prizant et al., 2006), I would describe Emily's emerging verbal communications as transitional steps toward the language partner stage (using first words and word combinations). These advances followed her earlier steps in the social partner stage (using nonspeaking signals such as gestures, facial expressions, and vocalizations).

Echolalia? Behavior Modification?

Was her language use echolalia? In other words, did her speaking consist of scripted repetitive verbalizations which are sometimes categorized as perseverations? I view her use of words as interactive communication rather than as the insistent repetition of a word or phrase. During "Row, Row, Row Your Boat," Emily was speaking the next words of the song, not echoing the same words I sang. She was completing the lyrics to two alternate songs, coordinating her timing, adjusting to my quick shift from one song to another. She was maintaining shared attention to the back-and-forth exchanges, and she was directing the microphone back to me as if inviting me to continue my part of the song. Emily was involved in more than simply the mechanical echoing of sounds.

Nor was our primary focus on instructing Emily to repeat back target words when systematically prompted by an adult in a one-to-one drill, often part of the process of behavioral modification in prevailing autism treatments. Instead, she vocalized sounds and words within a music group where adults and children were influencing each other. Her energetic self-chosen vocalizations prompted adult teachers to suggest a favorite song. Then Emily's subsequent speaking of the song's words sparked me to introduce another song and another invitation to take a turn in a "duet" of verbal and musical communication.

Developing interpersonal communication and relationships consists of more than behavior modification of a child, assert infant-caregiver researchers like Jaffe et al. (2001). It involves adults and children mutually modifying each other's behavior as they coordinate and change their responses in evolving and bidirectional interactions. During the "Microphone Song," Emily and I synchronized and adjusted our actions and words in response to each other. Her vocalizations and the teachers' suggestion of "She'll Be Comin' 'Round the Mountain" shaped my subsequent responses.

I think that these interactions with Emily were examples of the useful role that music therapy can play in facilitating and motivating children's active contributions in their own development, as Emily took advantage of the freedom and musical opportunities to surprise us with her initial self-chosen sounds and subsequent spontaneous back-and-forth exchanges. This provided a needed complement to the structured consistency and replicability of behavioral approaches. Children on the autism spectrum, like typically developing children, need multiple opportunities to take initiatives, make choices, and lead as well as follow in order to develop cognitively, socially, and emotionally.

Partners in Change

The SCERTS model has emphasized the importance of adult helpers growing in their ability to give interpersonal "transactional supports" to children. Supportive partners do this by attuning to a child's emotion and pace, responding to children's interests, offering choices nonverbally or verbally, and expanding on a child's play and nonverbal communication. During the past 2 years, the teachers and I were regularly learning to adjust our approaches to meet Emily's needs and those of each of the children. I introduced new objects, like the microphone, to increase Emily's motivation and ability to engage in vocal communication. Furthermore, to balance adult requests for her to follow, the teachers and I tried to create more opportunities for her to take the lead

in speaking, singing sounds, and exploring instruments. I also increasingly mirrored and expanded upon her play in improvised moments
before and during the class.

Over time in our music therapy group, and during this May 18th session, I witnessed communication and social interaction emerging through
initiatives from the children and teachers, in synthesis with my initiatives
as a music therapist. When I thought my job was to "get" responses from
the children, they appeared to be more withdrawn and avoidant, and I
was more frustrated. When I shared participative songs that I discovered
were enjoyable for our group—incorporating the microphone, movements, drums, parachute, and voice-output communication aids—the
communication and interactions within the group developed more naturally and cooperatively, and we became partners in change.

SUGGESTIONS FOR REFLECTION

- **What might help you foster musical and spontaneous
  exchanges** as bridges to interpersonal connection and vocal
  communication with children?
- **Could you re-envision goals** less in terms of unilaterally
  modifying children's behaviors and more in terms of learning to
  cooperate and play together as partners in change?
- **What sparks Emily to engage in self-chosen vocalizations**
  (playing with speech-like sounds) and then subsequently
  progressing toward back-and-forth verbal exchanges of whole
  phrases like "gently down the stream" and "life is but a dream"?
- **What nurtures collaboration with the classroom teachers
  and aides** when leading and following children during a music
  group? When we as classroom leaders notice and follow up on
  the in-the-moment suggestions and reactions of other classroom
  staff and participating children, this often facilitates the greatest
  shared engagement with the children, peers, and adults.
- **What alternative steps can we take to support the
  communication development of children who are
  nonspeaking or preverbal** if 30% of children on the
  spectrum may remain minimally verbal, even after a range of
  interventions and educational supports are provided (Tager-
  Flusberg & Kasari, 2013)? Offering musical instruments
  and movement activities can enable alternative ways of
  communicating other than through words alone. Affirming

and responding to nonverbal gestures, body movements, eye gaze, sounds, and facial expressions can expand avenues of communication with class members.

- **In your experiences with picture systems, augmentative and alternative communication, voice-output systems, sign language, or object symbols**, which methods have noticeably helped class members, and which have been of limited use?
- **What resources can help you compare your classroom methods with others' educational and therapeutic approaches?** Who might be able to assist you—either online or in person—in refining your understanding of the paths of development with children in the early stages of communication and social interaction? What might you learn by looking into the SCERTS model, the Communication Matrix, and other resources created to assess and enhance the social, interpersonal, and communication abilities of young children diagnosed with autism?

CHAPTER 14

Emily and the Drum; Gabriel and the "Toombah Song"

June 1

It is an early June morning, the last day for music therapy sessions in the preschool class. Six children are here: Emily, Gabriel, Jonathan, Talan, Shen, and Carlos. Teachers David, Elizabeth, and Rachel are also in the circle of class members.

SAY AND PLAY YOUR NAME

I'm bringing a drum in front of the children, one by one, during the "Hello Song" and encouraging them to "say and play your name with the drum." Jonathan has taken the first turn. He verbally says his first name, while playing three clear and strong beats on the drum, mirroring the three syllables "Jon-a-than." This is just what I'm hoping to encourage—the children actively using the drum to add some enjoyment and physical action to the process of saying and playing their names.

As Talan starts to take the next turn, I ask his name. Emily quietly says his name out loud, "Ta-lan." Then she reaches toward the drum and says, "Eh," the first syllable of her own name. It is as if she is trying to complete his turn and begin hers. But my attention is still on Talan, so I don't switch my focus to Emily's interjected sounds yet.

She tries again. She looks up toward my face and says, "Em-lee ba." Is this an approximation of her full name or some variation? Her second attempt to speak, and catch my attention, seems to be an example of her emerging ability to try to repair a missed connection in communication. In hindsight, I wished that I had more clearly heard and affirmed the quiet talking that she initiated—the sounds of her own name, while anticipating and verbalizing her next steps in the "Hello Song." Previously, in working with Emily, I had questioned whether her nascent verbalizations would be considered echolalia by other observers. But in this moment, she is not echoing adults or peers—because she begins saying the sounds of her name before we verbally ask her to do so.

After completing Talan's turn, I then transition toward Rachel's because I include the teachers in the musical turn-taking routines. They help model the communication and social interaction that I am trying to foster with the children, and they often add a motivating vitality to our music activities.

Emily doesn't express frustration while waiting for Rachel's turn. Instead, Emily gazes intently toward her. And after a few moments, Emily verbalizes her name, "Rachel." It's great to see Emily's active attention and to hear her speaking other group members' names!

Now it's time for Emily's own turn, and I move closer to her to give her the mallet and hold the drum in front of her. She is already reaching out her hands to get them.

"And let's say hello to Em-i-ly," I sing, strongly accentuating each syllable of her name. I pass her the mallet.

"Boom—boom—boom" she beats out three syllables (corresponding with her name, Em-i-ly), on the drum. She then lifts the mallet up and pauses momentarily.

"Goooood!" I say, with a long emphasis. Then I gesture my fingers toward my lips, and I urge her to speak too: "Can you say 'Em-i-ly'?" I ask.

Just to pause in my writing, I want to reiterate that my intention in offering the drum during the "Hello Song" is to give children an extra impetus to communicate verbally and nonverbally. In the past months, many of the class members are seeming to take an added interest, and the drum is providing a way for several of the children with limited speech to participate and beat the syllables of their names. But I am also learning that simultaneously playing and saying their names can have difficulties for some children. Will an invitation to drum and verbally communicate at the same time help Emily speak her name, or will this combined opportunity confuse or hamper her?

Emily responds by continuing to play the drum, reaching forward and rapping it several more times.

I invite her anew to say her name. I move nearer, trying to communicate my intention. "How 'bout you?" I say, touching my fingers to my mouth again and vocally trying to prompt her: "Em-i-ly."

I pause. No sound.

"Eh" I start to cue again. But she is already starting to talk.

"E-mi-ly," she says. She says her name!

"Yeah!! Good job!" I celebrate, with a feeling of elation.

Emily is reaching her arm out once more, indicating she wants the mallet again. So, I give it to her. She resumes her drumming, and then I begin to sing the song's chorus, starting to signal a transition to the next child's turn.

"That was awesome! Emily said her name!" I say, wanting to share my excitement with the rest of the group members.

"Yeah!" says Elizabeth.

And, in a tiny sing-song voice, Emily says "[muffled sound, then] morning . . . I said her name."

Re-listening to Emily

Afterward, I continued to re-listen to the audio-video recording of these moments to try to hear accurately what Emily said. I've been surprised by some of her quick, quiet verbalizations that I hadn't recognized initially—the sounds of her name before her turn and, afterward, the softly uttered words of "morning" and "I." This was one of the first times that I had been aware of her using the word "I" to refer to herself, which she intermixed with the pronoun reversal "her."

What was significant about her utterances? Saying the sounds in her own name, and playing her name's three syllables on the drum, represented additional steps in her emerging communication. During the past 2 years, her participation had moved along a continuum from early silence, to nonverbal vocalizations, and then to speech that was adult-directed and imitative. And, in this session, she engaged in self-initiated verbal communication (saying the syllables "Em" and "Em-lee ba" of her name before her turn and before we had asked her), and later with a first-person pronoun (*I*) and word variations (*morning*). She was using more spoken communication than previously: She was more willing and able to speak and to express herself during the "Hello Song," while also voicing an awareness of peers (saying Talan's name) and teachers (saying Rachel's name). Emily's peer awareness and attention to adults in the class were particularly significant when compared with last year's instances of appearing to avoid or look away from attempts to interact with her.

Relating Emily's Changes to the Nordoff-Robbins Evaluation Scales

Music therapists Paul Nordoff and Clive Robbins (2007) created three evaluation scales to attempt to measure the development of relationship, communication, and musical activity with children on the autism spectrum, or with differing developmental delays. Emily's emerging steps in communication—during the past 2 years in the music therapy group—corresponded with the descriptive terms and increasing levels of participation outlined in the Nordoff and Robbins Scale II Musical Communicativeness. This assessment tool defined seven successive levels of development in musical communication: moving from early "unresponsive non-acceptance" to subsequent "fragmentary, fleeting" contact, and toward gradually "more sustained" intentional "interactive musical communication" and increased involvement in vocal and rhythmic expression and movement (p. 396). Rather than Emily's musical communication level remaining unchanged during her years in the group (e.g., she could have continued to look away and stay detached from interpersonal interaction and communication), Emily moved from initial Level 1 inactivity to subsequent Level 6 communicative expressive involvement in music activities.

Nordoff and Robbins (2007) also envisioned that "music communication is realized in therapy through three modes of activity: Instrumental, Vocal, and Body Movements" (p. 398). Emily in her final "Hello Song" of the year was expressing herself using each of these three forms of active participation in music—playing an instrument (drum), communicating with her voice, and making body movements (grasping and swinging the mallet in beating the drum).

I mentioned earlier that inviting children to simultaneously drum and speak might have been too difficult for some class members. However, it also seemed that combining opportunities for instrument playing, vocalizing, and movement with the "Hello Song" enhanced Emily's motivation and participation. Her eye-gaze alternation between me and the drum and her expectant leaning-forward body posture indicated an eagerness to continue to play the drum, which I felt contributed significantly to her verbally expressing her name when I requested it. To me, this seemed an instance of tapping into the "musical motivation"

(p. 400) that Nordoff and Robbins saw in interactions with children. The motivating power of music played a central role in my current interactions with Emily and others during these sessions. The opportunities to move and play instruments could become catalysts for the children's communication and interactions within the group.

THE "TOOMBAH SONG"—GABRIEL'S BEEN DOING IT AT HOME

I will now resume describing our June 1st music session. After the "Hello Song" and a subsequent parachute song, I say to the group, "All right, it's time for Toombah!" This is a song for dancing and moving together. I have previously told the children that during this song we can pretend to be monkeys and move our arms, shoulders, and torsos back and forth.

As I prepare to start the song, Rachel says, "Lucia [Gabriel's mother] came in one day and asked, 'Are you singing a song about a duck?'" Lucia then showed a series of back-and-forth shimmying and swinging motions that she'd seen Gabriel doing at home recently.

"A song about what?" I laugh, and David and Elizabeth smile too.

"A duck!" Rachel laughs again. "Because she thought he was sort of doing like this [Rachel mimics his back-and-forth motions], and I said no, that's our song 'Toombah, Toombah, Toombah' . . . Gabriel's been doing it at home!"

The teachers and I begin expressing excitement that Gabriel is remembering the song's movements and is dancing them beyond the school day. We are finding delight in the news that he's sharing our "monkey" song with his mother nonverbally in such a way that she perceives he might be pantomiming an animal—whether the wiggling back-and-forth motions playfully represent a monkey or a duck!

When I announce the Toombah song, Emily seems to anticipate the coming actions of the song, and she stands up moments before I ask the group to do so. She puts her index fingers at the corners of her mouth (one of the motions during the song) and vocalizes just before the song starts. Like Gabriel, her actions show that she is remembering the coming movements of the song, and she is starting to do them before being asked.

I invite the rest of the group to join Emily, "All right! Let's stand up!"

Thinking out loud, I say, "Is that right? [Gabriel's been doing it at home?] That's great to know!"

Group Play and Coordinated Movements

Soon the class members are standing up and beginning to do the motions of the Toombah song. Gabriel is marching his feet, bending his waist, and moving his arms side to side. Carlos, Emily, and Jonathan are also moving their arms. They are swaying their bodies and shoulders back and forth in time with the adults' singing and movements. Gabriel's motions are very lively this morning, and his happiness and energy are so transparent that Rachel laughs happily and says, "Look at him! . . . Go, Gabriel!" Jonathan starts to move more vigorously and excitedly too, in seeming response to Gabriel's energy and the positive comments and other signs of active enjoyment in the group.

Then we do the next motion in the song's sequence, putting our index fingers at the corners of our mouths, and making wide upturned smiles. We sing, "Dearie-don, Dearie-don, Dearie, Dearie, Don!" Curiously, the silly sounds and the quaint oddness of smiling-very-widely often have the effect of causing somebody to actually start smiling or laughing, which helps build a good mood in the group. Carlos, Gabriel, Emily, and Jonathan join in these "Dearie-don" motions—elbows bent, fingers on cheeks, looking up, paying attention. Only Talan remains still, one hand bent behind his head, scratching the back of his neck, while watching.

During the third sequence of motions, we begin to turn circles in place, like tops, as we sing "Na na na na!" Jonathan laughs and wiggles as he turns around. Carlos and Emily are also each mirroring this turning motion without adult assistance, and they imitate the additional accompanying movement of placing one hand on the top of their heads as they turn in a circle.

Amidst cheers and praises when we finish the song, Gabriel smiles, laughs, and looks directly at Emily. I have the feeling that he is expressing social interest in Emily again by looking toward her. I note that his attention toward a peer follows his involvement in movement to the song's melodies and rhythms, as he takes actions that he's comfortable with and adept with.

The majority of the children today, in varying ways, moved, joined in, and played with me and the teachers and peers during the Toombah song. It wasn't only Gabriel who was lively. In the different sections of the song, Jonathan had swayed, jiggled excitedly, and laughed. Emily and Carlos had turned around in coordination with the group while simultaneously keeping a hand on their heads, and they had both vocalized. Talan eventually spun in a circle with my assistance and then smiled and made eye contact with me.

The children had given attention to the group activity, socially inter-acted by joining in the movements of classmates and leaders, and commu-nicated through smiles, eye gaze, and vocalizations. They were engaging in three crucial abilities in children's learning and development—shared attention, interaction, and communication.

Corresponding Developments in the DIR and SCERTS Models

The DIR model of Greenspan and Wieder (2006), introduced in Chapter 4, has outlined three similar fundamental abilities in their six levels of de-velopment with children on the autism spectrum:

1. *Shared attention and regulation* emphasizes the development of shared attention as a critical initial step.
2. *Engagement and relating* focuses on early social interactions and interpersonal relationships.
3. *Intentionality and two-way communication* describes children's growing communication.

The SCERTS Assessment Process of Prizant et al. (2006) also speci-fies milestones in joint attention and reciprocal social interactions that contribute to a child's transition from early idiosyncratic communica-tion to emerging socially conventional and purposeful communication. As Gabriel, Carlos, Emily, and Jonathan smiled, vocalized, and gazed at me and other group members, they were engaged in the early steps in joint attention outlined in the SCERTS Assessment Process: "JA2.1. Looks toward people" and "JA3.2. Shares positive emotion using facial expressions or vocalizations" (p. 167). As the children imitated a suc-cession of movements in sync with the song and the other members of the group, they actualized steps related to the early use of symbols in communication: "SU1.2. Imitates familiar actions or sounds when elicited immediately after a model" (p. 170) and "SU4.7. Uses sequence of gestures or nonverbal means" (p. 173). Moreover, Gabriel's at-home reenactment with his mother exemplified "SU1.4. Spontaneously imi-tates familiar actions or sounds at a later time" (p. 170).

It has been encouraging for me to realize that the DIR and SCERTS models of therapeutic and educational supports for autism emphasize a number of the same key ideas about shared attention, interpersonal interaction, and communication which I've experienced as crucial in children's development. These are abilities that I believe music therapy has special potential to help motivate and promote.

"IT'S TIME TO SAY GOODBYE"

After three more songs during this June 1st session, it was time for good-bye. It would be the ending song of this year, and my final contact with this group of teachers and children with whom I'd worked for 2 years.

Elizabeth looked at me and said, "We had a nice long music today . . ."

"Yeah," I said quietly, starting to feel wistful about my last moments with the children and teachers.

"But we're very sad," said Elizabeth, as if she'd been feeling something similar.

"I know . . ." I said, looking to her.

She added, "Half-way through this, I thought, 'I'm very sad.'" Her voice and gaze seemed to register humorous acknowledgment, as well as sorrow, possibly about the coming ending of her working relationship with David and Rachel, as well as the finishing of the music therapy group.

I looked toward David, and we both glanced down wordlessly.

Then I gazed around the class circle and said, "I know, it seems unbelievable . . ." I also tried to use a lighthearted tone, while wanting to express my gratitude for the children and adults in this group.

There was a pause, and I could hear the children vocalizing quietly, blending into this conversation.

I said to all of them in the circle, "Yeah. I've loved working with this class, thanks a lot for . . ."

"We've loved having you, it's . . . ," said Elizabeth.

David said, "It didn't occur to me when you walked in this morning this was going to be it."

Elizabeth said, "I did, as I said . . ."

Almost simultaneously Rachel said assertively, "I'm not even going to *think* that!"

Elizabeth said, "She doesn't do . . . [endings]{laughter}."

"Yeah," I said. "Well, hopefully . . . even this month, I'm going to try and come back and visit you guys . . . if you don't mind . . ."

"Oh good!" said Elizabeth.

I said, "Cause I, I feel like I always had a lot to learn from you. And even though I was leading the music group I wished I could be here more . . . to learn from what you're doing."

I looked out at the circle of children again—seeing Emily, Gabriel, Carlos, Talan, Shen, and Jonathan, and remembering Dylan, and thinking about all that I learned and experienced with the children and teachers over the past 2 years.

I paused, smiled, and I played the chime once, and began to sing, "It's time to say goodbye," for one more time.

SUGGESTIONS FOR REFLECTION

- **Offering multiple ways to join in the "Hello Song" through drum playing, speaking, singing, and gestures like waving hello** can help stimulate the participation of students like Emily, as it did in this June session, as well as give children avenues for nonverbal and verbal communication, play, and social interaction.
- **Similarly, drawing on the combined power of dance/ movement and music** in songs like "Toombah" gives children a range of opportunities for whole-body movements and gestures in sync with peers and teachers, while joining in a shared activity with the class group.
- **Music and movement activities like the "Toombah Song" can lead to carryover of learning.** Gabriel was demonstrating at home—in a one-to-one interaction with his mom—steps that he had learned at school in a group setting with a music therapist and his teachers and peers. This good-humored Toombah song encouraged his abilities to move rhythmically and communicate with facial expressions, and this contributed to his ability to enjoy, remember, and later share these forms of affective expression and movement play with his family.
- **The children's smiles and energetic participation in the dancing and gestures during the song** remain some of the most memorable parts of this last session. These actions are welcome for their own sake, and they also point to the powers of music and movement for helping motivate children's focus, emotional expressiveness, and social engagement.

Conclusion

As I bring this book to a close, I want to synthesize the findings from 2 years of leading a music therapy group with children on the autism spectrum in a public preschool. In the following pages, I will focus not only on the experiences of three of the children—Dylan, Emily, and Gabriel, who participated in the group for the majority of both years—but also on my own learning as a music therapist, with the intention of sharing insights with others who seek to nurture children on the spectrum.

INITIAL CHALLENGES

There were multiple difficulties that the children and I faced during the music therapy sessions. Dylan's participation included a perplexing endearing mix of ebullient ability (sight-reading words or laughingly declaring that his name was the teacher's name, David) as well as moments of complete withdrawal from social contact and communication with others.

Early on, Emily did not show the demonstrative flashes of ability that Dylan had, but instead she seemed somehow absent while present. When her body remained still, her face almost expressionless, and her gaze apparently directed off into the distance, I was initially unsure what she was absorbing or understanding during our music therapy sessions. Yet, as the weeks continued, I also began to see Emily engage in quick bursts of motion and visual attention to people and objects. Sometimes she seemed more active and interested during her classmates' turn taking, although she became almost silent and immobile during hers. This made me feel that she might be quietly following classroom events while keeping one step removed from personal engagement. Behind her appearance of remoteness, I sensed an alert awareness.

I found it harder to discern what was going on with Gabriel. He alternated between agitation, lethargy, and quiet onlooking, and I often could not tell why his mood or state of arousal changed. Sometimes I questioned: Were his changes in behavior related to events in the music group, or were they more a reflection of some kind of ebb and flow in his own internal world? When I tried to connect with Gabriel, I often felt in limbo, hoping for a dawning of my greater awareness and clarity.

DEVELOPMENTS WITH THE CHILDREN

Over the course of 2 years, the teachers and I witnessed a number of developments with the children.

Dylan

Gradually, Dylan began to show his interest in the rhythm instruments, the goodbye chime, the beanbags, and the pictures that accompanied songs like "At the Store." The songs and the objects, the weekly routines, and the supportive group environment contributed to his increasing contact and communication. He initiated interactions by reaching forward or asking to participate, saying, "Give it to me," and naming the numbers and colors of the beanbags, peering intently toward the pictures that accompanied songs, and laughing at the odd juxtaposition of fruit playing a flute. He became able and willing to express his own name in the "Hello Song," in addition to saying peers' names. During the "Microphone Song," he recalled and spoke phrases from both original and familiar songs that we had worked on 2 months before.

Autism researcher Simon Baron-Cohen (1995) wrote that the "mindblindness" of autistic individuals limits their social understanding of others' intentions, behaviors, or feelings. However, I felt keenly that Dylan was not blind in his social awareness of other people's intentions, emotions, and actions. His direct visual attention toward me and teachers and peers, his smiles, and his reintroduction of song phrases from our previous sessions suggested that he was recalling and referring to experiences that we had shared. This seemed similar to the times that typically developing children in other groups have reminded me of songs that we had performed before, either to request them again or simply to remember them. Dylan seemed able to apprehend and respond to the goals, emotions, and actions of his teachers, music therapist, and, at times, his peers. Perhaps most fundamentally, from my perspective, I was encouraged that Dylan became more interested in joining in the music activities and relating with the teachers and me during the course of my 2 years with the music group. He less frequently withdrew from us or evaded activities because of their difficulty or lack of appeal.

Emily

Emily surprised me by becoming one of the most attentive and interactive members of the music group. During the 2 school years, she began saying peers' names, reaching out to play the goodbye chime, smiling, and experimenting with small hand-percussion instruments. Several of these actions I did not anticipate after seeing her previous sometimes expressionless or motionless behaviors. She started verbally communicating her own name during the "Hello Song," and she imitated motions during action songs. Particularly during the second year, I shared moments with her that felt intimate and relational, such as when she came to the sessions before the other children, strummed the guitar, and vocalized in extended back-and-forth exchanges with me. In the "Microphone Song," she vocalized in varied ways, and also spoke/sang phrases of songs, alternating turn taking with me. Her ability and willingness to verbally communicate during the music sessions changed gradually from uncommunicative silence, to babble-like vocalizations, to spoken words, and then to spoken/sung phrases within songs. She progressed into new phases of development similar to those outlined in communication assessments such as the SCERTS Assessment Process (Prizant et al., 2006). I was probably most encouraged by her increased capacities and interests in interacting with me and other teachers while joining in shared activities. She rarely seemed absent or remote, and was often actively participating.

Gabriel

It was with some regret that I looked back on my work with Gabriel because I questioned whether I had been able to help in his development. My impression altered somewhat as I reviewed the videotapes and interviewed the teachers, who gave me perspectives that I had not perceived on my own. Where I saw a possible sameness in my interactions with Gabriel over time, the teachers noted that he was often more active and happier during music therapy sessions than at other times during his school day. Lead teacher David and assistant teachers Rachel and Elizabeth, each spoke about this in our interviews. Reviewing the video of Gabriel and his classmates dancing to my song, "Like This," David observed that Gabriel was the first student in the class to stand up and start moving when I invited the class to dance. He initiated and sustained a series of dance movements along with the music, and it seemed that he and one of the other children were noticing and, to some extent, copying each other's movements, while listening and smiling as the adults cheered them on.

David remarked, "[Gabriel's response] was surprising because I remember him being receptively . . . well, across the board, a very low energy kind of kid . . . and I was surprised . . . It was music that was motivating him and he liked the music and liked to dance . . . because he wasn't the kind of kid you would give a direction to and he would respond to it quite like that!" Elizabeth affirmed, "Gabriel loved music . . . That was where he blossomed." Rachel also observed that Gabriel often might not imitate or follow peer or adult actions, even with adult modeling and support, "Except for the music, he would imitate in the music."

During the "Beanbag Song," it was also the combination of music and movement that enabled Gabriel and me to find a shared way to interact through alternating and simultaneous motions with the song. When I mirrored Gabriel's motions, his attention and participation increased, as he led and I followed. Then he began to imitate some of my motions, and we ended by clapping our hands together at the same moment, in synchronicity. Balanced interactions, in which each partner has chances to lead and follow, have similarly resulted in increases in engagement and exchanges with children in studies by autism researchers and practitioners Koegel and Ashbaugh (2017), Prizant (2016), and others.

When Gabriel began to use the voice-output communication aid during the second year, he actively responded to opportunities, reaching forward to press the switch, and using a conventional pointing gesture to ask for more. In ways like this, I see that Gabriel was taking new steps to participate and communicate in the music therapy sessions. Because his language abilities remained very limited, and his level of arousal often appeared to be low, I may have been sometimes less able to attune with him. But given the substantial challenges that he and I faced in trying to interact, I appreciate how Gabriel was able to take advantage of opportunities—especially those involving movement and other nonspeaking means of interaction and communication.

Gabriel's mother also helped me realize that he was learning from what we introduced in the music therapy group when she reported that he was re-enacting the motions to the "Toombah Song" at home. He was, in some measure, generalizing the sequence of steps that he had learned in a classroom environment, at home at a different time and with additional people, his family members. His ability to learn these motions in music suggested a potential avenue for working with him to develop gestural or symbolic communication.

DEVELOPMENTS IN MY THINKING

In addition to highlighting the children's developments, I would like to describe some of the developments in my own thinking over the 2 years. In the coming pages, I'll address insights that I developed related to three concepts: peripheral attention, complex mixtures of emotions and behaviors, and children's latent abilities.

Recognizing Peripheral Attention

When Emily appeared uninvolved but then quickly answered a question that we had posed, she demonstrated that a child could be listening and paying attention without showing conventional attending behaviors such as direct eye gaze or body orientation toward a person. In differing degrees, I experienced this also with Dylan, Gabriel, and others in the group. I would term what I saw with Emily and classmates as peripheral attention or indirect attention. I hypothesize that other children demonstrate this way of indirectly orienting and relating with others in varied environments and with different people. Although children may be looking over to the side or downward, or appearing inert or restless, their subsequent participation can indicate that they were following what was being said and done. I have mentioned previously that indirectly attuning to people, sometimes without using eye contact, was familiar to me because my father was blind. By listening closely, he was able to pay attention and to understand without relying on eye gaze. I am not, however, asserting that each instance of a child's facing away or appearing not to interact with a caregiver or peer indicates peripheral attention. I am instead seeking to broaden an understanding of shared attention—in some instances, for some children like Emily.

I think that peripheral or indirect interactions can expand and complicate how shared attention has been understood and measured with children on the autism spectrum. If evaluations of attention are based on observing and counting direct eye gaze or body orientation, then children's indirect forms of attention may be overlooked in the resulting assessment. Although it introduces additional challenges in defining and measuring, it can enhance our understanding to include the alternative indirect ways that children may pay attention.

Working With Complex Mixtures of Emotions and Behaviors

Another related shift in my thinking occurred as I noticed that the children's resistance and participation, their disengagement and engagement, were sometimes intermingled and alternating within the same activity. I became more aware of this when I reviewed the videotapes of the children during the rhythm-instrument songs. At some moments, Gabriel, Emily, and classmates could be actively playing shakers and tambourines, while at other moments the same class members within the same song could be passive and not engaged with the instruments or could drop them or throw them to the floor. Later, I began to see that theoretically opposite behaviors were present together in a number of other activities with the children over time. Researchers Capps et al. (1993) wrote of "incongruous blends" (p. 475) of negative and positive emotions observed in affective expressions during their study involving children on the spectrum. I would affirm this, and add to their framework, and propose that incongruous blends, or what I might also call unconventional mixtures of behaviors, could appear in the children's vocalizations, movements, and instrument playing within a range of activities. I witnessed these mixtures during the songs that I led and in the activities that the teachers led.

Music therapists Paul Nordoff and Clive Robbins (2007) thought it was vital to understand that "resistiveness" and "participation" developed together. Their first evaluation scale ("the child-therapist relationship in coactive musical experience") was designed to assess changes in levels of participation and resistiveness side by side:

> Paralleling the ascent of the levels of participation, resistiveness is seen to move from shutting out the therapy situation, withdrawing from it, or actively rejecting it, to appear in successively higher forms of evasion, manipulation, assertiveness, and expressions of oppositional competent independence. (p. 373)

Nordoff and Robbins emphasized that children's withdrawal or resistance arose along with active new involvement in music. These differing responses represented not aberrations or behaviors to be eradicated. Rather they often naturally happen during the development of musical contact and interplay.

A mixture of coexisting contrasting behaviors need not only be associated with children on the spectrum. This phenomenon has also been noted in other ages and populations. For example, a combination of low responsiveness and heightened agitation was cited as the most common phenomenon among seniors with dementia in a study by Buettner and Fitzsimmons (2006). Such evidence shows that contrasting mixtures are concurrently present among people with a range of differing health needs. This counterbalances notions that "everything is either 1 or 0" (Kerlinger, quoted in Miles & Huberman, 1994, p. 40) or "It cannot be A and Non-A at the same time" (Buber, quoted in Kirschenbaum & Henderson, 1989, p. 59). I believe that reality may be distorted when we assess behaviors by classifying responses into univalent (and sometimes opposite) categories without representing the complex and sometimes incongruous blends actually manifested.

Because music has a special potential for adjusting to and expressing complex mixtures of mood and sound, it is possible for music therapists to mirror, vary, and accompany their clients' contrasting behaviors, emotions, vocalizations, instrumental play, or movements. "The clinical intervention through music," wrote Kenneth Aigen (1996), "does not have to be either challenging or supporting, inviting or demanding, leading or following; it can simultaneously offer all of these things and thus support contact with the child's present functioning level while still providing an invitation to growth" (p. 18). These ideas raise the welcome possibility of a therapist who can respond musically to the complex mixtures and seeming opposites in people's experiences. During shared music making, therapists can offer participants chances to both lead and follow, to be nurtured and to be challenged, and to use present abilities and develop new skills and connections. Music therapy can also add to the variety of ways to teach and engage children on the spectrum. Autism researchers Lynn Koegel and Kristen Ashbaugh (2017) have emphasized "task variation" as a key strategy in teaching communication skills:

> Students do not like to be repetitively drilled, and research shows that is not the more effective way to learn. For example, if a child is learning how to use expressive communication, then intervention to help a child vocalize should include a variety of tasks, activities, or play. Varying the teaching activities will help children be more engaged and respond better. (p. 53)

To expand the variety of learning activities for children on the spectrum, music therapy can add a range of motivating ways to facilitate children's vocal and preverbal communication, social interaction, and movement, as I saw with Dylan, Emily, Gabriel, and their classmates.

Encouraging Latent Abilities

Another insight crystallized during the years in the class: When the teachers and I encouraged preschoolers in expressing some of their latent capacities in social exchanges and communication, new possibilities came to life. In the research literature, I had read so many categorical statements about the fundamental *in*abilities of children on the autism spectrum that I began to question myself. Was I asking children to do things that they weren't capable of? Yes I was, at times, with some children. But particularly with Dylan and Emily, I also felt instinctively that they were able to do more than they initially revealed. In addition, Gabriel's capabilities in imitative movement and early preverbal communication also began to surface over time. During the 2 years, with each of the three children, we witnessed the growth of abilities that had earlier appeared absent or blocked.

What helps foster the emergence of capabilities that are not yet visible? Educator Caroline Heller (1997) sparked my thinking about this question when she asked, "Are you creating the kind of relationship that would make [new] communication possible?" Yes, I think that the relationships that we developed in the class music group over time did play an important part in the emergence of latent capacities for social communication. The children's own maturation also brought forth new capacities, and the songs, movements, materials, and actions and interactions of teachers and peers helped motivate and support the use of previously unseen capabilities. I was heartened to discover related research that articulated that a key to autistic children's development was connecting with seemingly "dormant" abilities. The authors Koegel, Vernon, and Koegel (2009) describe

> a specific intervention strategy that appears to be particularly effective with children who demonstrate very low levels of social engagement during intervention . . . [This approach] may have theoretical implications, as it suggests that the ability for social interaction were present all along. Developing methods for tapping into "dormant" social areas may hold a key. (p. 1249)

Our preschool music therapy group also sought to tap into not-yet-expressed potentials, aiming to nourish these within the class members and in ourselves as adult leaders.

DEVELOPMENTS IN MY INTERACTIONS
WITH THE CHILDREN

In my 2 years with the preschool class, there were developments in the overall way I worked and played with the children that I want to review in the following sections.

Learning and Creating Multimodal Ways to Promote Interaction

First, I was able to learn and create additional ways for the children to participate in the songs—incorporating visual and tactile materials such as pictures, photographs, beanbags, a parachute, a stretch band, a microphone, and voice-output communication devices (switches). The "Microphone Song," for example, provided an additional motivating opportunity, and it recognized and encouraged different kinds of sound-making vocalizations as well as verbal communication. In collaboration with the teachers, I introduced free dancing during "Like This" and other tunes, and I concocted additional structured-action songs and chants.

Developing multisensory dimensions in music therapy (visual, tactile, kinesthetic, auditory) helped make the activities more accessible and appealing. I also experimented with adaptations to the reoccurring components of the music therapy session. I incorporated opportunities to play a hand drum or use a switch during the "Hello Song" or tap a chime during the "Goodbye Song." I introduced photographs and drawings to accompany specific movement songs, and I created a picture schedule representing each part of the weekly session.

Perceiving and Responding to Potential Early Steps

Second, I became more experienced in perceiving and responding to the children's earlier possible signs of communication and social interaction. These beginning steps were often nonspeaking and could be hard to discern. Yet the relationships and musical history that the children and I developed in the group over 2 years had honed our ability to detect when each other's actions were intentional and interpersonally communicative. For example, I am remembering when I caught sight of Gabriel's subtle beginnings of his motions during the "Beanbag Song." As I described earlier in Chapter 6, I began to mirror his body movements, and his facial expression showed a spark of recognition that he was being mirrored. He increased his movements and began to switch roles and join me in my motions too. Then we both slowly brought our hands together in a simultaneous clap. I am also thinking of the moments when I was able to perceive Emily's incipient signals that she wanted to play the guitar before the group session. She subsequently used preverbal vocalizations to call for my attention, and we both began vocal turn taking and interplay.

In emerging interactions like these, the children and the teachers and I were drawing on the ability of music "to do what it does best: make connections, person-to-person . . . [and] to build musical bridges" (Lane, 1994, p. 180). I so admire the work and writing of music therapist Deforia Lane, who wrote these words. I have also experienced that music creates bridges of connection that contribute to the development of abilities and relationships among the participants.

USEFUL CONCEPTS FOR UNDERSTANDING EARLY RESPONSES AND INITIATIVES

Through my research, I gained insight into, and reformulated, several concepts and classifications to assist in analyzing and reflecting on the experiences in the music group.

Three Crucial Abilities: Shared Attention, Interaction, and Communication

One finding of my research was that the three concepts of shared attention, interpersonal interaction, and communication formed a useful framework for understanding what we were observing in the music therapy sessions. These concepts helped me identify and describe some of the early crucial and challenging dimensions of development with children on the spectrum in the classroom. The three terms encompassed and connected in a continuum children's early nonspeaking implicit ways of relating, along with children's later verbal or conventional explicit ways.

By synthesizing ideas from related research about children diagnosed with autism who also benefit from intensive additional supports, I have hypothesized that the preschoolers were engaging in these crucial abilities in five fundamental ways: through eye gaze, affect/facial expression, body movements/gestures/postures, vocal/verbal expressions, and sound making by manipulating instruments. As I reviewed video recordings of the music therapy sessions, the five categories of observable actions were useful in discerning specific moments of shared attention, interaction, and communication with the children.

Forms of Participation in Music Therapy

People participate in music therapy in three primary ways—through vocal expression, instrument play, and body movement—according to innovative music therapists Paul Nordoff and Clive Robbins (2007). As I studied the many particular instances of children's involvement in our music group over 2 years, I came to newly appreciate the simplicity and the encompassing scope of the three primary forms of participation in music therapy that Nordoff and Robbins identified. Multiple initially unclear interactions in the group could often be seen, upon reflection, to be variations of participation in one of these three primary forms. For example, Emily's widely varying vocalizations and verbalizations over the 2 years could be understood as interrelated points along a continuum of participation in vocal expression, one of the primary modes of expression in music.

My experiences in the preschool group, and with Emily in particular, led me to want to extend the framework of Nordoff and Robbins (2007) to include "listening" as a fourth form of involvement in music. Music educators David Elliot and Marissa Silverman (2015) have written that individuals experience music's distinctive qualities and joys when they develop their musicianship and listenership, their music making and listening capacities. Elliot and Silverman's introduction of the term *listenership* kindled my own sense that listening was a potent, though not always transparent, form of interaction. To introduce a possible neologism, "ear contact" seemed a critical early form of participation in music, one that often developed into the three forms of vocalizations, instrumental play, or body movements.

Idiosyncratic listening with atypical body postures and facial expressions was not easy to distinguish from disengagement or inattention. However, there were many instances when Emily and other apparently inattentive class members suddenly took well-synchronized actions to join the group activity. I began to newly appreciate that listening, both conventional and unconventional, was often an early and important step in children's engagement. So, I have found it helpful to identify four primary forms of music therapy participation in working with children on the autism spectrum: listening, vocalizing, instrument playing, and body movements/dancing.

A CONTINUING QUESTION AND THE CHILDREN'S
ONGOING NEEDS

The following paragraphs outline a central question first and then give examples of the children's continuing needs. This will provide a way to acknowledge the significant ongoing challenges that remained, alongside the developments that we witnessed.

How could I better facilitate specific, structured, motivating opportunities for the children to interact with each other during the music therapy sessions? This question was on my mind during the research and has remained with me afterward. I have realized that I need further help and ideas to foster peer-to-peer interactions. This is a challenging task with children with intensive levels of autism, particularly in a group not structured to pair autistic children with typically developing peer partners. In the future, I aspire to continue to learn and develop additional cooperative musical activities that incorporate specific ways (passing objects, using peer photos, or peer audio/video recordings, and other approaches) that might enhance the development of peer awareness and interaction.

Next, I'd like to examine a few examples of the children's continuing needs.

Dylan

A school report filed near the end of my research stated that Dylan had begun to eat only a limited selection of food for lunch. He was no longer eating a sandwich but was eating only certain crackers or snacks. His restricted eating habits hinted at a wider continuing issue with him: Could he grow in his ability to try new things in other areas of his life such as in his social interactions and communication with others? I felt it was pivotal, for example, that he keep learning how to perceive, accept, and respond to others' social bids, in addition to initiating contact on his own terms and in his own time. Relationships develop more fully when an individual responds to others' attempts to connect and not only to one's own interests and impulses.

If continuing to work with him had been possible, I would have attempted to encourage him to gradually move toward more-sustained exchanges with other people in addition to his quick-entry-and-exit sequences. Although Dylan was more social with school adults than many of the other children in the group, I would have liked to learn additional ways to promote and support the development of his rela- tionships with his peers too, as I alluded to earlier. His communication goals could include extending his use of word combinations and sen- tences, and he could work toward increasing his spontaneous relevant expressive language with adults and classmates.

Emily

Over time, Emily had begun to use language and to engage adults in her play. Remaining challenges included continuing to support her in expanding her social interests and abilities. How could we help her to further engage in direct, personal, commonly recognized ways of relating (using language, eye contact, expressive affect) in addition to her indirect ways of attuning with other people? Extending her use of words, word combinations, and sentences could have broadened her communication. If it had been possible, I would have loved to work and play with her in further vocal/verbal give-and-take exchanges and to support her spon- taneous self-initiated communication. Like Dylan, school reports noted that Emily had become observant of her peers but did not often use lan- guage to interact with them. Building relationships with peers was an important potential area of development for her too.

Gabriel

Gabriel shared several continuing needs with Dylan and Emily— establishing his relationships with peers and expanding his social and communicative abilities. But there were a few additional challenges that Gabriel was facing. I believe that he was at an earlier stage of de- velopment than the other two children. If I had been able to continue offering school service to him, I would have liked to support him in more clearly establishing intentionality in communication through the development of gestures, voice-output communication aids, or other alternative methods. He did not usually use verbal communication in a manner that a new listener would understand. I think it would be ben- eficial to help him more clearly express both his preverbal and verbal intentions in order to convey his wants and needs to listeners. So, use- ful communication goals with Gabriel would include supporting him in developing his abilities in intentional communication and, to the extent possible, in symbolic and vocal/verbal communication. Lastly, school reports indicated that Gabriel enthusiastically and happily participated in movement activities. He did so during occupational therapy clinic, music therapy sessions, and in the classroom. While moving, he became more alert, sometimes verbalized (e.g., "up, up, up"), and he attempted to make initial contact with peers. However, he also continued to often manifest significant under- and overarousal in a variety of contexts, so helping him find additional ways to reach a more optimal balance of arousal was another continuing area of need.

COLLABORATION WITH THE TEACHERS

Psychologists Barbara and Philip Newman (2017) have asserted that "behavior must be interpreted in the context of relevant settings and personal relationships" (p. 5). The children's behaviors and learning during the class were not simply caused by an individual adult manipulating the correct variables to produce a desired result. In the preschool music therapy group, the children's actions and experiences, and mine, were decisively influenced by our personal relationships with the teachers David, Elizabeth, and Rachel and the classroom environment they helped create. The teachers' active participation and collaboration during the majority of sessions over 2 years fundamentally nourished and strengthened the music group.

I'd like to touch on a few examples of the personal qualities, abilities, and knowledge that the teachers shared in the group. In the first year, David led a class-favorite activity as one part of every music therapy session, and he modeled approaches that the classroom staff were using to engage the children. This helped give me a clearer idea of the children's capabilities and struggles. Throughout the 2 years, Rachel's ease and rapport with Elizabeth and David, her sense of humor, and her enthusiastic interest in instruments like the shakere, drums, and the voice-output communication device added a playfulness and vivacity that were contagious to children and adults in the group. Elizabeth's affection for the children and active support helped a number of the children become involved in activities. For example, it was Elizabeth who first suggested that the children get up and dance to the song, "Like This," which led to increased participation and interaction with Gabriel, Dylan, James, and other children. It was Elizabeth who helped me understand, when Emily said, "Gently down the stream," which enabled and extended more give-and-take exchanges with her. In so many ways, the classroom teachers played a vital role in recognizing and facilitating children's developments within the group.

The teachers also expressed a mutual appreciation for the attention and engagement that I was able to help foster with the children through the songs, activities, materials, and ideas that I contributed. They pointed out that several of the children, unprompted, came to sit in the circle of chairs before the music therapy sessions, and that they remained in the circle after the goodbye song, as if somehow lingering in the positive group climate. The following paragraphs transcribe two of the assistant teachers' comments, which communicated how they valued the contributions of the music therapy sessions in their classroom. As part of the final stages of my research process, I met with each of the teachers after the 2 school years were over. I showed them a number of the video excerpts that I was examining and analyzing in my research. I asked them to describe difficulties or developments they noticed in reviewing these particular moments. My goal was to record their perspectives as I reviewed the video excerpts and then to discuss their analyses and interpretations and compare ideas. Below is a transcription of Elizabeth and Rachel's comments while reviewing a video excerpt from the second year. This video centered on Gabriel's and Emily's vocalizations and an extended vocal exchange between Emily and me. As the video recording was showing the back-and-forth vocal exchanges with Emily, Elizabeth interjected:

"Just shows how fantastic music is!" she remarked.

"Why do you say that?" I asked.

Elizabeth continued, "That engages them, always has, always . . . It's repetitive, it's familiar, and look what it pulls out . . . It pulls out her *playing* with you, and *engaging* you, and pulling *you* in . . . It's always been music's been the best."

Rachel added, "And she's looking at the schedule [the picture schedule of upcoming activities] . . . she was looking at it, anticipating what was going to happen, she was *ready* for what was going to happen, she was *excited* about what was going to happen."

Elizabeth turned to Rachel and said, "And she was looking at Geoff, and doing the thing [vocalizations back and forth]."

Rachel said, "Well that's amazing! . . . Can we see that one again?"

I started to reload the video.

"And her [Emily's] mother was thrilled," Elizabeth said, "with her progress."

"Her mother was thrilled with your class?" I asked, trying to clarify what she had said at the end of the sentence.

"Yeah," said Rachel.

"Well, as she should be," I said. "You teachers were awesome!"

"No, but you're part of it, you're part of it . . . ," said Elizabeth. "It was a good team."

I was grateful to be part of this professional team. Collaboration has been described as working together in a supportive and mutually helpful relationship. When collaboration develops between a music therapist and classroom teachers, it is a very welcome development not to be taken for granted. As music therapist Nicole Allgood (2006) noted, relationships within a classroom do not always develop smoothly, and there can be misunderstandings—lack of involvement (off-task chatting and disinterest); rude, condescending, or irritated voices when talking with children; and other challenges when working in classrooms (p. 116). However, the teachers in our preschool class were one of the most cooperative and actively engaged classroom teams that I have had the opportunity to work with. In addition to creating an environment of collaboration and affinity, the members of this group, I felt, operated as "partners in care" (Hirschland, 2008, p. 4), consistently offering children the empathy, positive regard, and authenticity that Carl Rogers (1957) and others have described. Early childhood educator Deborah Hirschland (2008), writing about collaborative interventions for young children, touched on something essential, I believe, when she stated, "For at the heart of any approach must be the recognition that children rely on warm connections with caregivers in order to change and grow" (p. 4). I have treasured the moments when we were able to collaborate to share this kind of warmth and caring, and to offer motivating and engaging musical activities and facilitate interpersonal exchanges.

There were wider circles of collaboration that were much more circumscribed during my research and work at the preschool. The music group would have been strengthened by my working in partnership with parents and other team members such as the speech therapist, physical therapist, behavior therapist, occupational therapist, and others. The part-time work that I undertook at the preschool, however, had been designed only to provide direct services to children, without any accompanying employment hours after classroom sessions to initiate and develop communication with parents or related-services providers. So, my contact with family members and related therapists was primarily limited to what occurred within my times in the classroom. This is an issue that may be faced by music therapists and related direct service providers in other settings: The potential benefits of enhanced reciprocal communication with family members, related therapists, and teachers may not be matched by the school's actual funding and facilitation of these (Harry, 1999).

FINAL THOUGHTS

Utilizing video recordings, teacher interviews, school written reports, and field notes, my practitioner research described and analyzed 16 video excerpts from a music therapy group in a public preschool class serving children on the autism spectrum over a 2-year period. The research centered on three of the children who participated in the music therapy group for the majority of both years: Dylan, Gabriel, and Emily.

I explored three areas of ability—shared attention, interpersonal interaction, and communication—as important dimensions in describing and analyzing specific moments of difficulty and development with children in the classroom. By synthesizing research literature findings, I identified five defining features involved in early shared attention, interpersonal interaction, and communication:

1. Use of eye gaze/eye contact
2. Affect/facial expression
3. Body movements/gestures/postures
4. Sound making through vocal/verbal expression
5. Sound making through manipulating objects/instruments

These criteria helped me recognize and analyze the varied particular instances of shared engagement in the music therapy session video excerpts.

The children participated in the music therapy sessions in four primary ways: through instrument play, body movements/dancing, listening, and vocalizations/verbal communication. I developed the term *peripheral attention* to describe instances of a child demonstrating indirect attention and then synchronized reactions, even though body posture and eye gaze had remained at an oblique angle. In addition, I observed that partial or difficult-to-discern approximations, and idiosyncratic expressions of intention or engagement, preceded and often coexisted with children's emerging steps in verbal/vocal communication and interaction with others.

By incorporating picture schedules; augmentative and alternative communication devices; hand-percussion instruments; rhythm and percussion grooves; beanbags; parachutes; stretch bands; and other visual, tactile, auditory, and kinesthetic dimensions of music and movement, I introduced multimodal opportunities for shared interaction. The active participation and collaboration of the classroom teachers— David, Elizabeth, and Rachel—played a pivotal role in encouraging children's participation in the music therapy group. Session excerpts showed children and adults affecting and influencing each other in a shared process of learning and communicating.

In an interview, neurologist Oliver Sacks (2007) was asked why person-to-person relationships are so important in promoting growth and well-being. He said, "Every teaching or therapeutic relationship will work better if there's trust and affection" (as cited in Cooper, 2008, p. 19). Sacks brought attention to the caring qualities in relationships that were vital in meeting individuals' needs and supporting their development. He also emphasized some of the shared impact that music could have: "Music therapy as group therapy can have a tremendous bonding effect. . . . [participants] become conscious of and interact with each other. Music has great powers to both calm and animate people, to engage them and give them focus" (as cited in Cooper, 2008, p. 19).

In the preschool music therapy group, interactions in emerging relationships were developed during coordinated vocal interplay, turn taking and theme-and-variation exchanges, joint percussion and guitar playing, group dancing and movement sequences, and in reciprocal expressions of emotion. Taking inspiration from concepts in parent-child research, psychotherapy, education, and music therapy, I have described the interpersonal exchanges within the music therapy group as moments of meeting and musical attunement. Here at the completion of my research, I am aware again of my thankfulness for the opportunity to have met and come to know this group of children and teachers.

References

Adamson, L. B., Bakeman, R., Suma, K., & Robins, D. L. (2019). An expanded view of joint attention: Skill, engagement, and language in typical development and autism. *Child Development, 90*(1), e1–e18.

Adler, J. (1999). Who is the witness? In P. Pallaro (Ed.), *Authentic movement: Essays by Mary Starks Whitehouse, Janet Adler and Joan Chodorow: Volume 1* (pp.132–159). Jessica Kingsley.

Adler, J. (2007). From autism to the discipline of authentic movement. In P. Pallaro (Ed.), *Authentic movement: Moving the body, moving the self, being moved, Volume 2* (pp. 24–31). Jessica Kingsley.

Aigen, K. S. (1996). *Being in music: Foundations of Nordoff-Robbins music therapy.* MMB Music.

Aigen, K. S. (1997). *Here we are in music: One year with an adolescent creative music therapy group.* MMB Music.

Aigen, K. S. (2014). *The study of music therapy: Current issues and concepts.* Routledge.

Allgood, N. (2006). Collaboration: Being a team player. In M. Humpal & C. Colwell (Eds.), *Effective clinical practice in music therapy: Early childhood and school age educational settings* (pp. 110–119). American Music Therapy Association.

Alvin, J. (1991). *Music therapy for the autistic child* (2nd ed.). Oxford University Press.

American Speech-Language-Hearing Association (ASHA). (2021). *Augmentative and Alternative Communication (AAC).* https://www.asha.org/public/speech/disorders/AAc/

Ansdell, G., & Pavlicevic, M. (2001). *Beginning research in the arts therapies: A practical guide.* Jessica Kingsley.

Ansdell, G., Pavlicevic, M., & Procter, S. (2004). *Presenting the evidence: A guide for music therapists responding to the demands of clinical effectiveness and evidenced-based practice.* Nordoff-Robbins Music Therapy Center.

Baranek, G. T., David, F. J., Poe, M. D., Stone, W. L., & Watson, L. R. (2006). Sensory Experiences Questionnaire: Discriminating sensory features in young children with autism, developmental delays, and typical development. *Journal of Child Psychology and Psychiatry, 47*(2) 591–601.

Baron-Cohen, S. (1995). *Mindblindness: An essay on autism and theory of mind.* MIT Press.

Black, K. R., Stevenson, R. A., Segers, M., Ncube, B. L., Sun, S. Z., Philipp-Muller, A., Bebko, J. M., Barense, M. D., & Ferber, S. (2017). Linking anxiety and insistence on sameness in autistic children: The role of sensory hypersensitivity. *Journal of Autism and Developmental Disorders, 47*(8), 2459–2470.

Boston Change Process Study Group: Bruschweiler-Stern, N., Harrison, A. M., Morgan, A. C., Nahum, J. P., Lyons-Ruth, K., Sander, L. W., Stern, D. N., & Tronick, E. Z. (2002). Explicating the implicit: The local level and the microprocess of change in the analytic situation. *International Journal of Psycho-Analysis, 83,* 1051–1062.

Botha, M., Hanlon, J., & Williams, G. L. (2021). Does language matter? Identity-first versus person-first language use in autism research: A response to Vivanti. *Journal of Autism and Developmental Disorders.*

Bottema-Beutel, K., Kapp, S. K., Lester, J. N., Sasson, N. J., & Hand, B. N. (2021). Avoiding ableist language: Suggestions for autism researchers. *Autism in Adulthood, 3*(1), 18–29.

Bottema-Beutel, K., Yoder, P. J., Hochman, J. M., & Watson, L. R. (2014). The role of supported joint engagement and parent utterances in language and social communication development in children with autism spectrum disorder. *Journal of Autism and Developmental Disorders, 44*(9), 2162–2174.

Brewe, A. M., Mazefsky, C. A., & White S. W. (2021). Therapeutic alliance formation for adolescents and young adults with autism: Relation to treatment outcomes and client characteristics. *Journal of Autism and Developmental Disorders. 51*(5), 1446–1457.

Bronfenbrenner, U., & Evans, G. (2000). Developmental science in the 21st century: Emerging theoretical models, research designs, and empirical findings. *Social Development, 9,* 115–125.

Buber, M. (1937). *I and thou.* T. & T. Clark.

Buettner, L., & Fitzsimmons, S. (2006). Mixed behaviors in dementia: A new paradigm for treatment. *Journal of Gerontological Nursing, 32*(7), 15–22.

Burgess, S., Audet, L., & Harjusola-Webb, S. (2013). Quantitative and qualitative characteristics of the school and home language environments of preschool-aged children with ASD. *Journal of Communication Disorders, 46*(5), 428–439.

Bury, S. M., Jellett, R., Spoor, J. R., & Hedley, D. (2020). "It defines who I am" or "It's something I have": What language do [autistic] Australian adults [on the autism spectrum] prefer? *Journal of Autism and Developmental Disorders.*

Bybee, E. R. (2020). Too important to fail: The banking concept of education and standardized testing in an urban middle school. *Educational Studies: A Journal of the American Educational Studies Association, 56*(4), 418–433.

Canner, N. (1968). *And a time to dance.* Beacon Press.

Capps, L., Kasari, C., Yirmiya, N., & Sigman, M. (1993). Parental perception of emotional expressiveness in children with autism. *Journal of Consulting and Clinical Psychology, 61*(3), 475–484.

Case-Smith, J., Weaver, L. L., & Fristad, M. A. (2015). A systematic review of sensory processing interventions for children with autism spectrum disorders. *Autism, 19*(2), 133–148.

Cipani, E. (Ed.). (2008). *Triumphs in early autism treatment.* Springer.

Clayton, M., Sager, R., & Will, U. (2005). In time with the music: The concept of entrainment and its significance for ethnomusicology. *European Meetings in Ethnomusicology, 11*, 3–75.

Coast Music Therapy. (n.d.). How are music therapy IEP goals written? http://www.coastmusictherapy.com/how-music-helps/goal-areas/

Cochran-Smith, M. (2006). Taking stock in 2006: Evidence, evidence everywhere. *Journal of Teacher Education, 57*(1), 6–12.

Cochran-Smith, M. (2021). Rethinking teacher education: The trouble with accountability. *Oxford Review of Education, 47*(1), 8–24.

Cochran-Smith, M., Carney, M. C., Keefe, E. S., Burton, S., Chang, W. C., Fernandez, M. B., Miller, A. F., Sanchez, J. G., & Baker, M. (2018). *Reclaiming accountability in teacher education.* Teachers College Press.

Cochran-Smith, M., & Lytle, S. (2009). *Inquiry as stance: Practitioner research in the next generation.* Teachers College Press.

Coles, R. (1993). *The call of service: A witness to idealism.* Houghton Mifflin.

Coles, R. (1996). *The mind's fate: A psychiatrist looks at his profession* (2nd ed.). Back Bay Books.

Cooper, A. (2008). Unchained by melody. *Neurology Now, 4*(1), 16–19.

Cooper, J. O., Heron, T. E., & Heward, W. L. (2020). *Applied behavior analysis* (3rd ed.). Pearson.

Denac, O. (2008). A case study of preschool children's musical interests at home and at school. *Early Childhood Education Journal, 35*(1), 439–444.

Elefant, C. (2002). *Enhancing communication in girls with Rett Syndrome through songs in music therapy.* Aalborg Universitet.

Elliot, D. J., & Silverman, M. (2015). *Music matters: A new philosophy of music education.* Oxford University Press.

Fosshage, J. (2005). The explicit and implicit domains in psychoanalytic change. *Psychoanalytic Inquiry, 25*(4), 516–539.

Freire, P. (1970). *Pedagogy of the oppressed.* Seabury Press.

Goffman, E. (1964). The neglected situation. *American Anthropologist, 66*(6), 133–136. http://www.jstor.org/stable/668167

Goodman, K. D. (2007). *Music therapy groupwork with special needs children: The evolving process.* Charles C Thomas.

Grandin, T. (2006). *Thinking in pictures: My life with autism* (2nd ed.). Vintage Books.

Gray, J. (Host). (2020, Sept. 24). Autism and identity: Interrogating the language we use [Audio podcast episode]. In *ASHA Voices.* American Speech-Language-Hearing Association. https://leader.pubs.asha.org/do/10.1044/transvoices-2020-0924-ashavoices-laguage-autism-identity-person

Greenspan, S., & Wieder, S. (2006). *Engaging autism: Helping children relate, communicate and think with the DIR Floortime approach*. Da Capo Press.

Guralnick, M. J. (Ed.). (2001). *Early childhood inclusion: Focus on change*. Paul H. Brookes.

Hännikäinen, M., & Munter, H. (2018). Toddlers' play in early childhood education settings. In P. K. Smith, & J. L. Roopnarine (Eds.), *The Cambridge handbook of play: Developmental and disciplinary perspectives* (pp. 491–510). Cambridge University Press.

Harry, B. (1999). Building reciprocal family-professional relationships: Culture in special education. In *Research and Training Center on Family Support and Children's Mental Health, Portland State University*. http://www.rtc.pdx.edu/CP99inPDF/CPKeynote.pdf

Hayes, T. (2016). Music therapy in the context of the special school. In J. Edwards (Ed.), *The Oxford handbook of music therapy* (pp. 176–185). Oxford University Press.

Heller, C. (1997). *Until we are strong together: Women writers in the Tenderloin*. Teachers College Press.

Hirschland, D. (2008). *Collaborative intervention in early childhood: Consulting with parents and teachers of 3- to 7-year-olds*. Oxford University Press.

Jaffe, J., Beebe, B., Feldstein, S., Crown, C. L., & Jasnow, M. D. (2001). Rhythms of dialogue in infancy. In W. D. Overton (Ed.), *Monographs of the Society for Research in Child Development, 66*(2), 1–7.

Juslin, P. N., & Sloboda, J. A. (Eds.). (2010). *Handbook of music and emotion: Theory, research, applications*. Oxford University Press.

Kenny, L., Hattersley, C., Molins, B., Buckley, C., Povey, C., & Pellicano, E. (2016). Which terms should be used to describe autism? Perspectives from the UK autism community. *Autism, 20*(4), 442–462.

Kim, J., Wigram, T., & Gold, C. (2008). The effects of improvisational music therapy on joint attention behaviors in autistic children: A randomized controlled study. *Journal of Autism and Developmental Disorders, 38*(9), 1758–1766.

Kirschenbaum, H., & Henderson, V. L. (Eds.). (1989). *Carl Rogers: Dialogues*. Houghton Mifflin.

Koegel, L. K., & Ashbaugh, K. (2017). Communication and autism spectrum disorder. In H. M. Chiang (Ed.), *Curricula for teaching students with autism spectrum disorder* (pp. 47–70). Springer.

Koegel, L. K., Bryan, K. M., Su, P. L., Vaidya, M., & Camarata, S. (2020). Definitions of nonverbal and minimally verbal in research for autism: A systematic review of the literature. *Journal of Autism and Developmental Disorders, 50*, 2957–2972.

Koegel, R. L., & Koegel, L. K. (2019). Pivotal response treatment for autism spectrum disorders (2nd ed.). Paul H. Brookes.

Koegel, R. L., Vernon, T. W., & Koegel, L. K. (2009). Improving social initiations with young children with autism using reinforcers with embedded social interactions. *Journal of Autism and Developmental Disorders, 39*, 1240–1251.

Konstantareas, M. M., & Homatidis, S. (1992). Mothers' and fathers' self-report of involvement with autistic, mentally delayed, and normal children. *Journal of Marriage and the Family, 54*, 153–164.

Lane, D. (1994). *Music as medicine: Deforia Lane's life of music, healing, and faith.* Zondervan Publishing House.

Lane, D. (2016). *Music therapy and medicine: A dynamic partnership* [Video]. TEDxBeaconStreetSalon. https://tedxboston.com/videos/music-therapy-med icine-a-dynamic-partnership/

Laurent, A. C., & Gorman, K. (2018). Development of emotion self-regulation among young children with autism spectrum disorders: The role of parents. *Journal of Autism and Developmental Disorders, 48*, 1249–1260.

Lewin, K. (1947). Frontiers in group dynamics: Concept, method and reality in social science; Social equilibria and social change. *Human Relations, 1*(1) 5–41.

Lowry, L. (2016). *Common questions about questions.* Hanen Centre. http://www .hanen.org/Common-Questions-about-Questions.aspx

Lowry, L. (2018). *Encouraging joint engagement with children with ASD.* Hanen Centre. https://emergepediatrictherapy.com/wp-content/uploads/2021/05 /Printer-friendly_Joint-engagement-with-children-with-ASD.pdf

Maenner, M. J., Shaw, K. A., Baio, J. et al. (2020). Prevalence of autism spectrum disorder among children aged 8 years—Autism and developmental disabilities monitoring network, 11 Sites, United States, 2016. *MMWR Surveillance Summaries, 69*(4), 1–13.

McLaughlin, B., & Adler, R. F. (2015). Music therapy for children with intellectual disabilities. In B. Wheeler (Ed.), *Music therapy handbook* (pp. 277–289). Guildford Press.

Meier, D. R. (1997). *Learning in small moments: Life in an urban classroom.* Teachers College Press.

Miles, M. B., & Huberman, A. M. (1994). *Qualitative data analysis.* Sage.

Mohr, H. (1987). *How to talk Minnesotan: A visitor's guide.* Penguin Books.

Mossler, K., Gold, C., Assmus, J., Schumacher, K., Calvet, C. Reimer, S., Iversen, G., & Schmid, W. (2019). The therapeutic relationship as predictor of change in music therapy with young children with autism spectrum disorder. *Journal of Autism and Developmental Disorders, 49*(7), 2795–2809.

Mundy, P. (2018). A review of joint attention and social-cognitive brain systems in typical development and autism spectrum disorder. *European Journal of Neuroscience, 47*(6), 497–514.

Mundy, P., Delgado, C., Block, J., Venezia, M., Hogan, A., & Seibert, J. (2003). *A manual for the abridged Early Social Communication Scales (ESCS).* University of Miami.

Murray Law, B. M. (2016). Interpreting autism. *The ASHA Leader, 21*(4), pp. 50–54.

National Research Council. (2001). *Educating children with autism.* National Academies Press, Committee on Educational Interventions for Children with Autism, Division of Behavioral and Social Sciences and Education.

Newman, B. M., & Newman, P. R. (2017). *Development through life: A psychosocial approach*. Cengage Learning.

Newman, L., & Leggett, N. (2019). Practitioner research: With intent. *European Early Childhood Education Research Journal, 27*(1), 120–137.

Norcross, J. C. (2001). Purposes, processes, and products of the task force on empirically supported therapy relationships. *Psychotherapy, 38*, 345–356

Norcross, J. C., & Wampold, B. E. (2019). Relationships and responsiveness in the psychological treatment of trauma: The tragedy of the APA clinical practice guideline. *Psychotherapy, 56*(3), 391–399.

Nordoff, P., & Robbins, C. (2007). *Creative music therapy: A guide for fostering clinical musicianship* (2nd Ed.). Barcelona Publishers.

Paley, V. G. (1997). *The girl with the brown crayon: How children use stories to shape their lives*. Harvard University Press.

Paley, V. G. (2010). *The boy on the beach: Building community through play*. University of Chicago Press.

Patel, A. D., Iversen, J. R., Bregman, M. R., & Schulz. I. (2009). Experimental evidence for synchronization to a musical beat in a nonhuman animal. *Current Biology, 19*(10), 827–830.

Patterson, S. Y., Elder, L., Gulsrud, A., & Kasari, C. (2014). The association between parental interaction style and children's joint engagement in families with toddlers with autism. *Autism, 18*(5), 511–518.

Perry, B. D. (2021). *Attunement: Reading the rhythms of the child*. Scholastic.com. https://www.scholastic.com/teachers/articles/teaching-content/attunement-reading-rhythms-child/

Piaget, J. (1964). Development and learning. In R. Ripple & V. Rockcastle (Eds.) *Piaget rediscovered*. Cornell University Press.

Prizant, B. M. (2016). *Uniquely human: A different way of seeing autism*. Simon & Schuster.

Prizant, B. M., Wetherby, A. M., Rubin, E., Laurent, A. C., & Rydell, P. J. (2002). The SCERTS model: Enhancing communication and socioemotional abilities of children with autism spectrum disorders. *Jenison Autism Journal, 14*, 2–19.

Prizant, B. M., Wetherby, A. M., Rubin, E., Laurent, A. C., & Rydell, P. J. (2006). *The SCERTS model: A comprehensive educational approach for children with autism spectrum disorders* (Vols. 1–2). Brookes.

Prizant, B. M., Wetherby, A. M., & Rydell, P. J. (2000). Communication intervention issues for children with autism spectrum disorders. In A. M. Wetherby & B. M. Prizant (Eds.), *Autism spectrum disorders: A transactional developmental perspective* (Vol. 9, pp. 193–224). Brookes.

Rogers, A. G. (1995). *A shining affliction: A story of harm and healing in psychotherapy*. Penguin Books.

Rogers, C. (1957). The necessary and sufficient conditions of therapeutic personality change. *Journal of Consulting Psychology, 21*(2), 95–103.

Rogers, C. (1989). The interpersonal relationship in the facilitation of learning. In H. Kirschenbaum & V. Land Henderson (Eds.), *The Carl Rogers reader* (pp. 304–322). Houghton Mifflin.

Rogers, S. J., & Dawson, G. (2010). *Early Start Denver Model for young children with autism: Promoting language, learning, and engagement.* Guilford Press.

Rogers, S. J., Dawson, G., & Vismara, L. (2012). *An early start for your child with autism: Using everyday activities to help kids connect, communicate, and learn.* Guilford Press.

Rowland, C., & Fried-Oken, M. (2010). Communication matrix: A clinical and research assessment tool targeting children with severe communication disorders. *Journal of Pediatric Rehabilitation Medicine, 3*(4), 319–329.

Sacks, O. (2007). *Musicophilia: Tales of music and the brain.* Alfred A. Knopf.

Scambler, D. J., Hepburn, S., Rutherford, M. D., Wehner, E. A., & Rogers, S. J. (2007). Emotional responsivity in children with autism, children with other developmental disabilities, and children with typical development. *Journal of Autism and Developmental Disorders, 37*(3), 553–563.

Schulman, A. (2016). *Waking the spirit.* Picador.

Sharda, M., Tuerk, C., Chowdhury, R., Jamey, K., Foster, N., Custo-Blanch, M., Tan, M., Nadig, A., & Hyde, K. (2018). Music improves social communication and auditory-motor connectivity in children with autism. *Translational Psychiatry, 8*(1), 231.

Sherratt, D., & Peter, M. (2002). *Developing play and drama in children with autistic spectrum disorders.* David Fulton.

Shire, S. Y., Gulsrud, A., & Kasari, C. (2016). Increasing responsive parent-child interactions and joint engagement: Comparing the influence of parent-mediated intervention and parent psychoeducation. *Journal of Autism and Developmental Disorders, 46*(5), 1737–1747.

Shonkoff, J. P., & Phillips, D. A. (2000). *From neurons to neighborhoods: The science of early childhood development.* National Academy Press.

Simpson, P. R., Adams, L. G., Byrd, S. E., Smith Myles, B., Otten, K., Ganz, J., Cook, K. T., Griswold, D., Ben-Arieh, J., de Boer, S. R., Kline, S. A., & Adams, L.G. (2005). *Autism spectrum disorders: Interventions and treatments for children and youth.* Corwin Press.

Skinner, B. (1966). What is the experimental analysis of behavior? *Journal of the Experimental Analysis of Behavior, 9*(3), 213–218.

Smith, L., & Thelen, E. (2003). Development as a dynamic system. *Trends in Cognitive Sciences, 7*(8), 343–348.

Staub, J. C. (2019). *Wing over wing.* Paraclete Press.

Stern, D. N. (2000). *The interpersonal world of the infant: A view from psychoanalysis and developmental psychology* (2nd ed.). Basic Books.

Stern, D. N., Bruschweiler-Stern, N., Harrison, A. M., Lyons-Ruth, K., Morgan, A. C., Nahum, J. P., Sander, L., & Tronick, E. Z. (1998). The process of therapeutic change involving implicit knowledge: Some implications of developmental observations for adult psychotherapy. *Infant Mental Health Journal, 19*(3), 300–308.

Strain, P. S., & Hoyson, M. (2000). The need for longitudinal, intensive social skill intervention: LEAP follow-up outcomes for children with autism. *Topics in Early Childhood Special Education, 20,* 116–122.

Strain, P. S., Schwartz, I. S., & Bovey, E. H. (2008). Social competence interventions for young children with autism: Programmatic research findings and implementation issues. In W. H. Brown, S. L. Odom, and S. R. McConnell (Eds.), *Social competence of young children: Risk, disability, and intervention.* Paul H. Brookes.

Tager-Flusberg, H., & Kasari, C. (2013). Minimally verbal school-aged children with autism spectrum disorder: The neglected end of the spectrum. *Autism Research, 6,* 468–478.

Tager-Flusberg, H., Rogers, S., Cooper, J., Landa, R., Lord, C., Paul, R., & Yoder, P. (2009). Defining spoken language benchmarks and selecting measures of expressive language development for young children with autism spectrum disorders. *Journal of Speech, Language, and Hearing Research, 52*(3), 643–652.

Thaut, M. H., Leins, A. K., Rice, R. R., Argstatter, H., Kenyon, G. P., Mcintosh, G. C., Bolay, H. V., & Fetter, M. (2007). Rhythmic auditory stimulation improves gait more than NDT/Bobath Training in near-ambulatory patients early poststroke: A single-blind, randomized trial. *Neurorehabilitation and Neural Repair, 21,* 455–459.

Tronick, E. (2007), *The neurobehavioral and social-emotional development of infants and children.* W. W. Norton.

Tronick, E., & Beeghly, M. (2011). Infants' meaning-making and the development of mental health problems. *The American Psychologist, 66*(2), 107–119.

Vygotsky, L. (1987). Thinking and speech. In R. Rieber & A. Carton (Eds.) & N. Minick (Trans.). *The collected works of L. S. Vygotsky: Vol. I, Problems of general psychology* (pp. 37–285). Plenum. (Original work published 1934).

Wacks, K., & Klotz, N. (Directors). (1996). *Music therapy and medicine: Partnerships in care* [Film]. American Music Therapy Association & N.A.K. Production Associates.

Watson, J. (1913). Psychology as the behaviorist views it. *Psychological Review, 20,* 158–177.

Weisberg, D., Sexton, S., Mulhern, J., & Keeling, D. (2009). *The widget effect: Our national failure to acknowledge and act on differences in teacher effectiveness.* New Teacher Project.

Weiss, E. M., Rominger, C., Hofer, E., Fink A., & Papousek, I. (2019). Less differentiated facial responses to naturalistic films of another person's emotional expressions in adolescents and adults with high-functioning autism spectrum disorder. *Progress in Neuro-Psychopharmacology and Biological Psychiatry, 89,* 341–346.

Williams, D. (2017, Jan. 9). *Tricks of light.* https://blog.donnawilliams.net/2017/01/09/tricks-of-light-by-donna-williams/

Yalom, I. D. (2017). *Becoming myself: A psychiatrist's memoir.* Basic Books.

Yalom, I. D., & Elkin, G. (1974). *Every day gets a little closer: A twice-told therapy.* Basic Books.

Yalom, I. D., & Leszcz, M. (2005). *The theory and practice of group psychotherapy.* (5th ed.). Basic Books.

Yeats, W. B. (1921). *Michael Robartes and the dancer.* Cuala Press.

Index

About the Author

Geoff Barnes is a music therapist (MT-BC) and Licensed Mental Health Counselor (LMHC) who has been working and learning with children on the autism spectrum as well as adults with intellectual disabilities, Alzheimer's disease, and visual impairments. He currently offers music therapy with students ages 3 to 21 with complex health needs at the Campus School at Boston College. He is an assistant professor at Lesley University in the Division of Psychology and Applied Therapies.